STATE OF NEBRASKA

Office of the Governor
P.O. Box 94848 • Lincoln, Nebraska 68509-4848
Phone: 402-471-2244 • E-mail: mjohanns@notes.state.ne.us

Dear Reader:

For many years we have described living and working in Nebraska as "The Good Life." From our outstanding education system to the strong Midwestern work ethic to the dramatic landscape, Nebraska is a unique place to raise a family, start a business, or just call home.

Towns forged along the Missouri and Platte Rivers by pioneers more than a century ago serve as centers of commerce for Nebraska today—from Omaha in the east to Scottsbluff in the west. The waterways stretching across Nebraska and our plentiful underground water supply serve as vital resources for agriculture, Nebraska's number one industry today just as it was at the time of statehood in 1867. In the 21st century, ribbons of highway and fiber optics also connect Nebraska schools, businesses, and homes to one another and their counterparts across the nation and around the world. Our state's growing technology and telecommunications companies, cutting-edge health care facilities, and financial services companies are industry leaders. But it is Nebraska's people who make a difference in the Cornhusker State.

The work ethic of Nebraskans is well known. It extends from the workplace into our communities and homes. Nebraskans from Harrison to Falls City value a handshake and a hard day's work. They respect one another and adhere to the tenet of personal responsibility but rarely fail to offer a hand to a neighbor, or a stranger for that matter. Volunteerism and charitable giving have contributed greatly to our quality of life. The friendly attitude and determination of our people make for safe communities and neighborhoods.

Nebraska blends Midwest plains and rolling hills with the buttes and pine forests of the West. In between lie distant sandhills that stretch for miles, dozens of wandering rivers, dramatic reservoirs, and open prairies. The diversity of our state provides for varied hunting, fishing, boating, canoeing, and other outdoor recreational opportunities.

Nebraskans are very proud of "The Good Life," which is grounded in the values and determination of the pioneers with an eye on the promise of tomorrow.

Sincerely,

Mike Johanns
Governor

NEBRASKA

BRINGING OUR HERITAGE
INTO THE TWENTY-FIRST CENTURY

NEBRASKA

BRINGING OUR HERITAGE INTO THE TWENTY-FIRST CENTURY

JAMES A. CLEMON

CHERBO PUBLISHING GROUP, INC.
Encino, Calif.

DEDICATION

For Nebraska's pioneer teachers—past, present, and future.

ACKNOWLEDGMENTS

Special acknowledgment is made of the assistance and support of
Bill Arendt, LoAnn Irvin, and Vicki Krecek; the Greater Omaha Chamber of Commerce
research staff, including Anne Branigan, Dorothy Buckingham, and Pete Thompson;
the Nebraska Department of Economic Development; the Nebraska Travel and Tourism Division; and
Joe Pilmaier and Bob Reilly.

PRESIDENT **Jack C. Cherbo**
EXECUTIVE VICE PRESIDENT **Elaine Hoffman**
EDITORIAL DIRECTOR **Christina M. Beausang**
MANAGING FEATURE EDITOR **Margaret L. Martin**
FEATURE EDITOR **Brian K. Mitchell**
ESSAY EDITOR **Tina G. Rubin**
SENIOR PROFILES EDITOR **J. Kelley Younger**
PROFILES EDITOR **Diane M. Ver Steeg**
PROFILES WRITERS **Maria Collis, Beth Mattson-Teig, Marilee
    Moshier Miller, Nancy Smith Seigle, Stan Ziemba**

SENIOR PROOFREADER **Sylvia Emrich-Toma**
SENIOR DESIGNER **Mika T. Mingasson**
PROFILES DESIGNER **Mary C. Barnhill**
PHOTO EDITOR **Catherine A. Vandenberg**
SALES ADMINISTRATOR **Joan K. Baker**
ACQUISITIONS ADMINISTRATOR **Bonnie J. Aharoni**
PRODUCTION SERVICES MANAGER **Ellen T. Kettenbeil**
ADMINISTRATIVE COORDINATOR **Jahnna Biddle**
REGIONAL DEVELOPMENT MANAGER **Merle Gratton**
PUBLISHER'S REPRESENTATIVES **Dick Fry, John Lofgren**

Library of Congress Cataloging-in-Publication Data
Clemon, James A.
    A pictorial guide highlighting 20th-century Nebraska lifestyle and
    economic history.
        00-107524
        ISBN 1-882933-35-4

CORPORATIONS AND ORGANIZATIONS PROFILED

The following companies and organizations have made a valuable commitment to the quality of this publication. The Nebraska Department of Economic Development gratefully acknowledges their participation in *Nebraska: Bringing Our Heritage into the Twenty-first Century.*

Alegent Health, 153

Back to the Bible, 78

Behlen Mfg. Co., 108–09

Blair Memorial Community Hospital and
   Health System, 152

Borsheim Jewelry Company, Inc., 235

BryanLGH Medical Center, 150–51

Cargill Corn Milling, 58–59

Cargill Dow LLC, 60

Chief Industries, Inc., 104–05

City of Omaha, The, 168

Clarkson College, 154

Commercial Federal Bank, 172–73

ConAgra, Inc., 64–65

Creighton University, 214–15

DLR Group, 166

Enron Corp., 128–29

Excel Corporation, 61

Farmers Mutual Insurance
   Company of Nebraska, 182–83

First Data Corporation, 176–77

First National Bank of Omaha, 174–75

Gibraltar Packaging Group, Inc., 96–97

Grubb & Ellis/Pacific Realty, 200–01

HDR, Inc., 198–99

Insul-8 Corporation, 90–91

John Day Company, 62–63

Kawasaki Motors Manufacturing
   Corp. U.S.A., 106–07

Leo A Daly, 194–95

Lincoln Electric System, 122–23

Linweld, 98–100

Malnove Incorporated, 94–95

Marriott Worldwide Reservations, 228–29

Methodist Health System, 144–45

Metropolitan Community College, 216

Metropolitan Utilities District, 126–27

Midlands Packaging Corporation, 110

Millard Lumber Inc., 196–97

Mutual of Omaha Companies, 184

Nebraska Department of Economic Development, 167

Nebraska Health System, 142–43

Nebraska Public Power District, 130–31

Oak View Mall, 232–33

Omaha Public Power District, 124–25

OMNI Behavioral Health, 148–49

Paxton & Vierling Steel,
   A Division of Owen Industries, Inc., 92–93

Peoples Natural Gas, 132

Pfizer Inc, 102–03

Rockbrook Village, 234

Saint Joseph Hospital, 146–47

Sandhills Publishing Company, 74–77

Southeast Community College, 217

Standard Digital Imaging, 79

Sterling Software Information Technology Division, 80

University of Nebraska, 210–13

Valmont Industries, Inc., 101

Werner Enterprises, Inc., 120–21

West TeleServices Corporation, 164–65

Woodmen of the World,
   Omaha Woodmen Life Insurance Society, 180–81

CONTENTS

PART ONE: A REGIONAL SAMPLER: REGIONS AND LIFESTYLES 2

NEBRASKA HIGHLIGHTS 4

CHAPTER 1   OMAHA AND THE NORTHEAST: THE RIVERFRONT AND THE LAND OF LEWIS AND CLARK 8

CHAPTER 2   THE PLATTE VALLEY: THE GREAT PLATTE RIVER ROAD 26

CHAPTER 3   NORTH CENTRAL: SANDHILLS CATTLE COUNTRY 32

CHAPTER 4   THE SOUTHEAST: LAND OF THE PRAIRIE PIONEER 36

CHAPTER 5   SOUTH CENTRAL: PRAIRIE LAKES COUNTRY 40

CHAPTER 6   THE PANHANDLE: PINE RIDGE AND TRAILS WEST 44

PART TWO: VISTAS OF OPPORTUNITY: INDUSTRIES AND PROFILES 48

CHAPTER 7   PANTRY ON THE PLAINS: AGRICULTURE AND FOOD PROCESSING 50

CHAPTER 8   BIG COUNTRY, MANY VOICES: COMMUNICATIONS AND THE MEDIA 66

CHAPTER 9   FACTORIES AMONG THE FIELDS: MANUFACTURING 82

CHAPTER 10   MOBILITY AND POWER: TRANSPORTATION AND ENERGY 112

CHAPTER 11   HEALING IN A NEW CENTURY: MEDICAL TECHNOLOGY AND HEALTH CARE 134

CHAPTER 12   SUSTAINING A GROWING ECONOMY: FINANCIAL AND PROFESSIONAL SERVICES 156

CHAPTER 13   HOME AND WORK IN A NEW CENTURY: RESIDENTIAL AND COMMERCIAL DEVELOPMENT 186

CHAPTER 14   FROM SODDIE TO CYBERSPACE: EDUCATION 202

CHAPTER 15   PLEASURABLE PURSUITS: HOSPITALITY, TOURISM, AND RETAIL 218

PART THREE: REFLECTIONS AND VISIONS: ESSAYS 236

BIBLIOGRAPHY 244

INDEX 246

PHOTO: *A tepee on the western Nebraska prairie, © Tom Bean/Corbis*

ESSAYISTS

ELECTRIC ENERGY   238
William R. Mayben, President and Chief Executive Officer, Nebraska Public Power District

FINANCIAL SERVICES   239
Bruce R. Lauritzen, Chairman, First National Bank of Omaha

HIGHER EDUCATION   240
Gladys Styles Johnston, Chancellor, The University of Nebraska at Kearney

MANUFACTURING   241
Anthony F. Raimondo, Chairman and Chief Executive Officer, Behlen Mfg. Co.
Richard F. Casey, Senior Vice President–Administration, Behlen Mfg. Co.

TRANSPORTATION   242
Clarence L. Werner, Chief Executive Officer, Werner Enterprises

PHOTO: *Oregon Trail marker, Ash Hollow State Historic Park, Garden County, © Tom Till*

FOREWORD

I bought my first stock at the age of 11 with my 14-year-old sister—six shares at $38 apiece. The price dipped, and on the subsequent recovery, I quickly sold my shares for a meager $5 profit. After that, it soared to $200. I developed a long-term philosophy of "buy and hold" from that experience.

It's far better to buy a wonderful company at a fair price than a fair company at a wonderful price. I guess the same thing could be said of selecting a state in which to live and work. It's better to settle on a wonderful state at a fair price than a fair state at a wonderful price.

Nebraska is a wonderful "buy and hold" state. I started my first business here when I was 11. A friend and I published a handicapping sheet by the name of *Stable Boy Selections.* To this day, Nebraska is the site of my business operations. I manage Berkshire Hathaway from an office in Omaha.

I choose to stay in Nebraska because it has a great deal going for it. For one thing, Nebraska's pro-business climate makes real economic sense for any type of business. And, of course, there are all those characteristics we are known for here in Nebraska: clean air, low crime rate, good schools, and midwestern work ethic.

I always say that investors should act as though they had a lifetime "decision card" with just 20 punches on it. Persons seeking a location for a business, or for an enjoyable and prosperous life, are other types of investors. If any one of them elects to locate in Nebraska, that decision would cost one punch, but it would be one of the smartest decisions that person could make.

Obviously, for the last many decades I could have lived any place in the country that I'd wanted to and conducted business from there—and I've never given a thought to being any place but in Nebraska.

Warren E. Buffett, Chairman, Berkshire Hathaway Inc.

PART ONE

A REGIONAL SAMPLER

You can still grow up to be a cowboy in Nebraska. Or a researcher on the front edge of medical science. Or a digital explorer pushing back the frontiers of communications technology. Lives led here are as varied as the landscape. From the vast quiet of a Sandhills ranch to the vibrant bustle of Omaha's Old Market, Nebraska's heritage of human and geographical diversity provides a virtually limitless choice of endeavor and entertainment. It is the legacy of Mormon emigrants and French fur trappers, of Native American visionaries, Irish railroad workers, Czech farmers, and countless others.

Generations of Nebraskans have worked together to build a society that validates the vision of the pioneers—one with uncrowded lifestyles, safe and comfortable communities, excellent schools, stable employment, and room to grow in every direction. Each distinctive region was shaped by different influences; yet all are united by traditions of sound education, sturdy work ethic, enriching cultural expression, and pride in knowing that in the Cornhusker State, life is longer and better.

A natural landmark for travelers on the Oregon, California, and Mormon Trails, Scotts Bluff National Monument today preserves the memory of nearly half a million brave pioneers who made the difficult journey west from the 1840s to the 1860s.

NEBRASKA HIGHLIGHTS

The most important of Nebraska's many great commodities may be its leaders. Pathfinders and innovators, whether they be natives or transplants, have always thrived here. Following is a mere glimpse of their ranks—from generals and peacemakers to scientists and poets—along with some of their accomplishments.

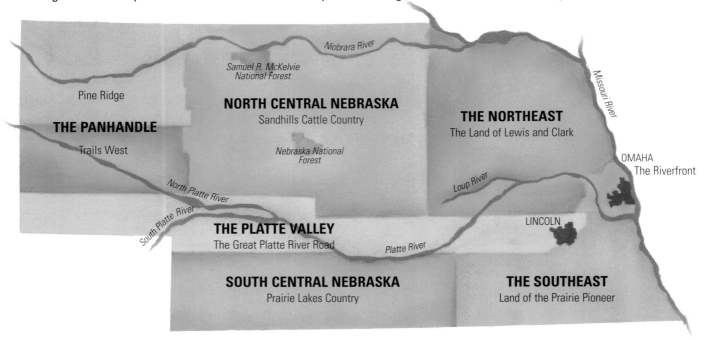

Niobrara River

Samuel R. McKelvie National Forest

Pine Ridge

NORTH CENTRAL NEBRASKA
Sandhills Cattle Country

Missouri River

THE NORTHEAST
The Land of Lewis and Clark

THE PANHANDLE
Trails West

Nebraska National Forest

OMAHA
The Riverfront

North Platte River

Loup River

South Platte River

LINCOLN

THE PLATTE VALLEY
The Great Platte River Road

Platte River

SOUTH CENTRAL NEBRASKA
Prairie Lakes Country

THE SOUTHEAST
Land of the Prairie Pioneer

AREA: 77,358 square miles
POPULATION: 1,666,028 (1999 est.)
CAPITAL: Lincoln
MOTTO: "Equality Before the Law"

STATEHOOD: Admitted as the 37th state on March 1, 1867
NICKNAME: The Cornhusker State
STATE BIRD: Western Meadowlark
STATE FLOWER: Goldenrod

FAMOUS SONS AND DAUGHTERS

FRED ASTAIRE (1899–1987)
Born Frederick Austerlitz in Omaha, Astaire started out in vaudeville with his sister, Adele. He made his movie debut in MGM's *Dancing Lady* in 1933.

His dancing artistry and debonair manner were showcased in a long series of hit musicals, including 10 with Ginger Rogers.

WILLIAM JENNINGS BRYAN (1860–1925)
Known as the "Great Commoner" for his populist beliefs and the "Boy Orator of the Platte" for his mesmerizing speeches, Bryan was a force in Nebraska and national politics for 30 years. The unsuccessful three-time Democratic presidential nominee served as President Woodrow Wilson's secretary of state, 1913–16. Bryan also was the special prosecutor in the famous "Scopes Monkey Trial" in Tennessee in 1925.

JOHNNY CARSON (1925–)
Born in Corning, Iowa, John William Carson moved with his family to Norfolk, Nebraska, in 1933. A graduate of the University of Nebraska–Lincoln, Carson got his big break at a Hollywood TV station by filling in for comedian Red Skelton on two hours' notice. He went on to emcee the

MEMORABLE MOMENTS IN THE HISTORY

1863

President Abraham Lincoln designates Omaha as the starting point for the transcontinental railroad.

1898

More than 2.5 million people attend the Trans-Mississippi and International Exposition in Omaha.

1904

The Kincaid Act, introduced by Rep. Moses P. Kincaid of O'Neill, allows farmers in western Nebraska to expand their homesteads to 640 acres.

game show *Who Do You Trust?* and from there to his legendary 30-year stint as host of *The Tonight Show.*

HENRY FONDA (1905–82)
Fonda, who was born in Grand Island, made his acting debut in 1925 at the urging of Marlon Brando's mother at the Community Playhouse in Omaha. He appeared in more than 80 movies, receiving an Academy Award for best actor in 1982 for *On Golden Pond.*

GERALD R. FORD (1913–)
Memorial gardens and a replica of his boyhood home honor the former vice president and president of the United States on the site of his birthplace in Omaha.

BOB GIBSON (1935–)
Born and raised in Omaha, the Hall of Fame pitcher played baseball and basketball for Creighton University. After touring briefly with the Harlem Globetrotters, Gibson *(above)* played for the St. Louis Cardinals, winning two Cy Young Awards (1968, 1970) and setting the major league season record for lowest earned run average (1.12).

MAKHPIYALUTA (RED CLOUD)
(1822–1909)
The Oglala Sioux chief was prominent in the Plains wars following the Civil War. As principal negotiator for his people, he signed the Treaty of Fort Laramie, accepting reservation status and thereby speeding the Native Americans' transition from warrior nomads to wards of the government.

GEORGE W. NORRIS (1861–1944)
Elected to Congress from McCook in 1902, Norris served in the House of Representatives, then the Senate, for 40 years. He was known as the father of the Tennessee Valley Authority, the federal rural electrification program, and other progressive legislation. He also was the architect and chief promoter of Nebraska's unique one-house legislature.

TOM OSBORNE (1937–)
Between 1972 and 1997, this native of Hastings and third-generation graduate of Hastings College coached the University of Nebraska–Lincoln football team to three national and 13 conference championships. After retiring as the winningest active coach in college football, with a .828 victory record, he ran for Congress in 2000.

JOHN J. PERSHING (1860–1948)
"Black Jack" Pershing was a cadet instructor at the University of Nebraska, and later won his nickname leading African American troops on the Plains. In World War I he commanded American forces in Europe, was made general of the armies in 1919, and became Army chief of staff in 1921.

SUSAN LA FLESCHE PICOTTE
(1865–1915)
Graduated at the top of her medical school class in Philadelphia in 1889, Picotte was the first Native American woman to become a doctor. She returned to Nebraska to serve as a government physician to her tribe, the Omahas, and later helped establish a hospital at Walthill.

LOUISE POUND (1872–1958)
A teacher, scholar, and athlete at the University of Nebraska for more than 50 years, Pound did her most important research and writing in the area of contemporary American English and was founding editor of *American Speech.* In 1894 she was the ranking U.S. female tennis player and was Nebraska's top woman golfer for 26 years. In 1955, at age 82, she became the first woman elected to the Nebraska Sports Hall of Fame.

TASHUNCA-UITCO
(CRAZY HORSE) (1844?–1877)
The Oglala Sioux chief became famous in his resistance to white settlement of the Plains and commanded, with Sitting Bull, the Sioux and Cheyenne who annihilated Gen. George A. Custer's force at the Little Big Horn River in Montana on June 26, 1876. He was killed by a soldier's bayonet while in custody at Fort Robinson in northwest Nebraska.

DID YOU KNOW...?

Fort Omaha was the scene in 1879 of a significant civil rights victory. In the trial of Standing Bear, a Ponca chief who resisted the removal of his people from Nebraska to Oklahoma, U.S. District Judge Elmer S. Dundy ruled that the Indian was a person in the eyes of the law, protected by constitutional guarantees of personal liberty. • While William F. Cody was employed to provide meat for railroad-building crews in 1867–68, he reportedly shot 4,280 buffalo in eight months. In a shooting competition with one Bill Comstock, Cody killed 69 of the animals to Comstock's 56, earning the nickname "Buffalo Bill." Cody's ranch in North Platte is now a state historical park and recreation area.

OF THE CORNHUSKER STATE

1918
Nebraskans buy a quota-busting $240 million in World War I Liberty Bonds and more war savings stamps per capita than any other state.

1922
Ground is broken in Lincoln for a new capitol, the 400-foot-high "Tower on the Plains," the only capitol financed entirely from current state revenue.

1934
Nebraska voters approve a constitutional amendment creating the nation's only unicameral (one-house) legislature.

GRAND SLAM

Nebraskans won a total of four Nobel Prizes in the 20th century: (left to right) Charles G. Dawes of Lincoln, for peace, in 1925; George W. Beadle of Wahoo, for physiology/medicine, in 1958; and Val L. Fitch of Merriman, for physics, and Lawrence R. Klein of Omaha, for economics, both in 1980.

PHOTOS (LEFT TO RIGHT): TOP, © Bettmann/Corbis; Courtesy, Archives, California Institute of Technology; © Princeton Univ.,

FIRSTS AND INNOVATIONS

Nebraska has always been a land of new ideas and pioneering innovations. Here are just a few:

1872: Nebraska City editor J. Sterling Morton *(right)* proposes a tree-planting holiday to be called Arbor Day.

1902: First trees are planted on the grassland for the Nebraska National Forest, which becomes the largest hand-planted forest in the nation.

1917: Father Edward Flanagan founds the Home for Homeless Boys, which is to become world-renowned Boys Town (now Girls and Boys Town).

1924: Two men from Lincoln, Republican Charles G. Dawes and Democratic Gov. Charles W. Bryan, run for vice president of the United States.

1927: Perkins Products Co. in Hastings introduces a powdered soft drink called Kool-Aid.

1933: State law enables Nebraska to become the only state whose entire electric output is generated by consumer-owned plants.

1937: First session of Nebraska's unicameral legislature, the only one in the nation, is held.

1948: Columbus's own Frank Zyback invents the center-pivot irrigator *(below),* called

the most significant mechanical innovation in agriculture since the tractor replaced draft animals.

1953: First National Bank of Omaha launches its First Charge, the nation's first bank-issued credit card.

1954: After Gerry Thomas of Swanson Foods in Omaha

comes up with the idea for a heat-and-serve meal, the company introduces the world's first TV dinner, which consists of turkey, dressing, gravy, peas, and sweet potatoes.

1955: Omaha becomes the nation's largest livestock center with more than six million head received.

1957: Nebraska is the first state to begin systematically developing foreign markets for wheat.

1964: Lincoln Telephone introduces an experimental version of the In-WATS calling service, first of its kind in the United States.

MEMORABLE MOMENTS IN THE HISTORY

1941

Kingsley Dam near Ogallala creates Lake McConaughy and a 170-mile network of canals and lakes that will irrigate western Nebraska farmland.

1957

The first contract is awarded for construction of Nebraska's portion of the interstate highway system, 478 miles from Omaha to the Wyoming border.

1968–69

Swift and Armour meatpacking plants in Omaha close; the city absorbs the blow as it makes the transition to a more balanced and diversified economy.

1965: Clarkson Hospital in Omaha performs the first kidney transplant in the Midwest.

1971: Omaha completes the first street-paving project to use "glasphalt," a locally produced blend of crushed waste glass and asphalt.

1973: Willy Theisen opens Godfather's Pizza in Omaha, one of the first restaurants to offer take-out pizza.

1974: The first nuclear power plant operated by a publicly owned utility goes on-line at Brownville.

1983: The National Parent-Teacher Association gives its first-ever endorsement of a television series to *Mutual of Omaha's Wild Kingdom.*

1983: Ag Processing, Inc., to become in 13 years the largest cooperative soybean processing company in the world, is formed in Omaha.

1986: Nebraska makes political history when Republican Kay Orr and Democrat Helen Boosalis oppose each other in the first U.S. gubernatorial election with women as the candidates of both major parties.

1995: Topping 5 million in sales each, the first two Christmas albums of the Omaha-based Mannheim Steamroller ensemble become the best-selling Christmas albums in history.

1997: With 16,000 workers in 13 Nebraska counties, Sitel, Inc., of Omaha becomes the world's largest telephone marketing and service company.

1999: University of Nebraska's Center for Human Molecular Genetics creates the world's first genetically engineered mouse model to explain how folic acid protects against human birth defects.

1999: University of Nebraska–Lincoln's baseball team sets three NCAA Division I offensive records, defeating Chicago State 50–3 in seven innings.

1999: *Forbes* magazine's list of the world's 100 wealthiest people includes three Omahans: Warren Buffett, J. Joe Ricketts, and Walter Scott Jr.

LITERARY PIONEERS

Often acknowledged as America's foremost woman writer, Willa Cather (1873–1947; left) was born in Virginia and moved to Nebraska in 1882. Her notable books, many set in and around her hometown of Red Cloud, include *O! Pioneers, My Antonia, Death Comes for the Archbishop,* and the Pulitzer Prize–winning *One of Ours.* • The prolific Bess Streeter Aldrich (1881–1954) of Elmwood produced 11 novels and 160 short stories, mostly about prairie pioneer families, and sold every one she wrote. Her books include *Miss Bishop, Mother Mason,* and *Rim of the Prairie.* • Named Prairie Poet Laureate of America in 1968 and Nebraska's Poet Laureate in Perpetuity in 1982, John G. Neihardt (1881–1973) completed his major work, the five-volume *A Cycle of the West,* in 1941. His best-known single book is *Black Elk Speaks.* • Mari Sandoz (1896–1966), historian, biographer, novelist, story writer, teacher, and authority on Native Americans of the Plains, is best known for works such as *Old Jules,* a biography of her pioneer father; *Cheyenne Autumn; Crazy Horse;* and *Slogum House.* She was born on Mirage Flats south of Hay Springs and is buried on a hillside overlooking the Sandoz Sandhills ranch near Gordon.

OF THE CORNHUSKER STATE

1971

Under Coach Bob Devaney, the Nebraska Cornhuskers win their first National Collegiate Athletic Association national championship in football.

1986

The state legislature deregulates telecommunications rates and services, strengthening Omaha's presence as an 800-number capital.

1996

For the first time, the number of Nebraskans living in the Lincoln and Omaha metropolitan areas exceeds the population of the rest of the state.

CHAPTER ONE

OMAHA AND THE NORTHEAST

THE RIVERFRONT AND THE LAND OF LEWIS AND CLARK

Preposterous. A town of barely 100,000, less than 50 years old, planning a *world's fair* in the midst of a paralyz-ing depression, in Nebraska of all places. Well, *Omaha* is a Native American word meaning, among other things, "against the current"; Omahans were used to swimming upstream. In 1898 their "preposterous" Trans-Mississippi and International Exposition opened on a 184-acre tract on Omaha's north side. It drew more than

2.6 million visitors, including President William McKinley, and sent a message that Omaha had arrived, not only as an industrial and transportation center, but as a serious player in the explosive growth of the West.

A HERITAGE OF OPTIMISM AND DETERMINATION

The community on the Missouri River muscled into the 20th century wearing on its rolled-up sleeve a heritage of optimism and determina-tion—"go-aheaditiveness," as a journalist of the time put it.

That heritage is alive and working as the Omaha metro area—Nebraska's riverfront—enters another new century and a new millennium. The city's population is 371,291, while the metro area is home to nearly 700,000, and a 50-mile circle drawn around Omaha would include more than one million. Business and industry, including more Fortune 500 companies than Kansas City, Denver, or Phoenix, provide expanding opportunities for the area's workforce of more than 400,000. Nearly 18,000 enter-prises, ranging from the Union Pacific Railroad and the Mutual of Omaha Companies to ambitious start-up firms in computing and telecommunications, bolster the

economic base and provide a diversity of employment. Prosperous farms and giant feedlots dotting the hills and plains around the 2,500-square-mile urban center give substance to Nebraskans' love of the land and nourish the agrarian roots put down by the pioneers.

Another sign that go-aheaditiveness remains a defining spirit of the area is the current $2 billion–plus commercial and public investment in infrastructure, including a 32-acre, $181 million business park down-town; a new convention cen-ter and arena on 104 acres; a 40-story tower built by First National Bank of Omaha; a $100 million expansion by the *Omaha World-Herald;* and a $70 million informa-tion science, technology, and engineering institute at the University of Nebraska at Omaha. This expansion and renewal reinforces growth that brought 1,000 net new jobs per month in 1994–99.

ABOVE: *Franz Johansen's* Handcart Pioneers, *at the Mormon Trail Center at Historic Winter Quarters, depicts a 19th-century family braving the Great Migration.* OPPOSITE: *The ConAgra campus in Omaha looms through the mist of the Heartland of America Fountain.*

THE GOOD LIFE

In one of the state's unofficial mottos, Nebraskans style theirs "the Good Life." The Omaha metro area provides its version of this essential livability in a cost of living about six points below the national average, a commuting time rarely more than 20 or 30 minutes from the farthest suburb to downtown, and 10,500 acres of green space in city parks, forests, and wildlife areas. Its young people share and contribute significantly to Nebraska's enviable educational records, which include one of the highest rates of high school graduation in the United States and student scores on college aptitude tests that are consistently above the national average.

In this comfortable setting, Omahans and visitors relax in myriad ways reflecting both the low-pressure lifestyle and the area's tradition of excellence and diversity in recreation and entertainment. The Omaha Community Playhouse is the largest theater of its kind in the nation in size and subscriptions, and the area supports more than two dozen other active performing arts organizations, from the Omaha Symphony Orchestra to the Nebraska Shakespeare Festival to neighborhood playhouses and dinner theaters. Ten museums, including the prestigious Joslyn Art Museum, the Durham Western Heritage Museum, and the Strategic Air Command Museum, featuring an outdoor display of generations of American fighting aircraft, offer attractions from the historical to the contemporary. The Henry Doorly Zoo is home to a world-class walk-through aquarium and an indoor rain forest ranked as the best zoo exhibit in the United States.

LON MILLER President and Chief Operating Officer, Insul-8 Corporation

Since its establishment in 1924 in the heart of the Old Market, Insul-8 Corporation, formerly Industrial Electric Reels, Inc., has deeply entrenched roots in Omaha.

Lon Miller, president and chief operating officer of Insul-8 Corporation, began his career at Insul-8 in 1986 as company controller. Though born in Iowa, Lon, his wife, Elizabeth, and their three children call Gretna, Nebraska, home.

Insul-8's headquarters are now located in the prime industrial area of southwest Omaha. "More important than the building are the terrific people working inside," says Miller. "Insul-8 products are well-known and used worldwide based on the expertise we cultivated here in the heartland."

OPPOSITE: *A produce market is among the galleries, restaurants, and specialty shops that enliven the cobblestoned streets of Omaha's Old Market quarter.* BELOW: *The Union Pacific Railroad uses one of the* nation's largest fiber-optic networks to control rail traffic from its headquarters in Omaha. The city's link with technology dates to the 1860s, when railways and the telegraph first spanned the continent.

The NCAA College World Series has been played at Omaha's Rosenblatt Stadium for 50 years, ranking annually as one of the hottest sports tickets in the Midwest. Creighton University and the University of Nebraska at Omaha draw fans to NCAA sports; the Omaha Lancers, Golden Spikes, and Omaha Beef offer ice hockey, Triple A baseball, and arena football excitement; and to indulge the urban taste for a truly western sport, championship rodeo is a centerpiece of the region's annual River City Roundup, a festival celebrating Omaha's and Nebraska's pioneer heritage.

A little-publicized testament to the area's attractiveness as a place to live and make a living is this: At last count, it was home to half a dozen billionaires, 130 hundred-millionaires, and 15,500 millionaires. What makes them want to stay at home when they can live

LOUIS W. BURGHER, M.D. President and CEO, Nebraska Health System

The dramatic changes that have taken place in the business of health care in the past few years have required a hybrid type of leadership that involves both clinical and financial management. I have always enjoyed combining medical and business pursuits and welcomed the challenge of leading Nebraska Health System (NHS), a merged partnership of two renowned, independent entities, Clarkson and University Hospitals.

Now, three years later, NHS is going strong and proving that institutions can achieve more together than apart. Nebraska offers the opportunity for progressive business growth and a lifestyle that supports family and community involvement.

Extraordinary Care

NHS NEBRASKA HEALTH SYSTEM
CLARKSON HOSPITAL • UNIVERSITY HOSPITAL
A Partner with University of Nebraska Medical Center

JOHN D. FONDA President and CEO, John Day Company

The John Day Company feels very proud to be a part of the history of Nebraska.
My great-grandfather, John F. Day, started the company in 1909 from the basement of his home in Omaha.

The John Day Company continues to believe in Nebraska and its people. The entire state, we believe, has shown a strong commitment to the arts, our zoo, universities, and our young people. Nebraska's continued emphasis on strong family values and work ethics will enable businesses statewide to have a reliable and strong workforce for the next century.

OPPOSITE: *Every June, the NCAA College World Series fills Omaha's Rosenblatt Stadium for a week. The tournament and related festivities bring as many as a quarter of a million visitors to town.*

BELOW: *Given to the people of Omaha in 1931 by Sarah H. Joslyn in memory of her husband, newspaper magnate George A. Joslyn, the Joslyn Art Museum boasts an encyclopedic permanent collection.*

anywhere they choose is perhaps summed up best by one of the community's exemplars of go-aheaditiveness, investor Warren Buffett: "Everyone has to decide where they want to spend the rest of their lives, and for me, no question about it, it's Omaha."

ALONG THE PATH OF TRADITION AND DISCOVERY

In some outward respects, Nebraska's northeast quadrant—the Land of Lewis and Clark—has changed little since the explorers passed through in the summer of 1804. The timeless Missouri River embraces this corner of the state on the north and east, flowing past the same silent wooded bluffs along its 500-mile course as Nebraska's eastern boundary. And the heritage and spiritual traditions of such peoples as the Poncas, who lived here since the beginning of recorded history, are nurtured

Originally a volunteer ensemble, the Omaha Symphony Orchestra now attracts and retains talented career musicians thanks to the area's quality of life and strong community support for the arts.

by Native Americans who still live along the path of the Lewis and Clark expedition and are immortalized in the words of such Nebraskans as the late Poet Laureate John G. Neihardt of Bancroft.

Inland from the river, in an area north from Omaha and extending across nearly one-third of Nebraska's breadth, lies a land which early explorers, who dismissed it as "the Great American Desert," wouldn't recognize today.

The country is filled with cornfields and huge feedlots, which help give the state one of its unofficial mottos, "the Beef State," and allow the town of Wisner to call itself "the Livestock Center of Nebraska." With

STEPHEN D. LONG, FACHE President and CEO, Methodist Health System

During the 29 years I have worked in the health industry in Nebraska, it has been obvious to me that this state provides a very favorable environment for almost any business. We are blessed with outstanding primary- and secondary-level school systems. Our colleges and universities are excellent and provide a broad range of curricula that produce well-trained students, ready to join the workforce in virtually all professions. Best of all, we seem to keep the majority in our state. We also are blessed throughout the state with outstanding health care professionals and facilities.

Combining the above with a stable economy and excellent transportation systems makes Nebraska a very attractive place to live and work.

ROBERT E. OWEN President, Paxton & Vierling Steel, and Chairman, Owen Industries, Inc.

Founded in 1885 as an iron foundry and machine shop, Paxton & Vierling Steel is now a division of Owen Industries, Inc., a family-owned corporation that is still proud to call Omaha its home.

Owen Industries has become one of America's leading processors of steel, employing over 400 people and generating annual sales of over $100 million. With strategic partners in Europe and the Pacific Rim, Owen Industries is now a global supplier.

BELOW: *Just off a highway through the Elkhorn River Valley, quiet woods and dandelion meadows provide an escape from workaday cares. Silvan retreats like this are now accessible via the Cowboy Recreation and Nature Trail, which follows U.S. 275 west from Norfolk. When finished, Nebraska's first recreational trail will stretch 321 miles, all the way to the Pine Ridge country.*

this bounty of feed and livestock at every hand, it's natural that the largest private employer in the region, and one of the largest in Nebraska, is Iowa Beef Processors, Inc., at Dakota City.

The people who farm the land, finish the cattle, and populate northeast Nebraska's tidy communities are in large part the descendants of European settlers who

Printmaker Lucas Weber created this engraving of Nebraska's first permanent white settlement, Bellevue, from a painting by Swiss-born artist Karl Bodmer, who visited the region in 1832–34.

established homesteads and broke the sod in the 19th century. Oakland, where visitors can take a "Troll Stroll" in the park, vies with Stromsburg in central Nebraska for

PAUL MALNOVE Chairman, Malnove Incorporated

Our company has operated in the state of Nebraska since our founding, more than 50 years ago. Many of the factors that contributed to our early success are still quite important to us today. Nebraska people possess a superb work ethic and take great personal pride in their contributions to our business success.

The state's positive business climate, as well as the excellent quality of life offered to our associates, has allowed us to grow and prosper over these many years. From this central location we have been able to expand our business throughout North America.

J. RICHARD STANKO President and Chief Executive Officer, Saint Joseph Hospital

Saint Joseph Hospital is on the leading edge of medical research, technology, prevention, and treatment. The hospital has attracted authorities in many specialty areas, such as Cardiology, Hereditary Cancer, Osteoporosis, Trauma, Orthopaedics, Women's Health, Neonatology, Bloodless Medicine and Surgery, and Primary Care.

At Saint Joseph Hospital today, the tradition of teaching is as strong as ever. We continue to serve as the primary teaching hospital for the physicians and allied health care professionals of Creighton University's various medical programs. Within the hospital today, students grow to understand that healing extends beyond the physical, to the mind and spirit.

SAINT JOSEPH HOSPITAL
AT CREIGHTON UNIVERSITY MEDICAL CENTER
Tenet HealthSystem

ethnic honors as the most Swedish town in the state, while O'Neill has been designated by two governors and the state legislature as "the Irish Capital of Nebraska." Dana College at Blair is America's only Danish-related four-year college.

Crisscrossing this region of more than 10,000 square miles are state highways linking peaceful little towns with larger communities and trade centers such as Wayne, Columbus, South Sioux City, and Norfolk, and leading to unusual places where Nebraskans celebrate their heritage and offer their widely known brand of hospitality. From the 859-acre Ponca State Park on the north to restored Fort Atkinson, first U.S. Army post west of the

Dawn creeps over the Omaha skyline, reflected in the tranquil waters of a man-made lagoon in Gene Leahy Mall.

Missouri, in the south, the area boasts both reminders of Nebraska's colorful past and opportunities for fun and relaxation at every bend in the road.

Ashfall Fossil Beds State Historical Park near Royal, one of the world's great archaeological finds, displays what *National Geographic* has described as "the Pompeii of prehistoric animals." The Cuthills Vineyards at Pierce,

Ten million years ago, wind-borne volcanic ash from what is now Idaho buried whole herds of rhinoceroses, saber-toothed deer, three-toed horses, and other animals. More than 300 complete skeletons are on view at Ashfall Fossil Beds State Historical Park.

the state's first winery, offers visitors prize-winning proof that Nebraska can grow grapes as well as grain. In proud

G. RICHARD "RICK" RUSSELL President and Chief Executive Officer, Millard Lumber Inc.

It has been both exciting and interesting watching our company grow from a small rural beginning to a company with locations in Omaha and Lincoln, Nebraska, and Des Moines, Iowa. As a second-generation family member, I greatly appreciate the foresight and dedication that my parents, George F. and Marjorie Russell, had to form the foundation and vision for our company.

Throughout the years we have been fortunate to have many great associates and customers, and it has been exciting to be part of the growth of our city and state. The atmosphere and ethics that exist in Nebraska and Iowa enable businesses like ours to grow and prosper.

homage to the state's railroading history, a dinner train from Fremont serves gourmet meals on a luxurious round-trip through the scenic Elkhorn River Valley.

And on the reservations of the Omahas, Winnebagos, Santee Sioux, and Poncas, annual festivals or powwows serve to both attract visitors and maintain a lasting link to the special heritage that has prevailed in

An estimated 60 million American bison once roamed the Great Plains. By 1900, only 500 to 1,500 were left. Managed herds such as this one on the Winnebago Indian Reservation are recalling the buffalo from the brink of extinction while reaffirming tribal ways.

northeast Nebraska since long before Meriwether Lewis and William Clark passed this way.

FIRST DATA CORPORATION Omaha, Nebraska

As one of the state's largest employers, First Data Corporation has a vested interest in a productive Nebraska. From our local roots we have created the world's leading credit and debit card processing company. Nebraska's friendly business environment has supported our growth through the years.

The state's excellent educational opportunities and quality of life make it a great place to live and do business. Our success, and that of our clients, is permanently linked to the human resources of Nebraska. It is with a sense of pride and satisfaction that employees of First Data call Nebraska home.

ABOVE: *Central Park Plaza has been a downtown Omaha landmark since its completion in 1982. Tenants in the twin 15-story towers include ConAgra, First National of Omaha's merchant processing operations, and other major businesses. Through decades of economic growth, Omaha has maintained the vitality of its urban core. About 90 percent of its office space was occupied in 1999.*

LEO A. DALY III Chairman and President, Leo A Daly

Leo A. Daly III—an architect licensed in 47 states, the District of Columbia, Australia, Guam, and the United Kingdom—is the third member of his family to head the Leo A Daly Company, one of the nation's largest privately held design firms. Following in the footsteps of his grandfather, Leo A. Daly Sr., and his father, Leo A. Daly Jr., Leo A. Daly III has continued to expand the Omaha-based firm's reach across the world.

Since becoming the company's chairman and president in 1981, Leo A. Daly III has established company offices in the United States in Atlanta, Georgia; Las Vegas, Nevada; Phoenix, Arizona; Austin, Texas; and Orlando, Florida; and overseas in Germany and Spain. He also engineered the firm's 1991 acquisition of Texas-based Lockwood, Andrews & Newnam, Inc., bringing the company's presence to Houston, Dallas, and San Antonio.

LEO A DALY
PLANNING
ARCHITECTURE
ENGINEERING
INTERIORS
EST.1915

ABOVE: *As one might expect in a place unofficially nicknamed "the Beef State," Nebraskans take their cuts of meat seriously. When it comes to steak houses, the best is a matter of debate. While* Gorat's, in central Omaha, is Warren Buffett's favorite, Johnny's Cafe, on the south side of town, has been around since 1922, and is considered one of the nation's top steak houses.

WILLIAM A. FITZGERALD Chairman of the Board and CEO, Commercial Federal Bank

Quality of life continues to be the leading reason so many companies and individuals are proud to call Nebraska home. Good schools, plenty of parks, wide-open spaces, clean air and water, affordable housing, and a low crime rate result in our state being consistently ranked by national publications as an ideal setting in which to raise a family.

Thanks to our stable economy, employment opportunities in major corporations are abundant, and conditions are fertile for continued small business growth. With roots firmly planted in Nebraskan soil, Commercial Federal Bank remains dedicated to helping people and businesses of this great state reach their financial goals.

WARREN STALEY President and CEO, Cargill, Incorporated

To Cargill, Incorporated, being a business leader means more than just marketing and processing agricultural and other commodities. It also means supporting efforts to enhance the communities where we operate. In Nebraska, Cargill has contributed more than $1 million during the last five years to nonprofit organizations and community initiatives. We have supported local fire and rescue programs, arts organizations like the Minden Opera House in Heartwell, and we have donated land to help Nebraska City develop a community center. Since 1995, Cargill has awarded $195,000 in scholarships to 169 college-bound Nebraska youth. In addition, Cargill employees have contributed thousands of volunteer hours. Being a good neighbor is a vital part of our business philosophy.

BELOW: *The popular food court at Oak View Mall overlooks an open, airy central court beneath a skylit dome. In addition to Oak View Mall, Omaha shopping destinations include Crossroads Mall,* *Rockbrook Village, and Westroads Mall. Together they offer dining and entertainment, personal services, and hundreds of top-name national chain stores and local retailers.*

A REGIONAL SAMPLER

C. L. WERNER Chairman, Chief Executive Officer, and founder, Werner Enterprises, Inc.

Nebraska is ideally situated at the crossroads of the nation, and it is a perfect location for a nationwide trucking company. With good proximity to major Interstate highways, it affords easy access for our drivers. Equally important, however, is the labor force of quality, hardworking people available to the company.

Since the pioneer days, Nebraska, and particularly Omaha, has served as a hub. Today, the state has a solid economic, regulatory, and political base for its transportation industry. These factors combine to make the choice obvious. Nebraska is the ideal place in which to do business.

BELOW: *Located in Omaha's handsomely restored art deco Union Station, the Durham Western Heritage Museum showcases the history of the city and surrounding areas with a multimedia presentation, an 85-foot-long model train layout, and vintage rail-cars. Life-size sculptures in the Main Waiting Room provide a glimpse of life in the 1930s, '40s, and '50s.*

ABOVE: *In the 1940s, Boys Town founder Father Edward Flanagan chose the image of two boys, one carrying the other, to symbolize the famous village outside Omaha that is now a haven for hundreds of abused, abandoned, and neglected children. Italian sculptor Enzo Plazzotta was commissioned in 1977 to create the* Two Brothers *statue, on which is inscribed the Boys Town motto, "He ain't heavy, Father . . . He's m' brother." In September 2000,* youngsters in the organization's care from coast to coast voted to apply the name Girls and Boys Town to its national programs and locations. OPPOSITE: *Starting in Ponca State Park and heading upstream, a 59-mile stretch of the Missouri is designated a National Recreation River. This part of Nebraska's northeastern shoulder offers vistas that Meriwether Lewis and William Clark must have seen when they first explored the region in 1804.*

CHAPTER TWO

THE PLATTE VALLEY

THE GREAT PLATTE RIVER ROAD

Nebraska takes its name (variant of an Otoe Indian term for "flat water") and much of its heritage from the wide,
shallow Platte River, which flows through the heart of the state to the Missouri River on the east. The Great Platte
River Road is one of the world's foremost natural highways, its broad, flat valley providing the way west in the 19th
century for the Oregon, Mormon, and California Trails, the Pony Express, and the first transcontinental railroad.

For many, the Platte Valley was not a route to the gold fields or the Pacific Northwest, but a destination in itself—a place to build a civilization of commerce, agriculture, learning, and living.

From the city of North Platte, where the two main branches of the river come together from Colorado and Wyoming, to the eastern urban areas of the state, the valley embraces a continuous sweep of cultivated land that has helped turn the arid prairies into the fifth largest global exporter of agricultural products in the United States. Along the way are colorful former frontier outposts such as Lexington, Kearney, Grand Island, Hastings,

York—each a landmark on the river road, most with roots intertwined with the Union Pacific Railroad, which operates the largest switching yard in the world at North Platte.

As the Platte River nears the Missouri, it flows midway between the state's two largest cities, Omaha and Lincoln. The latter is marked by the spectacular state capitol—"the Tower of the Plains"—and the University of Nebraska–Lincoln, an important research center and home of Nebraska's icon, the five-time national champion Cornhusker football team. Lincoln is one of the fastest

growing non–Sun Belt cities in the United States, its stable and diversified economy characterized by large employers in technology and information such as ALLTEL Corporation and the Gallup Organization, finance and insurance, pharmaceuticals, and traditional industries including Goodyear Tire and Rubber and the Burlington Northern and Santa Fe Railway (formerly the Burlington Northern Railroad). As befits a university city, Lincoln offers a variety of cultural experiences such as the Sheldon Memorial Art Gallery and Sculpture Garden, the prestigious Lied Center for the Performing Arts, and the State Museum of Natural History with permanent exhibits interpreting more than 12,000 years of plains life. The city is sprinkled with parks and lakes, and yields experiences as varied as

ABOVE: *The Great American Cattle Drive recalls Ogallala's historic status as the terminus of the Ogallala-Texas Cattle Trail. Ogallala meant payday for trail-weary cowpunchers, whose mischief sometimes earned them a plot on Boot Hill, the town's notorious cemetery.* OPPOSITE: *A wintry dawn over Duell County lends a bluish tint to the South Platte River's icy mantle.*

ABOVE: *Designed by Bertram Goodhue, the state capitol, with its 400-foot central tower, houses the nation's only unicameral legislature. Construction of the building spanned from 1922 to 1932, and* cost less than $10 million. OPPOSITE: *Every year from late February to early April, about 80 percent of the world's population of sandhill cranes gathers on the Platte River, near Kearney.*

SANDHILLS PUBLISHING COMPANY Lincoln, Nebraska

If you talk with more than a handful of people who make Lincoln, Nebraska, their home, you will hear the phrase "It's just right" more than once. Lincoln offers residents an appealing combination of metropolitan conveniences, a college town ambience, and small-city friendliness. Businesses find that Lincoln offers them an attractive mix, as well. Sandhills Publishing Company, which produces trade tabloids and consumer computer magazines, moved to Lincoln in 1985 because of the high quality workforce and storied midwestern work ethic. The central location also serves the company's shipping and telephone sales efforts well.

browsing the historic Haymarket district downtown or spending absorbing hours at the Children's Museum.

Lincoln is Nebraska's center for amateur competition. It annually hosts the boys' and girls' state high school championship tournaments for basketball and other school sports. Teams at the University of Nebraska are perennial national powers not only in football, but also in gymnastics, wrestling, women's volleyball, and other athletics. The Roller Skating National Museum is in Lincoln, as is Nebraska's State Fair, where blue ribbons for varied activities are abundantly awarded in late August and early September. There are also a few professional sports, headed by the Lincoln Stars in ice hockey and the Lincoln Lightning in arena football.

WHERE THE WEST BEGINS

Westward the Platte River Valley changes from gentle hills to flat expanses of prime irrigated cropland, which give way in turn to dryland pasture and hayfields. Geographically, the West begins officially where the 100th meridian passes through the center of the town of Cozad. Immigrants who settled this region came from Germany, Denmark, Bohemia, the British Isles, Sweden, and other northern and central European nations. Many came to build a railroad and stayed to build communities. Those who went on west left their marks, too—sometimes literally, as in the handcart and wagon ruts still visible at various sites along the Mormon and Oregon Trails.

One of America's most spectacular natural sights can be seen in a 40-mile section of the Platte between Grand

OPPOSITE: *The largest body of water between the Great Lakes and Great Salt Lake, Lake McConaughy features 100 miles of shoreline— plenty of room for powerboaters, sailors, windsurfers, and anglers.*

Island and Kearney. Every year in late winter, up to half a million sandhill cranes use the river and bordering wetlands as a migratory staging ground, drawing thousands of visitors. Man-made attractions line the river also, including a number of museums that keep Nebraska's heritage alive—the Stuhr Museum of the Prairie Pioneer in Grand Island, which features a railroad town where three movies have been shot; the restored Fort Kearny near Kearney, encapsulating much of frontier life; an original Pony Express station and recreated sod house at Gothenburg; and Scout's Rest Ranch at North Platte, the Victorian home of one of the state's most storied citizens, William F. "Buffalo Bill" Cody. In Ogallala, Boot Hill cemetery and Front Street, a re-creation of an Old West cattle town, preserve the character and pungency of cowboy life at the end of the trail. Mankind and nature collaborated just north of town to create resort-studded Lake McConaughy, a 35,000-acre impoundment of the North Platte River.

The flavor of life along the valley can be captured in one word: outdoor. From the State Fair in Lincoln to the annual Nebraskaland Days in North Platte, at rodeos, festivals, trail rides, campgrounds, and well-tended recreation areas in between, Nebraskans and their guests savor wide skies, fresh air, nature up close and personal. They taste fully the experiences and traditions of the travelers and settlers who laid the Great Platte River Road through the heart of America.

TERRY L. BUNDY Administrator and CEO, Lincoln Electric System

As a service provider, employer, corporate friend, and neighbor, the Lincoln Electric System (LES) is dedicated to providing energy and services of superior value and enhancing growth and development of the greater Lincoln area. The company provides a reliable supply of electricity—an essential component for growth—at some of the lowest rates in the nation. This assists in Lincoln's effort to bring new citizens, businesses, and industries to a city and state known for its neighborly ways and the good life it provides. LES has a strong foundation and possesses the strategies, infrastructure, and staff to help it remain one of the nation's leading utilities in the new millennium.

JOHN BRESLOW Chairman of the Board, Linweld

Nebraska offers a truly exemplary arena for business. From its central location to its attractive tax-incentive programs, this wonderful state continues to command the attention of companies from around the country.

But, without a doubt, true praise must be handed to Nebraska's dedicated, well-educated workforce. Our employees have defined and molded the favorable business environment of today and will continue to do so for future generations—a fact to which I attribute Linweld's success. Our employees believe in earning our customers' business every day. That says a lot for Nebraska.

CHAPTER THREE

NORTH CENTRAL

SANDHILLS CATTLE COUNTRY

You could hide Connecticut here. You could drive for days here and still miss many natural and man-made attractions. You could see everything that epitomizes the West, from ranches as large as 60,000 acres to restored frontier forts—and much that wouldn't seem to, from blues festivals to literary landmarks. You'd be in the storied Sandhills, some 20,000 square miles of north-central Nebraska comprising the largest dune field in the western

hemisphere. But you wouldn't see desert. The dunes are covered with a lush growth of grama grass, making the region Nebraska's most important cattle-grazing area. Far from being a Sahara, the Sandhills count abundant water resources as a primary asset. The countryside is sprinkled with hundreds of small lakes; it's refreshed by four rivers—the Niobrara, Snake, Dismal, and Loup—and sits atop 700 million acre-feet of water in the Ogallala Aquifer, the northern plains' enormous underground ocean. The land also supports two reserves of the Nebraska National Forest, at 325,000 acres the largest man-planted forest in the United States.

In the heart of the Sandhills is Cherry County, the biggest county in the nation, the size of Delaware and Rhode Island combined. Here the scenic Niobrara River, sporting virtually every kind of vegetation from cactus to alpine wildflowers, offers world-class canoeing adventures and other kinds of water-borne recreation. Near Valentine, the metropolis of the Sandhills with a population of 3,000, the Valentine National Wildlife Refuge provides shelter for nesting waterfowl, and the Fort Niobrara National Wildlife

Refuge preserves herds of bison and Texas longhorns in their natural habitat. Cherry County also boasts a long stretch of the bicyclist's daunting challenge, the Cowboy Trail, reaching more than 300 miles across northern Nebraska, the largest rails-to-trails conversion in America.

One of the region's most scenic attractions almost seems out of place among the endless vistas of grassland: Smith Falls, in a state park near Valentine. The sparkling, spring-fed cascade tumbles 75 feet from a forested canyon rim to the Niobrara River.

Traveling television personality Charles Kuralt said that State Highway 2, which skirts the Nebraska National Forest and carries motorists through such historic rangeland communities as Thedford, Mullen, and Hyannis, is one of the 10 most beautiful routes in the nation.

ABOVE: *Nebraska's most important cattle-grazing area sits atop a vast underground ocean, the Ogallala Aquifer, providing water for more native grasses than in any other state.* OPPOSITE: *Frosted sumac branches and tall pines frame the beauty of Snake River Falls, north of Merritt Reservoir State Recreation Area, in Cherry County.*

Every fall, the One Box Pheasant Hunt at Broken Bow draws sports-men from as far away as England. Hunting is allowed in season and with a permit in 300 state and federal areas throughout Nebraska.

AN HONORED WAY OF LIFE

It's only fitting that in a region where tending cattle is a principal occupation and an honored way of life, Nebraska's Big Rodeo held annually at Burwell is such a premier attraction that the grounds and arena have been designated a National Historic Site. Not as widely publicized, but no less fun, is the Cowboy Triathlon—golfing, calf-roping, and shotgun-shooting—staged at Hyannis every summer to raise money for charity. And among the many community celebrations, fairs, ethnic and historical observances, and western-flavored events held throughout the Sandhills, the town of Arnold contributes its bit of diversity in country-music territory with its annual blues festival.

For the people of the Sandhills, history is not a collection of events from the dim past. It's part of an unbroken, living continuum that now extends into a new century. You might expect to meet Old Jules, central figure in the fictionalized biography by Sandhills author Mari Sandoz, on a sidewalk in Valentine. You hear the echoes of bugles at Fort Hartsuff. At the Arthur Bowring Sandhills Ranch State Historical Park near Merriman, the past has vivid life in the present. The 12,000-acre spread, formerly the Bar 99, was donated to the state by the late Eve Bowring. While still a working ranch, its exhibits encapsulate the region, documenting the history of the cattle industry in Nebraska and the history and geology of the Sandhills. The ranch house displays an extensive collection of glassware and silver gathered on worldwide travels by Mrs. Bowring, who, among other attainments, was the first woman to represent Nebraska in the U.S. Senate.

What there is to do, see, live, and experience here is scattered like a handful of gems across the landscape itself—the tranquil oceans of rippling grass where time seems to stop. Nebraska folklorist Roger Welsch put it this way: "Any days you spend in the Sandhills are not taken off your lifetime allotment. It's so restful that God just gives them to you for free."

OPPOSITE: *Designated a National Scenic River by Congress in 1991, the Niobrara River is ranked among the top 10 canoeing rivers in the United States by* Backpacker *magazine.*

CHAPTER FOUR

THE SOUTHEAST

LAND OF THE PRAIRIE PIONEER

All of Nebraska properly could be called "the Land of the Prairie Pioneer," but the designation is particularly apt in the southeast where so much of the state's history and heritage is rooted and remembered. Magnificent Arbor Lodge in Nebraska City memorializes J. Sterling Morton, who originated Arbor Day in 1872, and Nebraska settlers who planted a million trees on the plains on the first Arbor Day. Arbor Lodge, one of the region's favorite

destinations for Nebraskans and tourists alike, was Morton's home for many years. Its meticulously land-scaped grounds reflect his commitment to turning Nebraska into "the Sylvan Queen of the Republic." The grounds, now a state historical park, include a 65-acre arboretum containing 260 varieties of trees and shrubs, a formal rose garden, and a garden of plants unique to the prairie. Centerpiece of the estate is Morton's 52-room neocolonial mansion, furnished mostly in Victorian and Empire style.

John Brown's Cave and Historical Village in Nebraska City marks the westernmost site on the Underground Railroad, a route established to help slaves escape the South in the period before the Civil War. Abolitionist John Brown is supposed to have visited the area several times in the 1850s. A cabin in the village, built in 1851, has been certified by the State Historical Society as the oldest building still standing in Nebraska. It's one of several historic structures in the village.

the Homestead Act took effect. The act of Congress would attract more than 100,000 settlers to Nebraska. The monument grounds include exhibits and audiovisual resources depicting the history and everyday life of the early homesteaders, including a restored one-room schoolhouse. A hiking trail meanders through the type of prairie lands and wooded areas that existed in the 1860s and past the graves of Freeman and his wife, Agnes, who lived on the homestead until Daniel's death in 1908.

Brownville, which began in 1854 as a steamboat landing, river crossing, and overland freight terminus, displays its colorful past in museums, historic homes and sites, galleries, theaters, and an imposing steamboat, the *Capt. Meriwether Lewis.*

ABOVE: *The federal Homestead Act of 1862 remained in effect until its repeal in 1976. It originally granted 160 acres to any adult head of a household who lived on and farmed the land, made improvements, and built a home, like this 1867 cabin at Homestead National Monument of America, near Beatrice.* OPPOSITE: *Stone Creek runs alongside one of many popular hiking and biking trails among the forests and bluffs of Platte River State Park, near Louisville.*

HOMESTEADERS REMEMBERED

A national monument near Beatrice stands on land claimed by Daniel Freeman on January 1, 1863, the day

The land is fertile and productive, supporting a thriving orchard industry near the Missouri River and yielding bumper crops of corn, soybeans, and alfalfa on fields spreading westward to the center of the state, north to Interstate 80, and to Nebraska's border with Kansas. Feedlots and dairy farms complement the crop-growing economy. While the region moves to the seasonal rhythms of agriculture, its commerce and industry provide jobs and nurture the state's reputation for progressive innovation. The Cooper Nuclear Power Plant near Brownville, one of the earliest installations of its kind, helps meet the region's and state's growing energy needs, and the little town of DeWitt is home to American Tool Companies, a worldwide industrial leader that began when a Danish immigrant blacksmith invented VISE-GRIP® locking pliers to help him in his work.

Nebraska owed much of its relatively rapid settlement to the influence of the railroads. This is apparent in this region, where on one stretch of the Burlington Northern and Santa Fe are towns named in alphabetical order—Clay Center, Deweese, Edgar, Fairfield, and so on—as the railroad promoted and organized settlements on its westward path. The trains, and earlier the covered wagons, brought a mixture of immigrants whose descendants still honor their

Southeast Nebraska's rich soil helps make the state a national leader in the production of alfalfa—shown here being harvested—as well as corn and soybeans. Roughly half of the state's 45.5 million acres of farmland is in crops.

cultural roots. The community of Wilber, for example, in 1987 was named by an act of Congress the National Czech Capital of the United States, and draws upwards of 40,000 visitors to its summer Czech festivals.

Between and all around the Fairburys, Wymores, Cretes, Genevas, and dozens of other communities that reflect the region's pioneer past, honor its diverse cultural origins, and energize its business and social life, lies the abundant land. A 19th-century promotional piece for the

Small hog farms like this one outside of Burr contribute an important share of Nebraska's livestock and livestock products, which account for about two-thirds of the state's agricultural income.

Burlington said of the soil: "You have only to tickle it with a plow and it will laugh a harvest that will gladden your hearts and make joyous your homes." The rich texture of life today in this Land of the Prairie Pioneer shows that that 1879 pamphleteer exaggerated only mildly.

RICHARD HINRICHS President and Chief Operating Officer, Gibraltar Packaging Group, Inc.

Our company's roots are in Hastings, Nebraska, and we can't think of a better place to be. Nebraska has provided our carton manufacturing company with opportunities and resources for growth since our founding in 1956. Our central location has allowed us to offer many value-added services to our customers, including manufacturing and warehousing of products to meet the just-in-time requirements of clients from coast to coast. But we feel it is the superior work ethic of Nebraska's people that allows us to continue our growth at or above our industry's average. We feel that these opportunities, and many others, make Nebraska the perfect place to start, build, and grow a business.

Great Plains Packaging
A Division of Gibraltar Packaging Group, Inc.

CHAPTER FIVE

SOUTH CENTRAL

PRAIRIE LAKES COUNTRY

Nebraska's most famous author, Willa Cather of Red Cloud, wrote, "By the end of the first autumn, that shaggy grass country had gripped me with a passion I have never been able to shake." Prairie Lakes Country and especially the Republican River Valley have been prominent settings in several of Cather's works—novels and stories which for much of the world were the first introduction to Nebraska.

This region, south of the Platte Valley and extending westward from the center of the state to Colorado and south to Kansas, is characterized by grassy hills and plains. Numerous large lakes, recreation areas, reservoirs, creeks, and rivers earn its reputation as a center for outdoor activities. Native Americans favored the area for hunting, and so did at least one international sportsman of the 19th century: The Camp Duke Alexis Recreation Area near Hayes Center offers its attractions on the site where in 1872 the Grand Duke Alexis of Russia came hunting bison and other game in a party led by William F. "Buffalo Bill" Cody and hosted by Gen. Philip Sheridan.

the present town of Benkelman. They were attacked at dawn by some 700 warriors led by Pawnee Killer. Custer ran from his tent into the thick of the battle. He escaped unwounded, to meet his fate nine years later at the Little Big Horn. Benkelman later was to be the hometown of another "cavalryman" — Ward Bond, who played John Wayne's sidekick in epic western movies and the wagon master in the television show *Wagon Train*.

This was prime buffalo country, and as such provided the setting for a rich share of Nebraska's Native American lore and history, which still echoes in such observances as the annual Massacre Canyon Pow-Wow, held at the site near Trenton of the final

RENDEZVOUS WITH DESTINY

Prairie Lakes Country provided the stage for another noteworthy encounter, between a group of Sioux and Cheyenne and a man whose name looms large in Plains history. In 1867 Lt. Col. George A. Custer and his men were camped on the Republican River just south of

ABOVE: *A prairie schooner crowns the entrance to Harold Warp Pioneer Village in Minden, where more than 50,000 historical items, displayed in 26 buildings, trace the building of a nation since 1830.*
OPPOSITE: *Loess cliffs carved by the Republican River in Webster County show how the sedimentary layer, deposited by wind during the Pleistocene age, maintains nearly vertical walls when eroded.*

Erected in 1883, the State Bank Building in Red Cloud is now occupied by the law offices of Garwood and Offner. The Willa Cather Foundation is restoring the 1885 opera house located next door.

battle between the Pawnee and Sioux. Descendants of the Plains settlers celebrate their own ethnic-cultural identity, too, with such fetes as the annual German Heritage Days and a yearly pageant of the American Historical Society of Germans from Russia, both in McCook.

A CROPLAND CORNUCOPIA

Wheat, corn, alfalfa, and oats are principal crops of the region; nonarable land is used mainly as cattle range. To illustrate the transformation of the open prairie into a cropland cornucopia, Phelps County in 1997 was one of Nebraska's top five counties in agricultural sales—a far cry from Cather's "shaggy grass."

From Holdrege in the east to Imperial in the west, the region is dotted with small communities, each serving as a market center for its surrounding area and each adding its unique cultural-social hue to the tapestry of south-central Nebraska. In McCook, for example, the High Plains Museum's collections offer a rare look at

"POW art"—paintings by some of the German prisoners of war who were housed in a camp between McCook and Indianola in World War II.

The prairie lakes, which give the region its flavor and make it a popular recreation destination, are to a large extent a reflection of Nebraskans' ingrained sense of stewardship. Many water features were developed as conservation and irrigation measures. Reflected also is the progressive spirit of McCook's George W. Norris, known as the father of the Tennessee Valley Authority and the Rural Electrification Administration, and named by the U.S. Senate as one of the five greatest members ever to serve in the body. McCook also has given Nebraska three governors—Ralph Brooks, Frank Morrison, and Ben Nelson.

Incidentally, the Republican River, natural centerpiece of the region, was not named as an exercise in partisan politics. It won its designation early in the 19th century from French fur traders and Spanish officials in Louisiana who thought that the Kitkehahki tribe in the valley showed a frame of mind that would be called "republican" in the European sense. The spirit lives on among today's Prairie Lakes residents who are proud to be dependent on soil, water, and little else.

ABOVE: *Sunset silhouettes a tractor and tank at the end of a long day of spring fieldwork. Nearly 95 percent of the land in the state is in agricultural use; except for the Sandhills, all of it is intensely cultivated.* BELOW: *The loess plains of south-central Nebraska contain some of the most productive soil in the world. Wheat fields like this one make this the nation's breadbasket.*

CHAPTER SIX

THE PANHANDLE

PINE RIDGE AND TRAILS WEST

Nebraska's Panhandle, comprising nearly a quarter of the state's area, can be characterized by a word familiar to

Plains dwellers: big. In the Pine Ridge country in the northwest corner of the state are immensities that have to

be seen to be comprehended, including the 22,000-acre Fort Robinson State Park, the 95,000-acre Oglala National

Grassland, and the 972-acre Chadron State Park. South of the Pine Ridge in Trails West territory stand Chimney

Rock, Scotts Bluff National Monument, Court House Rock, Jail Rock—towering geologic formations that signaled to early travelers that their trek across the endless plains was near an end.

FROM THE HISTORIC TO THE PREHISTORIC

The Panhandle's past is counted in millennia and recorded as well in historic events scarcely more than a century old. The Agate Fossil Beds National Monument south of Harrison exhibits remnants of animals extinct for 19 million years. A simple monument at Fort Robinson near Crawford marks the death there in 1877 of the great Chief Crazy Horse.

Unlike many frontier Army posts, Fort Robinson didn't go out of business when the Plains wars ended; it was an active military establishment from 1874 to 1948, serving as, among other things, a training center for the Army's equestrian team, a World War II K-9 Corps dog-training center, and a camp for German prisoners of war. A museum operated by the State Historical Society in the old post headquarters features exhibits spanning the entire history of the fort. Conspicuous by its absence, here and in all other Western museums, is any depiction of the region's most

famous figure, Crazy Horse. He never allowed himself to be photographed.

The area north of Crawford is home to two of the strangest archaeological sites in the West. The Hudson-Meng Bison Bone Bed contains the skeletons of some 600 bison that died at the same time about 10,000 years ago. Scientists have been unable to pin down what happened—a stampede over a cliff, a prairie fire, a winter storm. Nearby is the moonlike landscape of Toadstool Geologic Park, created when erosion sculpted the residue of prehistoric volcanoes into fantastic shapes. Fossilized footprints of ancient creatures still can be seen in the park.

A marker near Morrill commemorates one of the most significant events in Native American history, the

ABOVE: *Due to a scarcity of timber, pioneers built sod houses, using plows to slice the virgin grassland into bricks weighing as much as 100 pounds. Bound together with buffalo grass or bluestem, "soddies" have been known to last 70 years.* OPPOSITE: *A storm brewing over Oglala National Grassland hints at the extremes of weather in the Panhandle. Three-foot-thick walls insulated soddies and their occupants against both summer heat and winter cold.*

The center-pivot irrigator, shown here, was invented in Nebraska. The western portion of the state relies on irrigation to grow specialty crops such as dry edible beans and sugar beets.

gathering in 1851 of more than 10,000 Sioux, Blackfeet, Crow, Assiniboin, Mandan, Gros Ventre, Arikara, Cheyenne, and Arapahoe to conclude the first Treaty of Fort Laramie. It was the largest recorded assembly of native people in American history.

WIDE-OPEN SPACES—AND OPPORTUNITIES

Today, Trails West country is Nebraska's primary wheat-producing area and also yields crops of alfalfa and potatoes. Its irrigated acres, freshened by water from the North Platte River and giant reservoirs in Wyoming, provide a base for the state's sugar beet industry. Though the region's main industries are agriculture and tourism, since 1951 more than 1,400 oil wells have been developed in Kimball County.

Busy communities such as Alliance, Ogallala, and Scottsbluff offer business opportunities, employment, and retail development in the wide-open spaces. One of the region's most distinctive businesses is Cabela's, a world leader in outfitting. Headquartered at Sidney, the company ships its sporting goods and outdoor gear across the United States and to nearly 100 foreign countries.

Quality of life in the Panhandle is as rich and varied as its scenery of buttes, canyons, ridges, and prairie. Leisure-time activities range all the way from exploring the geology of Ash Hollow State Historic Park to bird-watching among the wetlands of Lake Crescent National Wildlife Refuge to rigorous mountain bicycling in mile-high Chadron State Park.

Wagon-train immigrants and early settlers realized when they reached Pine Ridge/Trails West country that they had not only arrived at a momentous milepost on the way west; they had reached a destination that could provide home, livelihood, and a uniquely free and open way of living that would endure into new centuries and a beckoning millennium.

The blacksmith shop and paddocks at Fort Robinson State Park are vestiges of its history as a cavalry post and quartermaster remount depot. During World War II, the fort kept a herd of 12,000 horses.

PART TWO

VISTAS OF OPPORTUNITY

Nebraska used its Trans-Mississippi and International Exposition of 1898 to say goodbye to one century and proclaim its vision for the next. Now at the close of another century and the beginning of a millennium, the Cornhusker State can inventory its achievements proudly and look ahead confidently to a new era of growth and prosperity.

Producing food for an increasingly crowded planet remains Nebraska's chief mission. But increased efficiency, new technology, and economies of scale in agriculture and food processing have enabled most Nebraskans to turn their resources and imaginations to nonfarm endeavors. Meanwhile, the state's and its communities' aggressive initiatives in economic development have helped open new vistas of opportunity. Manufacturing has become Nebraska's second leading industry, and it's anticipated that the largest growth in employment over the next few years will be in telecommunications industries.

Nebraskans have preserved prudently their natural treasures of fertile soil, abundant water, and clean air. They have established business incentives that have brought a resurgence of commerce and industry. And along the way they have created one of America's most livable and attractive places in which to do business and raise families.

Atop the 400-foot-tall state capitol, overlooking the city of Lincoln, sculptor Lee Lawrie's bronze statue The Sower *symbolizes Nebraska's chief industry, agriculture, and the duty of government to sow the seeds of prosperity and a better life for all.*

CHAPTER SEVEN

PANTRY ON THE PLAINS

AGRICULTURE AND FOOD PROCESSING

By the time Maj. Stephen Long of the Army engineers recorded his assessment of Nebraska in 1820—"of course uninhabitable by a people depending on agriculture for their subsistence"—he already had been proven wrong. The first Nebraskans developed a corn-and-bean horticulture starting about AD 1200; the early Pawnees, for example, were basically a farming people, raising pumpkins and squash as well as corn and beans.

Within 40 years of Long's and others' dismissal of this land as "the Great American Desert," settlers from the East had begun building what is today one of the world's leading centers of agricultural production. By the time of the Civil War, 120,000 acres of Nebraska soil were under cultivation, raising nearly 1.5 million bushels of corn a year. Less than 30 years later, Nebraskans had broken and tamed 15 million acres, and corn production had risen to 216 million bushels, fourth highest in America.

A BILLION BUSHELS OF CORN

Through drought, depression, and dust bowl, through floods and blizzards and the grasshopper years, the Cornhusker State has turned itself into a powerhouse of food production. As the second millennium came to an end, Nebraska had 46.4 million acres in farms, more than 19.4 million acres of it in crops yielding annually more than 1.1 billion bushels of corn, 86 million bushels of wheat, 181 million bushels of soybeans, 1.2 million tons of sugar beets, and 42.8 million bushels of sorghum grain. It was the nation's top producer of Great Northern beans, second in alfalfa meal, third in corn and sorghum

grain, fifth in soybeans, sixth in winter wheat, and eighth in sugar beets. The state also leads the nation in beef and pork production, slaughtering almost seven billion pounds a year.

Nebraska's livestock industry traces its beginnings to "road ranches" along the Platte River valley as early as 1859—ranches that raised working oxen and a few cattle. After the Civil War, substantial numbers of Texas longhorns began appearing in Nebraska, mainly as commuters, driven north to such Union Pacific railheads as Ogallala for shipment east. By the mid-1880s, the big cattle drives from Texas were coming to an end, victims of new quarantine and herd laws.

At about the same time, Nebraskans began raising cattle themselves, adding important new wrinkles of their own. The tough, rangy longhorns gave way to more palatable and marketable blooded stock—Shorthorns, Herefords, Angus—while the open range yielded to fenced pasture, feed supplements were added

This feed lot in Nemaha County supplies livestock for Nebraska's commercial hog slaughter, which increased to 6.4 million head in 1999, accounting for 6.3 percent of the national total.

to the grass diet, and cattlemen began raising large amounts of hay for feed. The beef census grew to 6.7 million head by 1999, second highest in the nation, and Nebraska counted more than three million hogs in its livestock inventory.

Fertile soil and abundant water have been dependable resources in building this dominant position in agriculture, and Nebraskans realized early the value of prudently husbanding their natural treasures. By 1950, all of the state's farm and ranch land was included in soil and water conservation districts. Irrigation began well before the end of the 19th century; in 1889 some 11,000 acres were being watered. The number grew to nearly three million by 1965, and to more than eight million by 1999. About four-fifths is pump-irrigated by ground-water, chiefly from the vast Ogallala Aquifer, and the rest

Nebraska is a leader in the development and application of new agricultural technology such as sophisticated weather sensor systems for regulating irrigation.

by surface water from reservoirs and such streams as the Platte, Loup, and Republican Rivers.

Finding new ways to conduct one of the world's oldest industries also has been a hallmark of Nebraska's agricultural growth. In many other respects a cautious and conservative people, Nebraska's farmers and ranchers have been quick to invent or adopt innovative approaches, often with the assistance and research leadership of the University of Nebraska, which opened its College of Agriculture in 1882 and its first experimental station four years later. Typifying the state's tradition of innovation was the invention in 1948 of the center-pivot irrigator, which revolutionized the nurturing of crops as the introduction of the tractor had revolutionized their planting and tilling. Today Nebraska is the nation's largest producer and user of these devices.

By the end of the 20th century, food and kindred products accounted for nearly $1 billion of Nebraska's exports to some 140 different nations; aggressive promotion by state

About 55,000 farms and ranches cover 95 percent of Nebraska's total land area; three out of four farms maintain livestock or poultry operations; and agricultural cash receipts exceeded $8.8 billion in 1998.

government, producers' organizations, and agribusinesses is expected to build foreign markets even further. Also expected to grow is the size of the average Nebraska farm: In 1982 it was 746 acres; in 1999 it was 844. The average farmer's investment in machinery and equipment grew from $68,000 in 1982 to $84,535 in 1997.

Control of the land has been a concern in Nebraska from the days when sodbusters squared off against cattlemen to the present era of farm consolidation and modernization. Nebraskans are explicit about maintaining their family-farm heritage: The state constitution contains a strong prohibition against corporate farming, a measure intended to discourage food-producing monopolies and give future Nebraskans the opportunity to share in the bounty of the land.

Major Long, the explorer who wrote off Nebraska's future as an agricultural producer, might have tempered his remarks had he seen the prophecy of an even earlier observer. John Bradbury, the great English naturalist, wrote in 1817: "In the process of time, it will not only be peopled and cultivated, but it will be one of the most beautiful countries in the world."

FROM FARM TO TABLE

Growing in tandem with Nebraska's rise as an agricultural production power has been the state's capacity to process

Nebraska ranked first in the United States in commercial red meat production with a total of 6.9 billion pounds in 1999.

and sell its crops and livestock. Some of the largest and most profitable food processing businesses in the world are headquartered in Nebraska or have significant operations here, providing ready markets for farmers and livestock feeders and providing jobs in both large and small communities. Across Nebraska their large-scale enterprises are complemented by businesses providing a range of food products as diverse as organically

A POCKETFUL OF WHEAT

Nebraska owes its status as a leading wheat producer in part to smugglers— Mennonite settlers who came to the south-central part of the state from Russia in the 1870s and 1880s with small quantities of Turkey Red winter wheat seeds secreted in their clothing and household belongings. Turkey Red and other hard varieties further developed by the University of Nebraska, along with refinements in milling processes, made winter wheat a strong second crop, after corn, by 1899.

Although Francisco Vásquez de Coronado came to Nebraska in 1541 under the impression that it offered vast treasures of gold, mineral resources have not been among this agricultural state's chief assets—except for unique local versions of marble and coal. "Nebraska marble" was what early settlers called the bricks of turf with which they built sod houses, and "Nebraska coal" was the buffalo chips they used for fuel.

Nebraska, which produces and uses more center-pivot irrigators than any other state, has approximately 8.1 million acres of pasture and cropland under irrigation.

grown pasta ingredients, popcorn, party snacks, seasonings, and even items as exotic as ostrich jerky.

In the late 19th and early 20th centuries, the local flour mill was a centerpiece of Nebraska "agribusiness." This industry provided the beginnings of one of the state's—and world's—largest food conglomerates. In 1919, four local mills combined to form Nebraska Consolidated Mills, headquartered in Grand Island. Eighty years later, this modest enterprise has become ConAgra, an Omaha-based giant with more than 82,000 employees in 32 countries and net sales of nearly $13 billion in the first half of 1999.

The scale of its food processing industry is commensurate with Nebraska's leadership in agricultural production. For example, here are Ag Processing, Inc. (AGP), the largest cooperative soybean processing company in the world,

third largest supplier of refined vegetable oil in the nation, and third largest commercial feed manufacturer in North America, and major packing operations of IBP, Inc., world's largest producer of fresh beef and pork and the state's largest private employer. Nebraska also is home to large installations of such nationally known food processors as Cargill, Hormel, and Farmland Foods.

As Nebraska's farm- and ranch-based economy grows into the third millennium, it confronts the same variables that have characterized agriculture since the original occupants of the Cornhusker State planted their first seeds—weather, prices, market availability, inventing or adopting new technology. Nebraskans have no doubt that the imagination and hard work that transformed their "desert" into a prime source of food for a nation and the world will overcome any challenges a new age can bring.

In 1999 Nebraska ranked eighth among the states in production of sugar beets (1.3 million tons), and third or better in Great Northern beans, alfalfa meal, corn and sorghum grain, and pinto beans.

'HEROES OF THE PLANET'

Nebraska's Groundwater Foundation, begun in 1985 as a volunteer effort to raise public awareness of the necessity of safeguarding underground water resources, has grown into a global influence, counting members all across the United States and in 27 other countries. In 1999 the foundation and its originator, Susan Seacrest of Lincoln, were honored by *Time* magazine as "heroes of the planet."

AGRICULTURE/FOOD PROCESSING>>

CARGILL CORN MILLING

Grinding 170,000 bushels of corn daily to produce a variety of food, feed, and fuel ingredients, Cargill Corn

Milling has found great success with its corn wet milling plant in Blair.

Cargill Corn Milling's wet milling plant in Blair, Nebraska, opened in 1995 to process Nebraska and Iowa corn into food, feed, and fuel ingredients that reach consumers through thousands of familiar products every day. The gleaming white facility currently grinds 170,000 bushels of corn daily to make the following:

- High fructose corn syrup, used in products such as soft drinks, candy, cookies, canned goods, and fruit juices;
- Corn oil, which is further refined by food processors and vegetable oil manufacturers in the United States and abroad;
- Sweet Bran™60, a premium livestock feed utilized and in demand by customers across the Midwest;
- Corn gluten meal, produced for foreign and domestic manufacturers of poultry feed and pet food; and
- Fuel grade ethanol, which is blended with gasoline by refiners to make motor vehicle fuel more environmentally friendly.

The teamwork and spirit that make the facility a safe, pleasant, and productive workplace spill over into the Blair community through employees' volunteer activities. The people of Cargill's Team Blair donated more than 12,000 hours of charitable service in 1999 through such activities as visiting senior citizens, coaching kids' sports, and helping youth understand environmental issues through special programs. Team Blair also makes financial

Cargill Blair employees take a team approach to providing customer solutions.

grants to support educational, environmental, cultural, and social projects and organizations in the community.

Cargill chose the 650-acre site just south of Blair for its fifth U.S. corn wet milling plant because of the availability of corn, its easy access to highways and railroads, and its excellent pool of highly qualified people to train as operations technicians. In addition there has been—and continues to be—strong state and local government support for sustainable industry that enhances economic development in Nebraska.

RAPID GROWTH AND EXPANSION

At grand opening ceremonies in 1995, Cargill announced that it already had begun an expansion of the plant to increase corn processing capacity from 120,000 to 170,000 bushels a day. Since 1997, Cargill has formed 50/50 joint ventures at the Blair facility with four other global companies to manufacture products through the fermentation of dextrose acquired from the corn milling plant.

While joint venture partners bring technologies and market savvy to a variety of value-added products, Cargill Corn Milling's contributions are consistently based on the same core competencies—plant engineering,

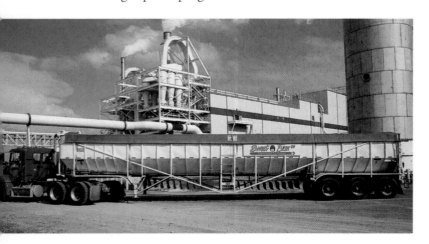

Sweet Bran™ 60 feed ingredient is used by Blair area cattle feeders.

construction and operation, fermentation capabilities, access to raw materials, risk management, and strong programs in quality, and food safety.

PGLA-1, a joint venture with the PURAC company of the Netherlands, opened a plant in 1998 at the Blair campus to make lactic acid, a naturally occurring organic acid that offers both food and industrial applications. A PURAC-owned plant next door uses lactic acid from the PGLA-1 plant to make such products as sodium lactate and potassium lactate for the food industry.

Another joint venture involves Cargill and Mitsubishi Chemical Company of Japan. This joint venture—M&C Sweeteners—opened its plant in 1999 at the Blair campus to make the new low calorie sweetener called erythritol.

Midwest Lysine, a joint venture with Degussa Hüls AG of Germany, opened a plant in 2000 at the Blair campus to produce Biolys^{R}60, a premium form of feed-grade lysine.

In January 2000, Cargill Dow Polymers (CDP), a joint venture of Cargill and The Dow Chemical Company, announced it would build a $300-million plant that will use corn-derived dextrose to make polylactide (PLA) polymers for the manufacture of clothes, cups, carpeting, plastic packaging, and other everyday products. This plant is expected to open in 2001.

The CDP plant will bring total investment at the Blair site to more than $825 million while increasing 1999 employment of 450 people by about 100. Cargill's ongoing search for new uses for corn is sure to mean continuing growth for the Cargill campus at Blair.

CARGILL IN NEBRASKA

Cargill came to Nebraska in 1927, when it opened a grain-buying office in Omaha. Today five different

High fructose corn syrup is an ingredient used in a variety of popular beverages.

Cargill businesses with 3,400 employees are represented in 31 Nebraska communities.

The animal nutrition business has feed plants in Grand Island and Duncan. The seed group has a distribution center in Grand Island and a service center in Seward. Excel Corporation, a Cargill subsidiary, has meat processing plants in Schuyler and Nebraska City. Cargill Corn Milling has a plant in Blair and is a partner in four joint ventures there, and the grain division has 14 elevators and nine fertilizer facilities in the state.

Since 1995, Cargill has contributed $1 million to support educational and quality-of-life programs in Nebraska communities.

CARGILL'S HISTORY

Cargill was founded in 1865 when William Wallace Cargill, the son of a retired Scottish sea captain, opened a small grain warehouse in northeastern Iowa.

Today Cargill Incorporated, based in Wayzata, Minnesota, near Minneapolis, is an international marketer, processor, and distributor of agricultural, food, financial, and industrial products and services with approximately 82,000 employees in 59 countries.

Cargill's vision is to raise the quality of living standards around the world by delivering increased value to producers and consumers.

Cargill's Blair plant is located near a cornfield just south of town.

CARGILL DOW LLC

Utilizing a revolutionary new technology, Cargill Dow LLC is creating a new method of producing common plastics and fibers with a most unlikely key ingredient—corn.

Cargill Dow is producing polymers created entirely out of Nebraska field corn.

Cargill Dow LLC, a 50/50 joint venture of Cargill Incorporated and The Dow Chemical Company, is revolutionizing the way businesses and consumers look at some of the most commonly used materials in the world—plastics and fibers. The company makes these materials out of annually renewable resources, such as corn. Cargill Dow has already broken ground for its first world-class production facility at the current Cargill site in Blair, Nebraska.

Finding new and innovative uses for corn has long been a goal of Cargill. This dream took a significant step forward when the company discovered how to make polymers out of natural plant sugars and then joined forces with Dow in 1997 to make the dream a commercial reality. The result was the formation of Cargill Dow, which has offices in Minnetonka, Minnesota; Midland, Michigan; Europe; and Japan. The company plans to use Nebraska-grown field corn as the base feedstock for its revolutionary technology, manufacturing the feedstock for use in a wide range of domestic and international markets.

The new technology, called NatureWorks™ PLA, uses corn-derived dextrose to make polylactide (PLA) polymers for use in natural-based fibers, plastic packaging, and many other everyday products. Cargill Dow is the first company in the world to offer its customers a family of polymers derived entirely from annually renewable resources, which are in turn, able to compete with

hydrocarbon-based fibers and packing materials on a cost and performance basis.

The new manufacturing facility will be located on the site of Cargill's corn wet milling plant in Blair and is set to come onstream in late 2001. The new facility will offer an annual capacity of 140,000 metric tons of NatureWorks PLA polymers. Cargill Dow's plant will enhance the already booming economic development impact of Cargill's Blair campus and will bring the total investment at the Blair site to more than $825 million.

What makes this new technology so exciting is its breadth of applications and the fact that it comes from an annually renewable resource. NatureWorks PLA offers the opportunity to truly develop sustainable business platforms because the raw material can be regenerated year after year, is cost competitive, and is environmentally responsible. In addition, it represents a new use for one of Nebraska's leading agricultural resources—corn.

Once operational, the new plant and technology are expected to grow and expand in conjunction with the dramatic global interest that is making NatureWorks PLA the breakthrough polymer of the 21st century.

Cargill Dow LLC
Where performance comes naturally™

Cargill's unique polymer, called NatureWorks™ PLA, can be used in a wide range of fibers and packaging applications.

EXCEL CORPORATION

One of the leading red meat processors in North America, Excel Corporation has been processing beef in Nebraska since 1975 and continues to offer premium quality beef for today's busy consumer.

Excel Corporation adds value to Nebraska agriculture by producing beef that meets the needs of today's consumers.

From Excel's fresh beef plant in Schuyler, Nebraska, come branded products such as Sterling Silver®. Served in five-star restaurants and sold at selected grocery chains, Sterling Silver is billed as great tasting beef time after time—addressing consumer demands for a consistently excellent eating experience.

At its Excel Specialty Products facility in Nebraska City, Nebraska, Excel produces fully cooked meats for the food service and retail food industries. In the retail category, Excel Specialty Products offers a line of precooked Butcher & Cook's brand entrees that fit the lifestyles of time-starved consumers.

Based in Wichita, Kansas, Excel is one of the leading red meat processors in North America. The red meat business division of Cargill Incorporated, Excel has processed beef in Nebraska since 1975, when it acquired its facility in Nebraska City. In 1987, Excel acquired and began operating the plant in Schuyler. Excel's other plants in the United States are located in Arkansas, California, Colorado, Georgia, Illinois, Iowa, Kansas, Texas, Missouri, and Massachusetts.

The Excel team in Schuyler is 1,950 employees strong. A major contributor to the area's economy, the payroll totals approximately $46 million a year.

Excel-Schuyler purchases about one million grain-fed cattle a year—an amount that represents an annual procurement of payments to cattle producers of approximately $900 million. Most of the cattle are purchased within a 200-mile radius of the plant.

Excel-Schuyler produces, in addition to many other products, fresh wholesale portions of beef and sells them to food service distributors and retail chains, who then cut the product into appropriate sizes to sell at restaurants and grocery stores.

A growing share of Schuyler's fresh meat is exported, and Japan is one of the major destinations. The export markets allow Excel to find the best price for all of the meat it produces, which in turn enhances the value of the cattle Excel purchases.

Excel Specialty Products in Nebraska City employs approximately 330 people—more than double the workforce since the new facility opened in 1995. Annual payroll totals $7.6 million.

Whether it's a great tasting steak from beef produced at Excel in Schuyler or a tender pot roast from Excel Specialty Products in Nebraska City, Excel is adding value to basic agricultural commodities by developing products that meet the needs of today's consumer.

The Butcher & Cook's line of cooked meat entrees is produced at Excel's Nebraska City plant.

Excel features a state-of-the-art meat processing facility in Nebraska City.

EXCEL®
A CARGILL FOODS company

JOHN DAY COMPANY

Committed to customer satisfaction, the John Day Company of Omaha, Nebraska, is a family-run business that sells agricultural, industrial, safety, and material handling tools, products, and services.

John Day Company's headquarters is located at 6263 Abbot Drive in Omaha, Nebraska.

With a philosophy of customer service that has endured through nearly a century, the John Day Company is a business that responds to industry changes by reinventing itself when needed.

John F. Day started his working career as a travelling salesman in an agricultural implement firm in Omaha in 1906. In 1909, with a little capital and a clear vision, he struck out on his own and began selling farm implements, which were then shipped by a factory he contracted with. It was a simple concept that provided the foundation to the flourishing wholesaler-distributor business that it eventually became.

Today, the John Day Company is headquartered in Omaha with offices in Lincoln and Columbus, Nebraska; Ankeny, Iowa; Milan, Illinois; and Redwood Falls, Minnesota. It now has 120 employees in five branches and represents more than 1,800 manufacturers. In addition, more than 55,000 SKUs (stock-keeping units) are featured in the John Day Company's extensive catalogs.

The Agricultural Division has provided the base for the John Day Company for more than 90 years. And for years, the John Day Company has focused primarily on serving high quality agricultural products and services to its customers, which include implement dealers, machine and welding shops, and short line equipment dealers.

What has helped make the John Day Company so successful is its capacity to help its customers before and after the product is sold.

GROWTH AND DIVERSIFICATION

Currently, the Industrial Division is the John Day Company's most rapidly growing division. The company has become increasingly diversified and now the Industrial Division's sales equal that of the Agricultural Division. The purchase of Sharp Edge Tool, Inc., based in Crescent, Iowa, has further diversified the company. Sharp Edge Tool is a full-service tool grinding and tool modification shop that serves the cutting and metal working industry by grinding customer's standard cutting tools to their exact specifications.

"In the field, our staff analyzes customer's problems and helps change the situation to solve that problem," says John Fonda, company president and CEO. "Basically, we make their tools last longer. This is an

John Day Company's Industrial Division provides complete tool resharpening services, using state-of-the-art CNC equipment.

added value benefit offered to our present customers. We sell the product and can also service that product later."

Cutting tools and abrasives are a large part of the Industrial Division. The John Day Company represents more than 50 different high quality manufacturers. The highly trained staff includes two cutting tool specialists. "Meeting the customer's expectations is a crucial component in assuring customer satisfaction. Our staff solves the problem and cuts costs by finding the best tool for each specific application," says Fonda.

The Safety Products Division was organized in 1997. Some of the items this division provides include personal protective clothing, respiratory devices, fall protection, industrial hygiene products, and environmental compliance products. The addition of this division has helped to further diversify the company.

CUSTOMER SERVICE AND SATISFACTION

John Day Company's Materials Handling and Power Transmission Division was created to assist in offering a more developed line of material handling and power transmission products and services. Additional services offered include layout and design of conveyor systems; belt fabrication and vulcanization; drive design; and industrial hose fabrication. Emphasis is placed on supporting the sales of motors, sprockets, belts, sheaves, reducers, bearings, hoists, pallet racking, shelving, and many other power transmission and material handling related products.

In addition to an enormous variety of products, the John Day Company delivers services that also assure customer satisfaction. One key service is called integrated supply and systems contracting. This service allows the company to efficiently implement and service integrated supply programs and innovative procurement solutions with its customers.

ADVANCING TECHNOLOGY

Technology is the clear and chosen path to the future for the John Day Company. A company that formerly handled all business aspects manually, John Day has implemented numerous technological advances. Data retrieval systems now enhance all levels of the organization. These sophisticated systems speed up communication between distributor and customer and enhance cost reduction efforts.

Two recent advances have included the use of bar coding and data mining. Bar coding has automated shipping and receiving while improving accuracy in compiling customer orders. Data mining is a computer process that allows distributors to work with multiple databases. The sales department uses data mining extensively to target potential markets, product groups, and customers, thus expanding the client base.

In the past decade, the John Day Company has reinvented the manner in which it satisfies its customers. This advancement has largely been accomplished through technological advances. "In the past five years, our business has been dramatically changing," says Fonda. "We can do so many more things than ever before. In 1992 my father, Jere Fonda, encouraged me to do what I needed with the company. He told me, 'Make your own footprints.'"

The fifth generation of the Day family now runs the business, which has continued to progress with the changing needs of the industry it serves. Technology is the impetus that will continue the success of this service-oriented family-run business.

TOP: *John Day Company's Agricultural Division provides equipment and replacement parts to implement dealers, machine and welding shops, and short line equipment dealers throughout the Midwest.* LEFT: *The company's Industrial Division distributes maintenance, repair, and operations (MRO) products, along with technical support, to manufacturers, municipalities, packing plants, food processors, contractors, and government institutions.*

CONAGRA, INC.

The second largest food company in North America and the fourth largest in the world, ConAgra, Inc., headquartered in Omaha, is a multifaceted industry leader that remains committed to its mission of feeding people better.

The 30-acre world headquarters campus of ConAgra, Inc., is located in downtown Omaha.

One of the world's leading food companies is headquartered in Omaha, Nebraska. ConAgra operates across the food chain and around the world. The company's products range from convenient prepared foods for today's consumers to supplies needed by farmers.

ConAgra is the second largest retail food supplier in North America and largest North American provider of products for restaurants, fast-food outlets, and other food-service customers. With operations in 34 countries and annual sales of approximately $25 billion, ConAgra employs about 80,000 people worldwide, including 6,500 in more than 50 locations across Nebraska.

ConAgra's well-known food brands are found on the shelves of nearly every section of the supermarket, along with hundreds of other food products made with ingredients supplied by ConAgra.

NEBRASKA HERITAGE

ConAgra was founded in 1919 in Grand Island, Nebraska, when four flour mills were consolidated and incorporated as Nebraska Consolidated Mills (NCM). In 1922, NCM relocated to Omaha for better access to Omaha's grain markets and its extensive railroad network. In 1951, NCM developed Duncan Hines cake mixes, named after a popular restaurant critic, and in 1956 it sold the business to Procter & Gamble. With the profit, NCM expanded by opening a flour and feed mill in Puerto Rico in 1957 and then entering the poultry processing industry in 1961. By 1971, NCM had become much more than a flour milling company and had outgrown its name. NCM became ConAgra, Inc., a derivation meaning "with the land" to signify the company's growth and partnership with the land. In the 1980s and 1990s, ConAgra expanded in the food products industry with numerous acquisitions and steady internal growth. Today the company has some 100 consumer brands, including 27 food brands that each produce annual retail sales of more than $100 million.

TRUSTED BRANDS, FAVORITE PRODUCTS

ConAgra is the good name behind the good names. Some of ConAgra's brands have been consumer favorites for a century or longer—Hunt's, Wesson, Armour, Swift. The long list of ConAgra brands also includes  Healthy Choice, Butterball, Act II, Banquet, Blue Bonnet, Eckrich, Fleischmann's, Hebrew National, Marie Callender's, Orville Redenbacher's, Parkay, Peter Pan, Slim Jim, Swiss Miss, and Van Camp's. In addition to its strong presence in supermarkets, ConAgra is the leading provider of products to America's food-service industry. ConAgra products are on the menus at restaurants and fast-food outlets across the country and around the world.

On ConAgra's downtown Omaha campus, the trading floor of the Global Trading Center is the size of a football field.

WORLD HEADQUARTERS

ConAgra's corporate headquarters is located on an expansive 30-acre campus along the Missouri River in downtown Omaha. Among the five buildings on the ConAgra campus are the Charles M. "Mike" Harper Product Development Center and the ConAgra Global Trading Center. The Harper Center is a state-of-the-art food product development lab and pilot plant facility. Inside the Harper Center, talented food technologists, chefs, dietitians, and marketers work to create food products that meet the ever-changing needs of ConAgra customers and consumers. The Global Trading Center, completed in 1999, is the bustling nerve center of ConAgra's international commodity procurement and marketing. Here, commodity buyers and traders work alongside experts in logistics, transportation, economic research, and risk management to create a sophisticated marketplace for ConAgra and its customers around the world.

ConAgra's many brand-name products offer limitless future expansion opportunities for the company. ConAgra is the nation's second largest retail food supplier and largest supplier of food products to U.S. restaurants, fast-food outlets, and other food-service providers.

In 1999, ConAgra announced a multiyear, multimillion-dollar initiative called Feeding Children Better, the nation's largest corporate initiative dedicated to fighting childhood hunger in the United States. A partnership with America's Second Harvest, the nation's largest charitable hunger relief organization (and the national network of food banks), Feeding Children Better is a comprehensive, multidimensional approach to helping end childhood hunger in the United States. There are three main components of the program:

- Kids Cafes—Kids Cafes are safe and nurturing places where kids can go after school for a free hot meal and a range of enrichment activities. The national Kids Cafes sponsor, ConAgra's Feeding Children Better program plans to open from 75 to 100 new cafes in the United States by 2003.
- Rapid Food Distribution System—ConAgra's Feeding Children Better is transforming the charitable food distribution system in America by funding computerization for food banks and transportation programs to move donated food farther, faster, and cheaper. The ConAgra Feeding Children Better Foundation plans to buy much-needed trucks for about half the food banks in the nation by 2003.
- Increasing public awareness—The third initiative is aimed at motivating people to become involved in helping to find solutions to childhood hunger in the United States. The ConAgra Feeding Children Better Foundation is sponsoring a multimedia Ad Council campaign about childhood hunger and is working in many other ways to raise awareness.

ConAgra employees in communities across Nebraska and across the United States are committed to the fight against childhood hunger. Feeding Children Better is working to ensure that *"no child should grow hungry."*

CHAPTER EIGHT

BIG COUNTRY, MANY VOICES

COMMUNICATIONS AND THE MEDIA

With its fleet horses and daredevil riders carrying mail between St. Joseph, Missouri, and Sacramento, California, in just 10 days, the Pony Express was one of history's most imaginative and romantic breakthroughs in communication. Shortly before the Civil War, California interests prevailed upon William H. Russell of Russell, Majors, and Waddell, the largest freighting company on the Plains, to establish a speedy horse-borne mail service

between East and West. On April 3, 1860, the first riders set out from St. Joseph and Sacramento, following the historic Platte River Valley route across Nebraska. Among its achievements, the Pony Express delivered a copy of Abraham Lincoln's first inaugural address to California in the record time of seven days and 17 hours.

Thus began a fabled era in Western lore. But it was to be extremely short, as eras go, because along the riders' route, Edward Creighton of Omaha was working on his own communications breakthrough—completion of a transcontinental telegraph line. The final wire was connected on October 24, 1861. Two days later, only 19 months after it started, the Pony Express officially ceased operations. One of its riders spoke the epitaph: "The telegraph does in a second what it took 80 young men and hundreds of horses to do."

E-mail and satellite signals work even better. Russell's riders and Creighton's telegraphers never could have envisioned the ways Nebraskans communicate with each other and the world in the 21st century.

"WIRED" FOR THE INFORMATION AGE

By 1995 Nebraska could boast more than 6,000 miles of fiber-optic cable connecting all but five of its 93 counties to national telecommunications networks, updating and

complementing the nearly one million telephone access lines crisscrossing the state and operated by firms ranging from the giant Qwest Communications (formerly US West) to small, modernized exchanges serving rural communities. At century's end, the state's classrooms were among the most "wired" in the nation for computer-assisted education, and the distance-shrinking technology of the information age offered the promise of more jobs, expanding business, and improved health care delivery to Nebraska's small towns and farm areas.

In the eastern urban area of the state, advanced network capability has its roots in the Defense Department's decision in 1948 to site Strategic Air Command (SAC) headquarters at Offutt Air Force Base near Bellevue. SAC built a wide and complex telecommunications infrastructure, including one of the nation's first fiber-optic networks, to support its global peacekeeping mission. The systems were designed to provide a large margin of overcapacity, and in the 1980s and 1990s, this technology began to be used increasingly by private companies.

They may be far removed from the itinerant "boomer" or "tramp printer" of 150 years ago, yet these skilled Web-site developers in Lincoln are very much a part of Nebraska's long history of leadership on the frontiers of communications and the media.

The region became the first metropolitan area in the United States to have total ISDN (integrated services digital network) coverage—an all-digital system carrying voice, data, facsimile, telemetry, video, and signaling information. Today more than 50,000 Omaha-area residents work in information technology and telecommunications fields, and the number grows steadily as new information-based enterprises continue to be founded.

Nebraska knows how to foster high-tech business. It has passed the nation's first law deregulating telecommunications and offers a range of tax-based incentives to encourage the formation, expansion, and relocation of communications and other enterprises.

Digital technology is reaching into the farthest corners of the state. In Imperial, for example, Internet

One of the largest employers in Nebraska, Qwest Communications (formerly US West) occupies a portion of Omaha's beautiful Landmark Center. Qwest provides telecommunications and other services to 25 million customers in a 14-state area.

STAR QUALITY

Soon after WOWT went on the air in 1949, the first television station in a five-state area, some of its most popular local programming was hosted by a young announcer whose imaginative zaniness sometimes furrowed the brows of station executives. Both he and the station survived, and he went on to entertain much larger audiences. His name: Johnny Carson. The popular entertainer grew up in Norfolk.

When you dial 1-800, you'll probably talk to a Nebraskan. The Omaha metro area is home to more than two dozen telemarketing firms, including giants such as ITI, West, and SITEL, and more than 30 million calls a year come into hotel reservation centers in Omaha.

provider Chase 3000, a nonprofit foundation called EIII, Inc. (focusing on education, environment, and economic development), and the federal government started a cooperative project in 1999 that will create a technology learning center and link some 400 households, hospitals, libraries, schools, and senior centers in southwest Nebraska and northeast Colorado.

CORNHUSKER AIRWAVES

Nebraskans also are linked by another kind of network, one that reaches every corner of the state every day to deliver a rich diet of entertainment, information, and long-distance learning. It's Nebraska Educational Telecommunication (NET), a multiple-channel satellite and fiber-optic system operating statewide over nine transmitters and 17 translator stations, plus a cable television service received by more than 221,500 households.

A partnership of the University of Nebraska–Lincoln and the Nebraska Educational Telecommunications Commission, NET had its start in 1954 when KUON-TV in Lincoln, still the flagship station, went on the air—only the seventh educational TV station in the nation. The present broadcast network was completed in 1963, giving Nebraska the first statewide system of its kind.

Four different systems compose NET: public television and radio broadcasting; a broadcast-quality channel providing statewide distribution of educational programming; a compressed video-audio service providing shared instruction and interactive communication; and a fiber-optic network linking groups of elementary, secondary, and college classrooms to share two-way instruction. At its main studios in Lincoln and Omaha, NET originates quality programs seen nationally on the Public Broadcasting System and is coproducer of the acclaimed *Reading Rainbow* series.

Commercial television also got off to a fast start in Nebraska, with WOWT and KMTV both going on the air in Omaha in 1949. In 2000, Nebraska is home to

26 stations in 16 communities that blanket the state and bordering areas with local programming and the network offerings of ABC, CBS, NBC, Fox, and PBS.

Perhaps in part because Midwestern speech patterns most closely reflect standard English pronunciation, Nebraska has given nationwide broadcasting more than one state's share of prominent voices. NBC News anchor Tom Brokaw, for instance, cut his journalistic teeth as a reporter for KMTV more than 30 years ago.

Cable television systems operated by more than 50 different enterprises—some local, some regional, some national—reach across the length and breadth of the state, serving as few subscribers as 12 in the little town of Elsie and more than 152,000 with Cox Communications in Omaha, one of several cable competitors in the metro area.

Foreshadowing the prominence of the University of Nebraska in educational television, the state's early ventures into radio also had a campus connection. Dr. John Jensen, professor of physics at Nebraska Wesleyan University in Lincoln, originated broadcasts in 1921–22 on a station called KCAJ. He and other wireless pioneers had few listeners; in 1920 there were no commercial stations in Nebraska and virtually no radios. But the new medium caught fire across the prairies, and within 10 years commercial broadcasting sent its signals across the state on such stations as WJAG in Norfolk, which went on the air in 1922; WOW in Omaha, 1923; and KMMJ in Grand Island, 1925. By 1930 about 40 percent of Nebraska farm homes had radios, mostly battery-powered.

Today, Nebraska radio counts nearly 150 stations in 51 communities, including such durable old-timers as KCRO (1922) and KFAB (1924) in Omaha.

SPECIAL EDITIONS

One of Nebraska's sturdiest journalistic traditions is of strong, locally owned newspapers that take a keen interest in their communities' advancement. Ironically, however, one of the most insistent voices in the state's early history was that of a paper published in Iowa. It was the *Council Bluffs Bugle,* edited by Joseph E. Johnson, a vigorous advocate of the establishment of the Nebraska Territory. His editorial policies were vindicated on May 30, 1854, when President Franklin Pierce signed the Kansas-Nebraska Act. Putting his money where his mouth was, so to speak, Johnson moved his operations to the new territory a few weeks later, founding the *Omaha Arrow.*

Less than a year later, J. Sterling Morton, founder of Arbor Day, began spreading his strong views in the *Nebraska City News.* The year after that, Robert W. Furnas established the *Nebraska Advertiser* in Brownville, a journal that helped establish the dominance of the Republican Party in Nebraska Territory.

One of the first television stations in the region, KMTV Channel 3 went on the air in Omaha in 1949. NBC News anchor Tom Brokaw got his start at the CBS affiliate, now owned by Lee Enterprises.

Anyone with Internet access can browse the Omaha World-Herald's *daily offerings at the click of a mouse. Delivering the news wasn't always so easy: until the mid-20th century, in rural areas some of the paper's carrier boys—and girls—made their rounds on horseback.*

And in 1865 Dr. George L. Miller started the *Omaha Daily Herald,* laying the foundation for what was to become the premier daily in Nebraska. In the post–Civil War era, Miller's *Daily Herald* gained a national reputation, and its influence multiplied when in 1889 it merged with Gilbert M. Hitchcock's *Omaha Evening World.* As a new century begins, the *Omaha World-Herald* has extended its reach across 107 counties in Nebraska and western Iowa, serving some 235,000 subscribers daily, nearly 300,000 with its Sunday editions, and an inestimable number of readers and advertisers through its Internet operations.

While the *World-Herald* is the state's most-read newspaper, its voice is by no means the only one Nebraskans hear. Second in size and influence is the capital city's *Lincoln Journal-Star,* with a local and state circulation of 80,000-plus. With a population of 1.67 million, the Cornhusker State supports 185 newspapers—18 dailies and 167 weeklies—with a total circulation of more than 800,000. According to the Nebraska Press Association, 91 percent of adult Nebraskans read a newspaper at least once a week.

Any profile of the printing and publishing industry in the state must give prominent mention to the University of Nebraska Press, a mainstay of Nebraska's literary and intellectual life. With operations in Lincoln and in London, England, it publishes serious works related to the military frontier, Native Americans, women in the West, and a host of other historical and documentary subjects. It also has been instrumental in establishing worldwide audiences for such authors as J. Frank Dobie, Mari Sandoz, Willa Cather, Dee Brown, John G. Neihardt, Merrill Mattes, and Bess Streeter Aldrich.

Also in Lincoln, just minutes from the University of Nebraska, Sandhills Publishing is helping to reinvent the business of information processing through the development of print publications and associated Web sites for specialized audiences. The company's leading product lines include *Truck Paper, Machinery Trader, Controller,* and *Smart Computing.*

Across Nebraska, many of the state's profusion of locally based commercial printers trace their roots to the early days of the "boomer" or "tramp printer," itinerant inksters who would show up in Nebraska Territory with a shirttail full of type and go into business producing broadsides, sale bills, and sometimes newspapers. Among the venerable practitioners is the Omaha Printing Company, which set up shop in 1858 and 142 years later has become the city's and one of the region's largest commercial printers.

OPPOSITE: *A printing press churns out a daily newspaper, which still has a vital spot in the changing world of communications.*

BIG COUNTRY, MANY VOICES

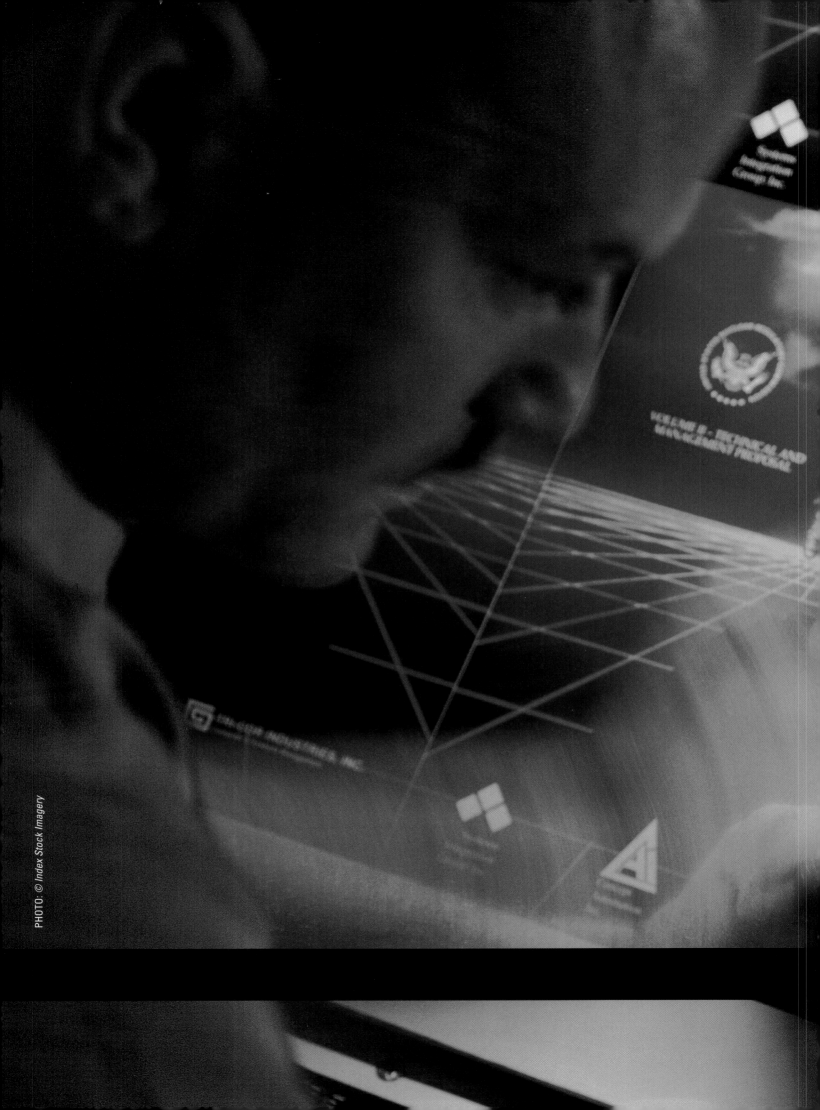

MEDIA/INFORMATION TECHNOLOGY >>

SANDHILLS PUBLISHING COMPANY

Sandhills Publishing Company reaches specific audiences with state-of-the-art print and electronic information

media including tabloid advertisement newspapers, magazines, and Internet resources.

After walking just 10 feet into the two main office buildings at Sandhills Publishing Company, in Lincoln, Nebraska, visitors understand the ideas that underlie the 22-year-old company. Filling the foyer of the administration building is a life-size statue of six Sandhill cranes rising into the air from a muddy Nebraska cornfield. The entryway of the multimedia building is a stone-floored atrium featuring a high ceiling supported by large wooden beams and four tiled pillars illustrated with petroglyph-style icons. The cranes and the pillars' icons symbolize the concepts that company owner and founder, Tom Peed, has made the foundation of Sandhills Publishing.

The company, which began in Webster City, Iowa, in 1978, is an information-processing firm. It produces tabloid advertisement newspapers for the heavy machinery, trucking, aircraft, and corporate computer markets, as well as computing magazines for consumers. Internet sites for each publication take the content, and the customer service behind it, on-line.

"Late Arrival," *a striking statue created by Thomas D. Palmerton, greets visitors in the main lobby of Sandhills Publishing in Lincoln with life-size representations of the company's symbol.*

SYMBOLIC SANDHILL CRANES

The Sandhill cranes are the company's best-known corporate symbol, and they were the inspiration behind its 1997 name change from Peed Corporation to Sandhills Publishing. Sandhill cranes migrate annually from winter homes in the southwestern United States to nesting grounds in Canada, Alaska, and even Siberia. A stretch of the Platte River in central Nebraska is a critical stopover in the cranes' migration pattern. Each year, from mid-February to mid-April, about 500,000 cranes stop along the river to gain weight through a rich diet of marsh-land wildlife and crops dropped in the fields during the previous season's harvest.

Icons on the multimedia building's four pillars represent the combination of ingredients that serve as strengths and guideposts for Sandhills. The pillars stand for what the company is and what it hopes to be.

Throughout the noisy, crowded rest stop, crane family units, consisting of adults mated for life and their adolescent offspring, remain intact.

The specially commissioned sculpture at the entryway of the Sandhills Publishing offices speaks of many company values that are embodied by Sandhill cranes. Loyalty, strength through teamwork, endurance, family structure, and reliance on Nebraska's resources are all principles that Sandhills emphasizes to its employees. The cranes' timeless reliance on the Platte River reflects the company's handling of information. The river acts as a natural fueling depot that the cranes visit in order to better continue their journey. Similarly, Sandhills Publishing is not an endpoint for any information, but rather a place where data stops over for improvements on its final journey to the customer.

Sandhills Publishing draws inspiration from the Sandhill cranes that stop each spring on Nebraska's Platte River during their long migration to nesting grounds. © Regal Images

CORPORATE CULTURE

The four tile and stone pillars in the atrium of the Sandhills Publishing multimedia building, built in 1995, represent a broad range of values and tools that Sandhills relies on. The pillars are decorated with icons of people (representing employees), hand tools (publishing tools), a cross (values and corporate culture), and a human eye (products). The pillars' support of the wooden beams in the atrium is to remind

The icons on the four pillars in the multimedia building represent (from left) tools, which are crafted from the latest technology available; people, the company's core asset; products, symbolized by an eye because of their visual nature; and values and beliefs, the defining force behind the company's culture.

visitors that the four concepts they represent support Sandhills Publishing itself. The icons on the pillar for products are especially intriguing. These images, which cover all four sides of each pillar, include windows, a lighthouse, a lightbulb, and eyeglasses. These evoke the visual products that Sandhills produces in the form of both print publications and electronic Internet sites.

The Sandhills entryways tell the heart of the company's story, but as visitors continue their walk through the multimedia building and the administration building, they see ongoing evidence of the unique Sandhills culture. Employees adhere to a formal business dress code, chosen to foster a professional attitude. The entire company has just a handful of offices. Employees and managers share large, open work spaces that encourage teamwork and ready communication.

A professional, open office environment encourages employees to share ideas and interact regularly on projects to find the best solutions.

MULTIMEDIA ENVIRONMENT

The location of the main corporate facility in Lincoln, rather than in a major, coastal metropolitan area, also is unusual in the publishing business. Peed moved the company to Lincoln when its needs began to outgrow the resources of Webster City. He chose Lincoln because of its ready supply of college graduates, its Midwestern work ethic, and its central location, which makes both shipping and phone calls convenient. The company is on a 68-acre campus on the northwestern edge of Lincoln, just minutes from the University of Nebraska, downtown Lincoln, and the Lincoln

airport. Its two office buildings are on either side of its state-of-the-art printing and binding facility, where all Sandhills publications are produced.

This publishing company thrives on a highly dynamic environment. It prides itself on finding a better way. No process endures simply because of tradition when employees discover a more efficient means of serving customers. This makes Sandhills Publishing a challenging and exciting place to work, a place where every employee is expected to propose new ideas and readily adapt to those that are adopted.

STATE-OF-THE-ART PRODUCTION

The company's production process is a prime example of its dedication to constant improvement. Sandhills has consistently been at the forefront of the publishing industry's efforts to develop direct-to-plate printing systems and custom-designed pagination software. The printing facility uses leading-edge printing equipment, such as Hantscho and Goss printing presses.

Sandhills Publishing is closely following the booming demand for electronic information delivery with its extensive Internet-based offerings. The company was a pioneer in E-commerce before the term even appeared thanks to the Peed Networks, an electronic system for international buying and selling of machinery parts, which is now *Machinery Trader*'s Fast Track service on the Internet. Each of the company's publications posts regular product listings or editorial content on its own World Wide Web site. The corporate Web site (www.sandhills.com) home page is the gateway to the company's on-line offerings and provides links to each publication's site.

ABOVE: *The Sandhills printing process uses cutting-edge technologies such as direct-to-plate production and customized pagination software.* LEFT: *Sandhills produces and binds all of its publications on-site, with equipment such as state-of-the-art Hantscho and Goss printing presses.*

The Sandhills facility in Scottsdale, Arizona, provides a data back-up center, which ensures that corporate Web services are always available.

The growing importance of on-line content created the need for Sandhills to expand its facilities beyond Nebraska to Scottsdale, Arizona. A center for data redundancy, built in 2000 in a Scottsdale office park, guarantees that Sandhills Publishing's on-line content and other data will be available even if weather or technical problems should hamper Internet servers at the Lincoln office.

PUBLICATIONS DESIGNED FOR SPECIAL AUDIENCES

The Sandhills Publishing business model centers on developing publications that are finely tuned to the demands of special audiences. Many of the company's publications, such as *Machinery Trader*, *Truck Paper*, and *Controller*, create streamlined markets where buyers and sellers exchange products. *Smart Computing* magazine, along with its three sister lines of single-topic special issues, delivers personal computing instruction and buying advice to performance-minded personal computer users in a unique plain-English style. Key Sandhills product lines include:

- *Truck Paper*—This industry-leading weekly covers the United States in seven regional editions, featuring full-color photos of heavy trucks and trailers (www.truckpaper.com).
- *Controller* and *Executive Controller*—Aircraft buyers and sellers rely upon these publications for the color photos and detailed descriptions of single-engine and twin-engine piston aircraft, featured in the weekly *Controller*, and turbine aircraft, in the monthly *Executive Controller* (www.aircraft.com).

- *Machinery Trader* and *Machinery Trader Marketbook*—The weekly *Machinery Trader* carries listings and photos of heavy equipment and related parts. The semi-annual *Machinery Trader Marketbook* is a definitive reference on prices in the machinery industry. *Machinery Trader* also provides Fast Track service on the Internet, which offers up-to-the-minute information on the buying, selling, and management of machinery equipment (www.machinerytrader.com).
- *Smart Computing*—This monthly magazine, along with its three special-topic issues (two monthly and one quarterly), provides plain-English computing instruction and product reviews that are among the computer industry's most trusted (www.smartcomputing.com).
- *Processor*—This full-color weekly publication gives corporate purchasers a comprehensive market for new and used computer hardware and software (www.processor.com).

Lists of products provide only limited insight into what Sandhills Publishing is about. Descriptions of buildings, photos of operations, and lists of accomplishments are similarly inadequate. Sandhills is a company about ideas, specifically those ideas that its artful cranes and pillars can sum up in a glance.

Sandhills Publishing's line of printed publications covers a wide range of consumer and business-to-business markets.

BACK TO THE BIBLE

With offices in 13 countries and programming in 25 languages, Back to the Bible teaches the Bible on 1,500 radio outlets worldwide and also in print and on television, video, CD-ROM, and the Internet.

The international headquarters of Back to the Bible is located in Lincoln, Nebraska. The ministry utilizes radio, television, literature, and the Internet to teach the Bible in 25 languages, spoken by half the population of the world.

BACK TO THE BIBLE

Sponsoring media ministries in 25 languages spoken by 50 percent of the world's population, Back to the Bible provides Bible teaching through more than 1,500 radio stations worldwide and also in print and on television, video, CD-ROM, and the Internet.

Back to the Bible, headquartered in Lincoln, Nebraska, began in 1939 when its founder, a preacher named Theodore Epp, reached out to radio listeners and encouraged them to turn to the Bible for answers. His broadcast on Lincoln station KFOR 1240 AM has grown into a worldwide media ministry.

Epp began the *Back to the Bible* program because of his desire to impact the world with the Bible. In order to reach people everywhere, he supported missionaries and added short-wave radio broadcasts and additional stations until his death in 1985. Today, Back to the Bible utilizes radio as well as television, video, literature, CD-ROM, and the Internet to teach what the Bible says, what it means, and how it applies to peoples' lives.

Back to the Bible's purpose is to lead believers into spiritual maturity resulting in active service for Christ in the local church, and to reach unbelievers with the Gospel of Christ by teaching the Bible through media.

Dr. Woodrow Kroll has led the organization since 1990. The ministry's signature radio program, *Back to the Bible*, is a 25-minute daily Bible-teaching program. The ministry also produces three additional programs: *Gateway to Joy, Confident Living for Midlife and Beyond*, and *The Bible Minute*.

The ministry's Web site, www.backtothebible.org, has received on-line visitors from more than 185 nations. Visitors can listen to the program with Real Audio and read program transcripts and inspiring daily devotionals. The daily devotionals are also available through E-mail subscriptions and on handheld devices through the Internet. Each year, Back to the Bible's publishing division releases a number of book, video, and CD-ROM products.

In 1954, the ministry opened its first international office in Canada; today, Back to the Bible continues to expand around the world. Nearly 50 national speakers produce radio programs in 20 different languages. Back to the Bible also produces and distributes Christian literature, sponsors camps, and impacts lives in unique and relevant ways.

The ministry continues to change as new technology becomes available, but Back to the Bible is more committed than ever to achieving its mission of leading people into a dynamic relationship with God.

The voices of Back to the Bible include (left to right) co-host Don Hawkins, associate Bible teacher Tony Beckett, and president and senior Bible teacher Woodrow Kroll.

STANDARD DIGITAL IMAGING

At the forefront of digital printing in Omaha, Standard Digital Imaging has used advanced technologies to meet the reprographic needs of architects, engineers, construction trades, and other businesses for more than eight decades.

Standard Digital Imaging provides its patrons with advanced reprographic services, supplies, equipment, and facilities management.

For more than 80 years, Omaha-area architects, engineers, and construction trades have been loyal patrons of Standard Digital Imaging, a company that offers reprographic services, supplies, equipment, and facilities management. Standard Digital Imaging still serves many of its original patrons and has expanded dramatically into other business segments with the advent of Large Format Color to provide courtroom exhibits for attorneys and trade show exhibits for all businesses.

Originally called "Standard Blue"—a nickname for Standard Blueprint—the company was founded in 1919 by the Swanson family of Omaha. Standard Blue changed its name in 1997 to more accurately reflect current technology offerings. The company's mission statement reflects its goal of meeting customers' needs: "Standard Digital Imaging is a customer-oriented organization, dedicated to providing a network of intelligent print-copy solutions and products. Our goal is to be your partner and the industry leader in reprographic services, supplies, and equipment. We promise to provide unequaled value through our trained, professional staff, state-of-the-art technology, and commitment to customer service. We remain ever mindful that we exist to serve you—our customer!"

According to its president, Peggy Bardouniotis, Standard Digital Imaging is known for its special niche in providing large or oversize printing for architecture and engineering companies. "Typical copy shops do not have the specialized equipment to produce drawings for architects and engineers," she says.

With blueprints a product of the past, the digital format is now becoming more common. Standard Digital was the first firm in Omaha to be involved in the new technology of digital printing, which produces a cleaner, faster, and better copy. Standard Digital has been involved with electronic submission for digital output since 1991—making every print an original.

"We've chosen to embrace technological changes rather than fear them," Bardouniotis says. "Standard Digital has always been on the leading edge. Providing digital products requires highly technological equipment and a sophisticated infrastructure to accept, manage, transfer, and digitally image for our clients. Our clients look to us for guidance from document creation to the final product."

Standard Digital Imaging is also involved in facilities management. "We design on-site, tailor-made print shops for clients where we provide the equipment, trained staff, materials, and accounting processes. This allows clients to focus all time, energy, and resources on their core business, and it provides cost savings!" says Bardouniotis.

While the future is here today at Standard Digital, technological changes are still on the horizon. Seeking innovative service advancements, responding to technological advancements such as Internet transfer and real-time image editing, and simply producing faster and better is clearly the path to the future.

The advent of Large Format Color has enabled Standard Digital Imaging to serve many additional customer sectors, creating such products as courtroom exhibits for attorneys and trade show exhibits for all kinds of companies.

STERLING SOFTWARE INFORMATION TECHNOLOGY DIVISION

Sterling Software Information Technology Division specializes in providing information technology services

to a wide range of customers, from government to commercial to weather agencies.

Sterling Software Information Technology Division provides business and government with software and services, including network integration, document management, work group solutions, and electronic commerce.

Formed in 1984, Sterling Software Information Technology Division (ITD) has grown to become the largest private employer in Sarpy County, Nebraska, with more than 300 employees.

A division of Sterling Software, Inc., one of the 15 largest software companies in the world, Sterling Software ITD is headquartered in Bellevue, Nebraska.

Sterling Software ITD, Bellevue, focuses on providing software products and professional services for commercial customers as well as for all levels of government—local, state, and federal.

Key services offered by this division include: enterprise document management and work group solutions, outsourcing electronic commerce solutions in deregulated electricity and gas markets, network integration services from mainframe to the desktop, client/server technology, and object-oriented software development.

While most contracts awarded in the infancy of Sterling Software were related to the Department of Defense, recent contracts have expanded the focus of the business. As a result of working with Nebraska government offices, Sterling has signed contracts with the Secretary of State, Department of Health and Human Services, Department of Roads, and Nebraska Investment Council.

Sterling Software's modest beginnings in Nebraska parallel the information technology boom in the Midwest. "Sterling hired half of the information technology graduating class from the University of Nebraska at Omaha in 1982," says Douglas Pachunka, vice president. "New contracts necessitated a rapid expansion of Sterling's staff. The dedicated Nebraska work ethic enabled us to grow faster than our coastal counterparts."

Hiring highly skilled employees has always been a priority for Sterling Software dating back to the early days, when such employees were limited in number. To maintain its staff of well-trained employees, Sterling fosters close relationships with area universities, presenting to students its proven methodologies for software development and systems integration.

Sterling's success is based on its keen ability to solve customers' problems not only satisfactorily but also creatively. Working closely with each customer, Sterling partners to create innovative solutions in a wide variety of industries. With its financially strategic location in the Midwest, Sterling is better able to provide its services at the most competitive prices.

While many defense contractors are shrinking in size and scope, Sterling Software is standing strong and growing in Omaha. Top, well-trained professionals are attracted to the firm because of its stability, powerful growth, and diversity of work activities.

CHAPTER NINE

FACTORIES AMONG THE FIELDS

MANUFACTURING

"Manufacturing" in the Nebraska context often is taken to refer to the state's prodigious capacity for turning field crops and livestock into food for the table, but in reality, nonfarm industry in the 20th century grew into an economic force that in some respects matches or exceeds food processing in contributions to the state's prosperity.

Much of this growth has taken place in less than 50 years. In 1958 there were about 1,500 manufacturing businesses in Nebraska, employing 59,000 and producing about a half-billion dollars worth of goods. By the end of the century the state could count about 2,100 manufacturers with 118,000 employees and sales of more than $6.7 billion.

BUILDING INDUSTRIAL MUSCLE

The numbers represent in part the growth and output of such urban industries as Data Documents and the Lozier Corporation of Omaha. Data Documents is one of the nation's largest providers of products and services for the management of business information, including custom forms and form management systems. It has 11 manufacturing plants and more than 70 sales offices across the United States. Lozier, the nation's largest supplier of retail store fixtures and accessories, employs about 2,500 in more than 2.4 million square feet of manufacturing space in five cities. Lincoln-based manufacturing companies—ranging from Linweld, a premier supplier and manufacturer of industrial, medical, and specialty gases in the Midwest, to Kawasaki Motors Manufacturing Corp., U.S.A.—continue to expand, as well.

Nebraska's smaller communities also have played a large part in industrial development. For example, Valmont Industries, with its manufacturing facility in Valley, has become the world's largest maker of mechanized irrigation equipment for agriculture and a global leader in engineering, manufacturing, and marketing poles, towers, and metal structures for a wide variety of industrial and civil infrastructure uses. More than 10 million acres in the United States and other countries around the world are irrigated using Valmont's Valley® center-pivot and linear-move water-management equipment. With more than 30 plants in North and South America, Europe, and China, Valmont employs more than 5,000 personnel worldwide. American Tool Companies, which began in DeWitt as the originator of the famous VISE-GRIP® locking pliers, has grown into a global manufacturer of multiple lines of finely engineered hand tools and power tool accessories. Behlen Mfg. Co. of Columbus started making steel

Cargill Dow has found a way to make plastic from corn for a wide range of consumer applications, including clothing such as this jacket. Carbon and other elements in natural sugars are used to make NatureWorks™ PLA (polylactide) polymers for fibers, plastic packaging, cups, and other everyday products.

toe caps for work boots and clamps for egg-case lids and became a manufacturer of steel building systems and grain storage equipment for a nationwide market.

Cargill Dow, a joint venture of Cargill Incorporated and the Dow Chemical Company, has broken ground for its first production facility at the current Cargill corn wet milling plant in Blair. Cargill Dow's new $300 million manufacturing facility, scheduled to come onstream in 2001, plans to use Nebraska-grown field corn as the base feedstock for its breakthrough technology, called NatureWorks™ PLA (polylactide). Relying entirely on annually renewable resources, the revolutionary process uses corn-derived dextrose to make PLA polymers for a

Behlen Mfg. Co.'s world headquarters are located in Columbus, where the employee-owned company was founded in 1936. Since then, Behlen has evolved into a nationwide leader in the manufacture of livestock equipment and grain storage, drying, and handling systems, as well as metal building systems.

wide range of applications, including clothes, cups, plastic packaging, and many other products.

A GREAT PLACE TO DO BUSINESS

Among several considerations that influenced Cargill Dow's decision to locate in Nebraska were proximity to existing Cargill operations (Cargill Corn Milling and

SWEPT INTO HISTORY

A mint-condition sample of one of Nebraska's humblest yet most widely used household products has taken a place of honor in the Smithsonian Institution in Washington, D.C. It's a "Victoria" model broom manufactured at the Deshler Broom Factory in Deshler. Founded in 1890, the plant operated until 1998, and in the 1930s became the largest broom factory in the world, producing 400 dozen a day. The Smithsonian requested the "Victoria" for its National Museum of American History.

ABOVE: *Nebraska-based telemarketing firms conduct direct sales and customer service programs for manufacturers and other clients.* OPPOSITE: *Valmont Industries' corporate headquarters in Omaha were designed by the DLR Group. The world's largest maker of irrigation equipment, Valmont also provides poles, structures, and coatings services for the lighting, utility, and communication industries.*

Excel Corporation), availability of natural plant sugars, easy access to rail and highway transportation, and an excellent pool of labor. Adding to the state's attractiveness as a place to do business are essential "livability" qualities such as its family-oriented culture. Nebraska is one of the top five states in which to raise children, according to a

FACTORIES AMONG THE FIELDS

in the west, support manufacturing establishments with more than 10 employees.

A number of other factors have also contributed to Nebraska's rise in manufacturing. One of the most influential recent developments was adoption in 1987 of landmark legislation that changed the state's tax structure to grant sizeable incentives to businesses locating or expanding in Nebraska, targeted specifically to encourage an influx of capital and employment. In less than five years, this business-friendly policy was credited with attracting more than $3.1 billion in investment and creating 26,000 new jobs.

Nebraska has made a strong commitment to preserving its traditional pioneer work ethic and preparing its young people for productive enterprise. For example, in 1971 the legislature created a statewide independent system of locally governed technical community colleges at Scottsbluff, North Platte, Hastings, Norfolk, Milford, and Omaha, offering practical education in such fields as mechanics and electronics. Compared with the national averages, a higher proportion of Nebraska's high school students take the ACT and SAT college aptitude tests and get better scores.

1998 survey by the Children's Rights Council. It also ranks 11th among "kid-friendly" states in the 2000 *Kids Count Data Book.* Such incentives are not limited to one or two regions, and therefore, Nebraska's manufacturing base is widely distributed geographically: a dozen counties, from metropolitan Douglas in the east to Scotts Bluff

Lozier Corporation of Omaha is the nation's largest supplier of retail store fixtures and accessories, from showroom display shelving to backroom storage systems.

At its plant in DeWitt, American Tool Companies manufactures *VISE-GRIP®* pliers, which were invented in DeWitt in 1924 by Danish-born blacksmith William Peterson. With operations in 12 countries, American Tool boasts 16 other brands, including *MARATHON®* saw blades, *QUICK-GRIP®* clamps, and *IRWIN®* bits.

In addition to offering a well-educated, highly motivated workforce, Nebraska provides its employers with a wealth of infrastructure advantages—abundant water resources, low utility rates, and comprehensive transportation systems ranging from river barges to modern freeways to an established network of large-volume railroads.

Such bottom-line attractions have encouraged the growth and development of scientifically advanced industry, typified by Valmont's successful introduction of computer-controlled irrigation systems and the emergence of Lucent Technologies as a large-volume high-tech manufacturer. Lucent, at its Omaha installation, makes telecommunications hardware for a global market, employing 3,400 and reporting a billion dollars in annual sales.

Across the breadth of the Cornhusker State, manufacturers large and small are anticipated to continue expanding their sector of the economy at a steady rate. The Bureau of Business Research at the University of Nebraska–Lincoln has estimated that nonfarm employment, including manufacturing, will grow about 2 percent annually in 2000 and 2001—establishing "Made in Nebraska" as an even prouder and more familiar label in the new millennium.

WORK AND THE BOTTOM LINE

The Nebraska work ethic—born in the pioneers' struggle to survive, strengthened by immigrants' efforts to create a better life, and encouraged by the state's diverse opportunities to succeed—pays off in monetary as well as psychic rewards. In Omaha, for example, employers report a productivity edge of about $2,000 per worker per year over the national average.

MANUFACTURING>>

INSUL-8 CORPORATION

Backed by a history of innovation and excellence, Insul-8 Corporation has become an industry leader in the business of providing mobile electrification to a wide range of customers.

In business since 1944 and a member of the international corporation Delachaux, S.A. of France, Insul-8 Corporation continues to raise the standards for safely, effectively, and economically conducting electricity to mobile equipment and systems.

"Insul-8 designs and builds products that are at the heart of what makes material handling machinery and transit systems move," says Jolie Koesters, marketing manager for Omaha-based Insul-8. "From our customers' perspective, if it doesn't move, it doesn't work."

Insul-8 Corporation's roots are similar to those of its parent company, Delachaux S.A., founded by Clarence Léon Delachaux in 1902. Delachaux S.A. began as an innovative aluminothermic company specializing in rail welding and quickly became an international leader in several activities, including the business of supplying electricity to industrial equipment and transit systems. The founder's grandson, François Delachaux, currently heads the firm.

Working with a variety of electrification products, Insul-8 and its sister company Industrial Electric Reels, Inc. (IER), an electrical cable reeling equipment manufacturer, made great headway in the industry by the late 1940s. Both companies quickly blazed paths through their respective markets from their locations in Nebraska and California.

IER, established in 1924 in Omaha's Old Market area, gained recognition as a top quality manufacturer of cable and hose reels. IER reels run the gamut in size, from small commercial-use reels for powering hand tools to enormous custom-built reels for extremely demanding applications such as mobile missile launch towers and dockside cranes.

Insul-8 emerged as an industry leader by the late 1940s with its introduction of the original figure 8–shaped, covered metal conductor bar system. Now known universally

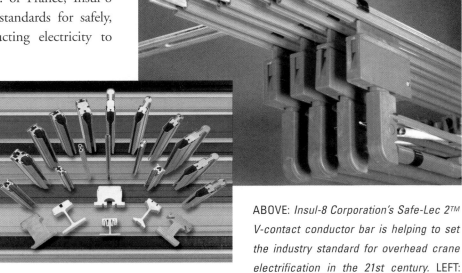

ABOVE: *Insul-8 Corporation's Safe-Lec 2™ V-contact conductor bar is helping to set the industry standard for overhead crane electrification in the 21st century.* LEFT: *Conductor bars in many variations designed and manufactured by Insul-8 exemplify the company's ongoing industry leadership.*

in the overhead material handling industry as "8-bar," this product is used to electrify cranes and other mobile machinery. Insul-8 was also the first to design and produce a stainless steel–capped aluminum conductor bar for the mass transit industry.

Insul-8 is helping to set the industry standard once more with its introduction of the Safe-Lec 2™ V-contact conductor bar. At the request of crane manufacturers and other customers, Insul-8 successfully designed the V-contact bar as an alternative to 8-bar systems. "Safe-Lec 2 bar provides superior performance and higher safety standards at an attractive price," Koesters says. The potential obsolescence of the 8-bar product that the company originally created doesn't seem to bother those at Insul-8. Rather, the people of Insul-8 are genuinely excited for the opportunity to take overhead electrification of cranes to a new level of performance.

Acquired by Delachaux in 1975, Insul-8 and IER were merged in 1996 under the name Insul-8 Corporation. Subsequently, all U.S. operations of Insul-8 and IER were moved to the Midwest. "As one company, Insul-8 has gained the opportunity to serve customers with one of the most diverse product offerings in the electrification industry," according to Lon Miller, president and chief operating officer of Insul-8 Corporation. In an ongoing effort to provide electrification in all forms, in 1999, Insul-8 acquired Drivecon Corporation, based in Illinois. Drivecon designs and manufactures motor drives and controls for the overhead crane industry, one of Insul-8's biggest markets. "Adding Drivecon to our group proved to be a key strategic move," says Miller. "We couldn't think of a better way to celebrate Insul-8's 55th anniversary."

Today, Insul-8 continues to have a strong presence in the Midwest, while maintaining its key position as the Delachaux arm in North and South America. The Omaha office employs 90 people in sales, engineering, administration, and production, while a second office in Harlan, Iowa, employs another 70 people in primarily manufacturing and engineering positions. Drivecon employs 25 people in Gurnee, Illinois. Insul-8 is dedicated to maintaining a multilocal position in the U.S. while reaching across four continents. Insul-8's main focus is North and South America, and its Omaha office also is headquarters for the Insul-8 offices in Australia, Great Britain, and Canada.

Over the years, the name Insul-8 has become synonymous with electrification. "Insul-8 has the most enduring presence in the industry," says Koesters. "Insul-8 is well established in nearly all areas of electrification. Our products are widely used by crane builders, electrical distributors, transit system designers, and port authorities and terminals." Insul-8 also has a lucrative and interesting niche market in the amusement park industry. One of Insul-8's best known references is the conductor bar

system that electrifies the monorail at Walt Disney World in Florida.

With many successes in hand, Insul-8 continues to look for new ideas and opportunities for development. "Latin America is a new area for future growth," Koesters says. "Insul-8 has been active in Latin America since the 1990s. We see terrific potential for this area and have set aggressive development goals."

"Insul-8 also is looking to the mass transit market for growth," says Richard Prell, manager of Transit Sales for Insul-8. "We have provided electrification for numerous public transit systems, ranging from the SkyTrain in British Columbia, Canada, to the LRT System II in Kuala Lumpur, Malaysia." Insul-8 also is well known for its work on airport monorail systems, such as those in place at Newark International Airport and Dallas/Fort Worth International Airport. "The entire transit industry offers great potential for continued sales growth through high-profile projects," adds Koesters. "We are well positioned with the right people and products in place."

Insul-8 products can show up practically anywhere. The company's slip rings are used on irrigation systems manufactured in Nebraska as well as on large power shovels used in South American mines. Its conductor bar systems are used on small cranes in local midwestern plants, as well as on immense transit systems in Asia. Insul-8's festoon systems and cable/hose reels are used worldwide, serving facilities that range from small warehouses to huge ports.

Insul-8's unique ability to provide a wide variety of electrification solutions from a single source cements the company's reputation as a leading manufacturer, not only in Nebraska, but also nationally and internationally. As Miller says, "Insul-8's mission is to attain and sustain growth not only by strategically marketing new products and adding value to existing products, but also by finding the best people available to make our goals a reality. Luckily, many of these people are right here in our backyard."

PAXTON & VIERLING STEEL
A DIVISION OF OWEN INDUSTRIES, INC.

Paxton & Vierling Steel is a leading supplier of unprocessed and processed steel in North America—for complex

buildings and bridges, from component parts and tool steel for many industries, to one-time cut-to-length sheets.

For more than a century, Paxton & Vierling Steel, a division of Owen Industries, Inc., has been a part of the structural history of Omaha and Nebraska. Throughout the area, the girders and beams that support numerous buildings and bridges attest to this long relationship. Paxton & Vierling played a pivotal role in erecting many of Omaha's landmark structures: the Ak-Sar-Ben Coliseum; Union Pacific Corporation headquarters; the main branch of the United States Post Office in Omaha; the Zorinsky Federal Building; the Mutual of Omaha complex; Woodmen Tower; and hundreds of highway and railroad bridges, including Abbott Drive bridge.

In 1885, an Omaha business pioneer, Billy Paxton, along with A. J. Vierling and his brother Robert Vierling, of Chicago, founded Paxton & Vierling Iron Works in Omaha, with 30 employees. The company made industrial ironware of all kinds, including most of the street lamps and manhole covers in Omaha. Many of the city's historic warehouses still have an iron threshold with the Paxton & Vierling Iron Works insignia.

The Owen family relationship with Paxton & Vierling began in 1930, when the Vierlings sent Fred H. Owen from their Chicago-based steel company to Omaha to help manage their struggling subsidiary. Fred was initially dividing his time between Chicago and Omaha, but he soon found that he needed to be in Omaha on a full-time basis. By 1943, with World War II raging on, Fred Owen was able to buy out the Vierling family interest in the company. His son Edward F. Owen also joined the

Robert E. Owen, president of Paxton & Vierling Steel and chairman of parent company Owen Industries, Inc., stands at the site of First National Center Tower in Omaha. Landmark Steel, an alliance of Paxton & Vierling Steel, Drake Williams Steel, and Davis Erection, is managing steel erection for the Tower, planned as the tallest office building in Nebraska and Iowa, using 8,000 tons of structural steel.

firm, beginning as a weekend watchman working for one dollar per day and rising through the company to become chairman. In 1979, Edward Owen handed the day-to-day responsibility of running the company to his eldest son, Robert E. Owen, who now is chairman of Owen Industries, headquartered in Omaha, and president of Paxton & Vierling Steel (PVS).

TOP STEEL PROCESSORS OF TODAY

PVS has become one of the top steel fabricators in the United States, dedicated to meeting stringent production and schedule requirements and setting industry standards for precision workmanship. PVS maintains large inventories of materials, uses advanced technology

Shown here is a light fabrication bay at Paxton & Vierling Steel, in Omaha, Nebraska.

Pictured are (left) a robotic welder and (right) a manufactured product with a powder coat finish. The finish was applied electrostatically at the Tri-City Fabrication and Welding division in Davenport, Iowa.

and equipment, streamlines logistics management, and operates its own fleet of trucks. As one of Owen Industries' divisions, its projects are supported by a network of steel service centers across the Midwest.

Owen Industries is now one of the nation's leading processors of steel for the manufacturing, railroad, agriculture, and construction industries. Its projects range from silos to power plants, from interstate highway light fixtures to bulldozers and tractor parts, from stadiums to railroad bridges. The company provides a full range of steel products and steel-processing capabilities and service. Service centers fill orders for long-term and just-in-time steel needs and provide extensive processing-plus capabilities. The contract manufacturing division produces steel products completed up to the fully painted stage for just-in-time assembly. The structural fabrication division handles projects of immense size and supplies products and services to satisfied customers worldwide. Project management teams oversee time lines and budget matters. Because of

corporatewide commitment to high quality standards, many Owen Industries divisions have received ISO-9002 certification.

A WORLDWIDE ARENA WITH OMAHA ROOTS
Owen Industries employs more than 400 people, and annual sales are more than $100 million. The company believes that its success relies on the development of all its employees and their abilities. The corporation has strategic partners throughout the Pacific Rim and Europe. Its arena is everywhere in the world, with its home court in Omaha.

Fred H. Owen and Edward F. Owen established a charitable foundation in 1959 that has generously endowed more than $4.5 million to various scholarships and more than 50 community groups in greater Omaha. The Owen family and the Owen Foundation also have made significant contributions to enhance the quality of life in the community, including tennis courts at Mahoney State Park; Camp Owen at Platte River State Park; improvements to the Omaha Community Playhouse; and new facilities for lions, tigers, seals, and giraffes at the Henry Doorly Zoo. The Owen family also is strongly committed to enhancing the cultural amenities of Omaha by supporting Opera Omaha, the Omaha Millennium Lights Display, and Boy Scouts and Boys & Girls Clubs of Omaha.

What does the future hold for PVS and Owen Industries? Robert Owen believes the range of services and value the corporation can provide to its customers is unlimited. "Our goal is to become our customers' supplier of choice when they need steel and steel processing," he says.

OWEN INDUSTRIES COMPANIES

Paxton & Vierling Steel and all companies of Owen Industries can be contacted via the Internet, and customers can make project commitments or inquiries. All are welcome to visit the Owen Industries World Wide Web site at www.owenind.com or contact Robert Owen via E-mail at reowen@owenind.com.

- Paxton & Vierling Steel, Omaha, Nebraska (www.pvsteel.com)
- Lincoln Steel Company, Lincoln, Nebraska (www.lnsteel.com)
- Northern Plains Steel, Fargo, North Dakota (www.npsteel.com)
- Missouri Valley Steel, Sioux City, Iowa (www.mvsteel.com)
- Tri-City Fabrication, Davenport, Iowa (www.tcfab.com)

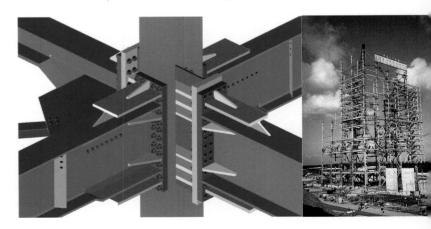

Paxton & Vierling Steel fabricated more than 10,000 tons of structural steel for the Quezon Power Project in the Philippines, diagrammed here with the Design Data CAD/CAM detailing package.

MALNOVE INCORPORATED

A national leader in the packaging systems industry, Malnove Incorporated continues to grow and prosper under the philosophy of providing premium quality folding cartons, excellent customer service, and competitive pricing.

Healthy Choice, Dolly Madison, Hostess, Fiddle Faddle, Puffs, Sara Lee—these brand names are far more recognizable than that of Malnove Incorporated, headquartered in Omaha, Nebraska. But Malnove Incorporated provides a key product vital to those famous companies—packaging. Malnove Incorporated is an Omaha-based company that converts paperboard into folding cartons to provide retail packaging for some of the most recognizable names in the American marketplace.

Malnove's primary plant in west Omaha encompasses 250,000 square feet and includes the company's manufacturing and corporate offices.

The company began 50 years ago when founder and CEO Paul Malnove and his Omaha-born wife moved to Omaha. With prior experience working at a paper converting company in New York City, Malnove decided to launch his own packaging systems business in Omaha.

Having outgrown the company's original facilities more than 20 years ago, the manufacturing operations moved to their current location in a 250,000-square-foot building at 13434 F Street in southwest Omaha. The company started by Malnove still maintains a strong entrepreneurial spirit and flourishes under the philosophy of providing high quality folding cartons, excellent customer service, and competitive pricing.

Omaha was the single location for the business until the early 1980s, when as a result of successfully serving a variety of larger national customers, the company decided to expand its operations. Two key acquisitions, one in Florida and the other in Utah, gave the company full access to national markets. The Clearfield, Utah, plant currently houses 120 employees and serves the growing business in the western states. The original plant in Jacksonville, Florida, was replaced in early 1998 with a greenfield state-of-the-art, 200,000-square-foot carton manufacturing plant with more than 200 employees. This facility serves a larger customer base extending throughout the eastern United States and the Caribbean.

ON THE CUTTING EDGE OF TECHNOLOGY

Malnove Incorporated of Nebraska employs 220 people and together they work three shifts, 24 hours a day, five days a week. New equipment has catapulted Malnove even farther into the area of cutting-edge technological advancements. An electronic prepress uses electronic proofs to decrease lag time in production and to guarantee more control on the quality of the end product.

Since customers expect consistent quality, Malnove Incorporated strives to decrease downtime and defects in the end product. To achieve this end, Malnove

State-of-the-art equipment helps assure Malnove's superior quality and competitiveness.

Incorporated has developed and implemented a comprehensive quality management program, which is monitored with the aide of personal computers installed on each piece of manufacturing equipment. Premier quality levels are also dependent on the capabilities of the equipment used. Malnove is aggressive in assuring that its printing and die-cutting machinery utilizes all the latest technological advances.

AT THE FOREFRONT OF THE INDUSTRY

In fact, technological innovation is what keeps Malnove ahead of its competition, at the forefront of the industry. In one recent case, a major manufacturer challenged Malnove to improve the complex packaging of its facial tissues. By designing and utilizing an equipment line unlike any other in the industry, Malnove was able to provide substantial quality improvements while at the same time offering dramatic savings to the customer.

The perishable baking product market is a large end-use customer for Malnove. Many of the packages demand the application of a clear window membrane for display of products such as donuts, cookies, and pies. Malnove recently developed a completely different concept of applying the window material to the package. This innovation has resulted in significantly higher manufacturing speeds, yielding a more competitive package for customers in the industry.

A commitment to staying ahead of competition is the foundation of Malnove's approach to its markets. When challenged by a customer to provide a high strength package that could easily be constructed at the customer's plant and reduce shipping costs, Malnove created the now patented StackRite™ packaging system. This system involves a unique paperboard design with supporting equipment. Premium gift products from well-known Harry & David's are packaged in Malnove's StackRite. Building on this success, Malnove has positioned its StackRite product line to package diverse products such as premium teas, golf balls, and frozen sandwiches and desserts marketed in club stores.

The combination of desirable properties of the StackRite design which significantly lower customer's costs through lower paperboard thickness, reduced carton blank size, and more efficient shipping storage and

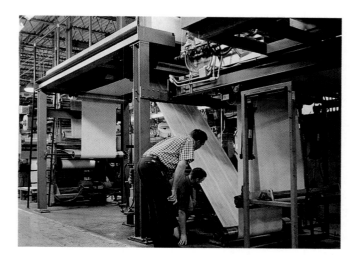

Malnove maintains a strong commitment to the ongoing training of its employees.

processing, have gained widespread interest for the products. Malnove is currently pursuing licensing opportunities for this system in the Americas, Europe, and Asia.

A BRIGHT FUTURE

Paul Malnove is philosophical about company growth: "I am always being asked about how big we want to be in the future. The answer is quite simple: We want to become as big as we think we should be to satisfy the needs of a consolidating industry. We are not putting a size limit on ourselves—the industry, as a whole, will determine that. To be prepared for growth, we must be able to afford the latest equipment. And we have to keep growing to offer our people better opportunities. Growth itself becomes the real challenge."

Innovations such as the Stack-Rite™ carton system allow Malnove to compete in the national and international arena.

GIBRALTAR PACKAGING GROUP, INC.

Gibraltar Packaging Group, Inc., headquartered in Hastings, Nebraska, manufactures product lines of folding, litho-laminated, and corrugated cartons, plus flexible packaging, at three strategically located facilities across the nation.

The products of Gibraltar Packaging Group include folding, litho-laminated, and corrugated cartons, as well as flexible packaging.

Packaging that speaks volumes without saying a word—that's the goal at Gibraltar Packaging Group, Inc., and each of its three divisions strives to meet that goal with every order produced. Gibraltar Packaging's national award–winning design staff and experienced customer service and production personnel ensure that this goal is kept at the forefront of everything the company does.

It all began in 1956 when the corporation's predecessor, Great Plains Packaging, was founded in Hastings, Nebraska. During its early years, the company mainly produced corrugated shipping containers, but also offered folding carton capabilities to its markets within western and central Nebraska. Through the years, the company built upon its historical successes by expanding its sales territories into the central and southern areas of the United States. As these regions flourished, so did the demand for folding cartons—which became the company's primary product line.

During the 1980s the company identified a growing need for "litho-laminated" cartons, which offer both the high quality graphics of a folding carton as well as the protective characteristics of a corrugated carton. Litho-laminated cartons were mostly being used in the rapidly growing markets of hardware, toys, and computer products, and entering into this product line offered additional growth opportunities for Great Plains Packaging.

In 1985, the company added laminating capabilities to its operations, which increased its product offering to three complementary product lines of folding, litho-laminated, and corrugated cartons.

This strategy for growth continued into the 1990s and today, the company, which originated as a small, corrugated print shop with four employees, is Gibraltar Packaging Group, Inc., a publicly held company that employs more than 475 people.

Gibraltar's corporate headquarters is located in Hastings, Nebraska, at its Great Plains Packaging facility. The corporation also consists of two additional divisions that add new and exciting dimensions to the company. These facilities, Flashfold Carton in Fort Wayne, Indiana, and Standard Packaging & Printing in Mount Gilead, North Carolina, are strategically located to position the company to serve larger national accounts.

Although folding cartons are the core of Gibraltar's business, the company also manufactures laminated and corrugated cartons from the Hastings, Nebraska, facility, as well as flexible packaging from its facility in Mount Gilead, North Carolina. The four product lines that Gibraltar's divisions manufacture complement each other and enable the company to provide multiple packaging products to its customers.

Gibraltar Packaging Group, Inc.'s corporate headquarters and its Great Plains Packaging facility are in Hastings, Nebraska.

Management and press teams inspect and verify output from the automated color control system to guarantee consistent, quality printing.

HIGH STANDARDS OF QUALITY

The philosophies that each division was founded upon mirror the overall goal of Gibraltar Packaging Group. Each division is committed to continual process improvement and to providing the best in quality packaging products. In this pursuit, the company's Great Plains Packaging division embarked on a journey to obtain certification to ISO-9001, the worldwide standard for quality management. Following an extensive review and documentation of procedures, processes, and work instructions, Great Plains Packaging received certification to the ISO-9001 standard in June 1996. With this achievement, Great Plains Packaging became the first manufacturing company with folding, laminated, and corrugated product lines under one roof to become ISO certified. Gibraltar continued this pursuit and in January 1998 its Flashfold Carton facility achieved ISO-9001 certification. This division also received the State of Indiana Quality Improvement Award in 1999 and 2000 for its efforts in ensuring the production of quality products. Standard Packaging & Printing also holds this philosophy for quality as it pursues ISO certification for its product lines of folding and flexible packaging. The dedication that these three divisions have to the ISO standards and overall quality management underscores the corporation's commitment to quality and customer satisfaction.

Great Plains Packaging
A Division of Gibraltar Packaging Group, Inc.

Each of Gibraltar Packaging Group's divisions strives to offer the most innovative packaging solutions found in the marketplace. The company has four structural designers on staff, who offer more than 70 years of combined industry experience and expertise to its customers. This design staff has received numerous national awards for its innovations in structural carton design. Gibraltar also has graphics support personnel who provide additional resources to its customers for translation of their graphics into quality carton printing.

DEDICATION AND EXPERIENCE

President and Chief Operating Officer Richard Hinrichs sums up Gibraltar's philosophies: "We at Gibraltar Packaging Group feel that the dedication and experience of our employees is unsurpassed by others within our industry. Our production, quality, customer service, sales, and management staff work in a team effort to ensure that our customers are provided with the best service, support, and products from our company. This dedication is at the core of our business, and has enabled our company to experience tremendous growth.

"We at Gibraltar Packaging Group know that it is our employees who have enabled the company to be successful since its beginning in 1956. It is this dedication that allows Gibraltar Packaging to be its customers' first-choice packaging supplier."

Designers at Gibraltar Packaging use CAD (computer-aided design) systems to create top quality packaging design for prototypes and products.

LINWELD

One of the largest welding supply distributors and independent processors of industrial, medical, and specialty gases in the United States, Linweld achieves growth by continually striving to exceed its customers' expectations.

From its modest beginnings with five employees and one truck, Linweld, based in Lincoln, Nebraska, has expanded to become a company with multiple sales, service, and manufacturing locations.
© *Edholm & Blomgren*

In 1945, David Breslow founded Linweld as the Lincoln Welding Supply Company to provide welding supplies and industrial gases to customers in Lincoln, Nebraska, and rural areas within a 100-mile radius.

At the time, the company's principal customers were small welding shops, farmers, construction companies, and a few medical care facilities. Gases, equipment, and supplies were delivered by a company-owned route truck—a real nod to customer service, since, at the time, most competitors relied on common carriers to deliver products to the same customers.

Four years later, in 1949, Lincoln Welding Supply Company expanded its gas and welding supply operations to Hastings, Nebraska. Then, in the mid-1960s, the company acquired equipment to deliver, handle, and store liquid oxygen. This successful venture broke traditional industry practice and led to added investments for the transportation and delivery of liquid oxygen and argon. High-volume customers were now able to realize the cost, safety, and supply benefits of bulk gases.

In 1975, after 30 years as a distributor for a major gas manufacturer, Linweld ended the relationship and began purchasing industrial and medical gases on the open market. This new venture allowed Linweld to remain competitive in the marketplace and enhanced its position as a major player in the liquefied gas market. In 1977, John Breslow made the transition from vice president to chairman of the board.

In 1982, Linweld distinguished itself from most U.S. welding supply distributors by building its first air separation plant in Waverly, Nebraska.

Breslow notes, "The building of this plant was a defining moment in the history of our company. We were able to generate significant growth because of the competitive prices and availability of the products we brought to the market. Although the project was a big financial risk, at the end of the day, it has been a great boost for Linweld and its customers." The plant in Waverly solidified Linweld's place in the liquefied gas market and positioned the company for significant future growth.

Linweld takes care to provide timely delivery services to its customers. The trucks shown here deliver Linweld high quality gas.

Linweld distinguishes its state-of-the-art automation solutions with "quality people, quality products, and quality service."

DIVERSE EXPANSION AND NEW TECHNOLOGIES

The late 1980s marked Linweld's diversification into robotic arc-welding systems. As an integrator and supplier of flexible and fixed automated cutting and welding systems, the company's reputation for outstanding customer service and technology-based solutions continued.

The advent of the 1990s brought with it growing concerns about air quality in the workplace. It also marked Linweld's introduction as a specialty gas manufacturer and supporter and seller of clean air equipment and technologies. In 1997, the company purchased its primary supplier of clean air products, Industrial Air Specialists, which enhanced the Linweld distribution of air cleaners and systems, large-capacity dust collector systems, filters and ventilation systems, commercial fans, and cooling equipment for the manufacturing industry.

Today, Linweld has manufacturing and sales facilities in more than 30 locations, serving Nebraska, Iowa, South Dakota, Minnesota, Missouri, Kansas, Colorado, and Wyoming. As a manufacturer, processor, and distributor, Linweld now delivers a diverse line of products that includes welding equipment and supplies, liquefied and compressed gas, automation systems, clear air equipment, safety, metalworking, and general industrial products.

In addition to its sales and service locations, Linweld operates its own cylinder distribution center, acetylene plants, specialty gas department, and air separation plant. The air separation plant converts large quantities of air into oxygen, nitrogen, and argon. Linweld is one of the few independent distributors and manufacturers of welding supplies and gases in the nation.

SUCCESS THROUGH SERVICE

Overall, the company employs more than 400 dedicated people who continually exceed the demands of diversified markets and customers in agricultural, health care, beverage, and high-tech companies, to name just a few.

"No one job at Linweld is more important than any other," says president Charles Canterberry. "We just all do different things. Our people define this company every day and are responsible for the success we have enjoyed throughout the years. Many of our managers and outside salespeople started here by working in the warehouse, at the counter, or driving a route truck. Employee-advancement opportunities have been a hallmark and a strength at Linweld since day one."

To better educate employees about its products and services, Linweld opened the David Breslow Training Center in 1995. Since then, a welding laboratory and an automation center have been added to provide product demonstration and integration space for Linweld's growing automated-solutions business. The

Staff engineers and chemists consult regularly with Linweld customers to help them maintain strict control of quality and costs.

primary focus of these training facilities is to raise the professional, technological, and solution-providing capabilities of employees and sales teams. Similar training is provided at the same facilities for Linweld customers.

The David Breslow Training Center is recognized as one of the finest facilities of its kind in the nation.

STRATEGIC GROWTH

Looking to the future, Linweld will build another facility that will include a cylinder distribution center, a specialty gas laboratory, and a medical and cylinder-filling site. The 85,000-square-foot facility, scheduled for completion in early 2001, will also house the Linweld safety and quality department. This facility will assist retail stores in serving such customers as hospitals, colleges and universities, emission-testing laboratories in power plants, large chemical plants, government and independent laboratories, food-blanketing and food-processing plants, and oil refineries.

Linweld also plans to open a new, larger air separation unit in fall 2001—a move that will position Linweld as a premier supplier and manufacturer of industrial, medical, and specialty gases in the Midwest. Specifically, the facility will produce high-purity oxygen, nitrogen, and argon.

With the recent acquisition of several Air Products and Chemicals, Inc., stores, Linweld has gained another acetylene plant and an additional cylinder distribution and pumping facility.

Another milestone in Linweld's long history of exceptional customer service is the company's Web site (www.linweld.com). Linweld's E-commerce functions make it possible for customers to obtain information on sales and service locations, management, and current company news. In the near future, Linweld customers will also be able to make on-line purchases of welding equipment and supplies, liquefied and compressed gases, automation systems, and air cleaning equipment and filters. Once again, Linweld displays its commitment to the customer.

Linweld is proud to be a leader in the welding and liquefied and compressed gas industry and continues to seek new markets and areas of expansion. The company's success and growth is attributed to employees who believe in earning their customers' business each and every day.

For more information, contact the Linweld corporate office: 2900 S. 70th Street, Suite 400, Lincoln, NE 68506; phone: 402-323-8450; Web site: www.linweld.com.

Linweld makes liquefied and compressed gases that meet the highest quality specifications, delivered on time and at a competitive price.

VALMONT INDUSTRIES, INC.

Serving clients worldwide, Omaha-based Valmont Industries, Inc., makes water-management equipment for agriculture

and steel and aluminum poles and towers, and provides protective coatings services for infrastructure development.

Valmont Industries, Inc., is a leading global manufacturer of irrigation equipment for the agriculture industry, and poles, structures, and coating services for the lighting, utility, and communication industries.

Valmont's heritage is deeply rooted in the land and its bountiful harvests. Starting as a small farm equipment manufacturer in a cornfield just west of Omaha, the company realized the potential and importance of a strange-looking invention it came upon that propelled a long pipeline, mounted on wheels, around a field, irrigating the crop with sprinklers as it went. The inventor agreed to license the patent to Valmont and soon center-pivot irrigation equipment was revolutionizing agriculture. Today, more than 10 million acres are irrigated using Valmont's Valley® center-pivot and linear-move irrigation equipment in the United States and more than 90 countries worldwide.

As an industry leader, Valmont continued to develop new technology and procedures to increase crop yields and reduce farming costs through efficient water management. Valmont pioneered the "corner system" to assist in irrigating square, rectangular, and odd-shaped fields. It also introduced low-pressure sprinkler systems capable of reducing energy costs by up to 80 percent and designed computerized controls that enable farmers to program and monitor irrigation equipment remotely, from their offices or homes.

After Valmont began to manufacture its own pipe for its irrigation equipment, the company's engineers designed and built machinery to make tapered steel poles. Valmont's

Valmont's infrastructure products help create safe, well-lit outdoor environments around the world.

development and use of a special, high-speed welding process led to the manufacture of tapered poles for outdoor lighting, traffic signals, and many other applications. Valmont now makes poles for the street lighting, traffic signal, utility, and wireless communication markets.

Another Valmont first was the application of hot-dipped galvanizing to its finished products to provide long-term corrosion protection. The demand for galvanizing as a protective coating continued to increase through the years and the company now has coatings operations throughout North America.

Today Valmont operates major facilities on five continents around the world. The company is headquartered in Omaha, Nebraska, and employs more than 5,000 trained personnel worldwide, with approximately 1,600 located in Nebraska.

As you travel in Nebraska and throughout the world, notice the lights that brighten your way at night, the electricity you use, the phone call you make, the water that nourishes the food you eat—there's a good chance Valmont products help produce, transport, support, or protect these products and services.

Valley® mechanized irrigation equipment, manufactured by Valmont, is designed to conserve water and increase food production and can be used in the application of fertilizer, chemicals, fresh water, and recycled wastewater.

PFIZER INC

Pfizer Inc's Lincoln Manufacturing Operations, a major supplier of biological and pharmaceutical products for animals, employs more than 800 people and ranks among Lincoln, Nebraska's top industrial employers.

Pfizer Inc's 145-acre Lincoln Manufacturing Operations campus is home to one of the world's most advanced technological centers for large-scale production of biologicals and pharmaceuticals.

After more than 80 years in business, the Lincoln Manufacturing Operations of Pfizer Inc is a major supplier of biological and pharmaceutical products to customers around the globe. The site's current international presence has its roots in the birth of the animal health industry that quietly began early in the 20th century and grew dramatically to the vital role it now plays worldwide.

It was 1919 when Dr. Carl J. Norden Sr., a young immigrant from Sweden, fulfilled his dream of starting an ethical drug firm selling its products to veterinarians. The company that would be known as Norden Laboratories for 70 years enjoyed steady growth through its first 40 years, first as a distributor and then by researching, developing, and producing its own biological and pharmaceutical products for livestock.

In 1959, Norden Laboratories became a subsidiary of Smith Kline & French Laboratories, a leading developer and producer of high quality pharmaceuticals for humans. At that time, Norden Laboratories was marketing approximately 60 biological and 165 pharmaceutical products. The merger provided the philosophical and financial resources for the organization to grow and thrive.

Norden Laboratories continued its tradition of achieving industry firsts in both its function and its method of development. The next three decades were an impressive period of growth for Norden Laboratories, when many new products for both livestock and companion animals were introduced.

In July 1989, SmithKline Beckman (formerly Smith Kline & French) merged with Beecham Group and the once–fully autonomous Norden Laboratories became an operating facility—the Lincoln plant. The plant was designated as the worldwide manufacturing center for all SmithKline Beecham Animal Health biological products and was chartered with the production of additional pharmaceutical products.

In 1994, a state-of-the-art plant to make biological products in bulk for vaccine production was completed and dedicated. Later that same year, the news came that the entire SmithKline Beecham Animal Health business was being purchased by Pfizer Inc.

Pfizer Inc is a research-based global pharmaceutical company that discovers, develops, manufactures, and markets innovative medicines for humans and animals. In 1999 Pfizer celebrated its 150th anniversary. Pfizer is committed to the pursuit of medicines that help ensure good health in every corner of the world, doing business in more than 150 countries.

A GLOBAL MANUFACTURING CENTER

Today the 145-acre Pfizer Lincoln property in northwest Lincoln, with manufacturing facilities of nearly 900,000 square feet, serves as a global manufacturing center for bulk biological antigens for livestock and companion animal vaccines, as well as biological-product finishing and packaging operations for vaccines. The facility also is a manufacturing center for animal health pharmaceutical products.

Biological products made at Pfizer Lincoln are regulated by the USDA and other international regulatory agencies. Annual production exceeds 550 million vaccine doses. Major biological products made at Pfizer Lincoln are: RespiSure®, BoviShield®, FarrowSure®, the Vanguard® product line, Felocell CVR®, and LitterGuard®.

Pharmaceutical products made at Pfizer Lincoln are regulated by the FDA and other international regulatory agencies. Production includes antibiotic drugs, anti-inflammatory drugs, parasiticides, liquid and tablet nutritional supplements, and anthelmintic pastes and suspensions. Annual production includes more than 500,000 liters of liquids, more than 1.5 million kilograms of solids, and more than 600 million tablets. Major pharmaceutical products made at Pfizer Lincoln are: Rimadyl®, Anipryl®, Pet-Tabs®, and Anthelcide EQ®.

DEDICATION TO SCIENCE, HEALTH, AND PEOPLE

Pfizer Lincoln considers its real strength to be found in its employees. The company employs more than 800 colleagues, and it ranks among Lincoln, Nebraska's top industrial employers. Pfizer's Lincoln Operations remains focused on manufacturing technology, combining scientific expertise with dedication to continual improvement.

Pfizer Lincoln is poised for the promise and challenge of the future. Pfizer is a world leader in research and development (R&D) dedicated to animal health. Product candidates in the pipeline have increased significantly in recent years. Current prospects include genetically engineered vaccines, general therapy products,

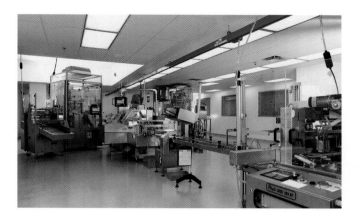

Pfizer pharmaceuticals are produced for both companion animals and livestock for the treatment of disease, parasites, and nutritional deficiencies.

and novel, easy-to-use medicines. Pfizer Lincoln is expected to become the manufacturing site for some of these new products.

In Lincoln, as in other communities where Pfizer operates, there is an emphasis on the need for both corporate and individual support of community. Pfizer Lincoln has repeatedly been the largest contributor to the Lincoln Lancaster County United Way/CHAD campaign. Pfizer Lincoln is a strong supporter of mathematics and science education in local schools, and employees participate in a wide range of volunteer activities, including the Paint-A-Thon, Junior Achievement, and reading with students at the plant's neighborhood school.

Pfizer Lincoln is particularly proud to have been the first recipient of the Mayor's Community Conscience Award, in 2000. Pfizer was recognized as an outstanding corporate citizen for its support of nonprofit organizations and its participation in building a healthy community.

NEAR RIGHT: *The fermentation process, by which some vaccines are produced, is completely enclosed to ensure purity and includes a permanent network of piping, which allows material to be transferred to progressively larger fermenters until production volumes are reached.* RIGHT: *Individual production units are isolated from each other. Each has its own air supply, and access to each area is limited to the technicians and other staff members involved in the operation of only that area.*

CHIEF INDUSTRIES, INC.

Chief Industries, Inc., is a diversified manufacturer of fabricated steel for grain handling, correctional products, pre-engineered buildings, wastewater treatment, electronic signs, truck chassis, factory-built homes, RV's, and ethanol.

The corporate headquarters of Chief Industries, Inc., is located in Grand Island, Nebraska.

Among the challenges facing today's entrepreneurs is to devise effective business models. How best to fulfill the needs and goals of customers and clients, employees and suppliers, and the multiple communities an organization serves and depends upon for success? From its corporate headquarters in Grand Island, Nebraska, during nearly a half-century of dynamic growth, Chief Industries, Inc., has refined its uncommonly strong corporate model of compatible and synergistic business units.

The strategy emerged soon after the company was launched, in 1954, as a small construction firm devoted to building and remodeling single-family homes. Chief soon added farm buildings and grain bins to its manufacturing mix. As the capable people at Chief steadily increased the company's reputation for high quality, superior product support, and competitive prices, the company expanded with a carefully balanced range of products. Sales and marketing resources were developed across the United States, then in Great Britain and France. Today, Chief is a thriving transoceanic network of 10 semiautonomous divisions and six subsidiaries.

With every corporate addition, the guiding principle remained that each Chief product should set a standard for its type. And so it has, from reliable bulk-handling systems and factory-built homes, to road-tough recreational

vehicles and intermodal trailer chassis, to distinctive, programmable message-display products.

PRINCIPAL OPERATIONS

A survey of the thriving operations at Chief Industries in the new millennium reveals the way a strategy of controlled growth balanced with insistence on quality and service marks progress for the company.

Agri/Industrial: Among the best-known products of Chief Industries are its Chief and York bins for farm and commercial grain drying and storage, complemented by Caldwell grain conditioning and handling equipment for nearly every grain storage and handling need. Agri/Industrial also manufactures and markets post frame buildings for farms and ranches.

Building: Durable pre-engineered buildings are designed and factory built with advanced technology to achieve low construction and maintenance costs. Chief designs and manufactures wide-span and low-rise building systems to suit individual client requirements; buildings range from service buildings to aviation hangars, from industrial plants to stylish offices.

Custom Products: Among the special products and services provided by this division are Chief correctional products, including doors and door frames, windows, and heavy-gauge steel furniture and accessories, all reinforced for durability in correctional institutions and other secure building settings. Also under the Chief custom-made products umbrella are Ecolo-Chief wastewater treatment systems, which are custom-fabricated for facilities not served by municipal sewage treatment systems; Concept Fiberglass, manufacturers of fiberglass components; and powder coating with Chief Powder Coated Tough™, an environment-friendly finish for metal that provides durable protection from corrosion, heat, abrasion, fading, and extreme weather for many kinds of products.

Ethanol Fuels: Chief is a leading maker of ethanol fuel, which combats air pollution from automobile engine emissions; Chief produces more than 60 million gallons of ethanol annually, and also markets the high-protein feed substance by-product to the cattle and dairy industry.

Electronics: Chief designs and manufactures programmable message-display products for point-of-sale or public communications information by institutions and commercial sites, from banks to shopping centers.

Fabrication: The Chief fabrication division supplies steel components and custom-made metal fabrication to other Chief divisions and other Midwest manufacturers. It also builds a patented intermodal trailer chassis that permits efficient load transfers between trucks, railroad cars, and ships.

Housing: A longtime leader in the design and construction of prefabricated houses, Chief builds well-made factory-manufactured modular homes with various floor plans and decors, at its two BonnaVilla Homes plants. The houses are marketed, in part, through four company-owned retail outlets, in Omaha, Kearney, and Grand Island, Nebraska, and Denver, Colorado, under the Eagle Crest banner.

Recreational Vehicles: Under its respected King of the Road marque, Chief produces fifth-wheel recreational vehicles in several size and floor plan options, all designed, engineered, and manufactured to the high standards of Chief craftsmanship and attention to detail.

International: Chief products are marketed abroad through the Chief international subsidiary and also through the international sales staffs of its various divisions. Strengthening its international presence, Chief acquired two existing grain bin manufacturing facilities in Europe: Chief Industries UK Ltd., in Maldon, Essex, England; and Phenix-Rousies Industries, S.A., in Rousies, France.

QUALITY, INNOVATION, AND COMPETITIVE PRICING

The nearly 2,000 skilled, imaginative, and dedicated men and women of Chief Industries at its plants and offices in Nebraska, across the nation, and abroad are responsible for the quality, innovation, and competitive pricing that distinguish every Chief product. These able people have built a strong and forward-looking company positioned to grow and to ably serve its many customers and communities with distinction well into the 21st century.

CHIEF INDUSTRIES, INC.
CORPORATE OFFICES • GRAND ISLAND, NEBRASKA

DIVISIONS

- Agri/Industrial Division
  Kearney, Nebraska; Fort Dodge, Iowa
- Buildings Division
  Grand Island, Nebraska; Rensselaer, Indiana
- Construction Divisions
  Chief Construction and Heartland Electric, Grand Island, Nebraska
  Bohnert Construction, Kansas City, Missouri
- Custom Products Division
  Grand Island, Nebraska
- Electronics Division
  Electronic Display Systems, Grand Island, Nebraska
- Fabrication Division
  Grand Island, Nebraska
- Housing Division
  BonnaVilla Homes, Aurora and Bradshaw, Nebraska
- Recreational Vehicle Division
  King of the Road, Russell, Kansas
- Intermodal Sales
  Grand Island, Nebraska

SUBSIDIARIES

- Chief Ethanol Fuels, Inc., Hastings, Nebraska
- Eagle Crest Homes, Inc., Omaha, Kearney, and Grand Island, Nebraska; Denver, Colorado
- Grand Island Contract Carriers, Inc.
  G.I.C.C. Brokerage, Inc., Grand Island, Nebraska
- Chief International, Inc., Grand Island, Nebraska
- Chief Industries UK Ltd., Maldon, Essex, England
- Phenix-Rousies Industries, S.A., Rousies, France

KAWASAKI MOTORS MANUFACTURING CORP., U.S.A.

Making its famous motorcycles and other products in Lincoln, Nebraska, since 1974, Kawasaki Motors Manufacturing

Corp., U.S.A. holds constant its commitments to top quality production, to its employees, and to its home community.

Few states in the U.S.A. can boast about being the home of a company whose products have become icons on the nation's highways, back roads, farms, and lakes. One of the few is Nebraska and the company whose products have become synonymous with the idea of quality in motion is Kawasaki Motors Manufacturing Corp., U.S.A.

Japan-based Kawasaki, one of the world's leading manufacturers of motorcycles, all-terrain vehicles (ATVs), Jet Ski® watercraft, utility vehicles, wheels, industrial robots, and engines for consumer products, has been an integral part of Nebraska's economy and a staple of the industrial complex of Nebraska's capital for more than a quarter of a century.

Having established its American manufacturing facility in Lincoln in 1974, Kawasaki has been a pioneer among foreign vehicle manufacturers who have established plants in the United States. It was, in fact, the first to do so, paving the way for such other well-known foreign vehicle makers as Toyota, Honda, Nissan, and Volkswagen, who followed in Kawasaki's footsteps. Far-sighted Kawasaki executives at the time reasoned that if a product is being sold in America, it could be built in America, too, saving time and shipping costs and making use of U.S. labor pool talent.

Mixed model production requires assembly line workers to perform multiple tasks, checking quality at each step.

For one thing, the company's facility in Lincoln, including manufacturing operations, offices, and warehouses, has undergone more than a dozen expansions, growing from 210,300 square feet in 1974 to nearly 1.3 million square feet in 2000, spread over a 335-acre campus. In addition, the Lincoln plant opened an auxiliary facility for the production of engines for consumer products in Maryville, Missouri, in 1989. Today, Maryville contains nearly 640,000 square feet of manufacturing, office, and warehouse space on about 114 acres. And there are plans for even

CONTINUED GROWTH

Like its adopted Cornhusker home, and its own parent company, which was founded in Japan in 1878, Kawasaki's Lincoln operation has undergone some dramatic changes during the past 26-plus years.

Kawasaki's ZX-11 Ninja® motorcycle set the standard for open-class sportbike performance for nearly a decade.

more expansions that will add up to another one-half million square feet of space to the Lincoln plant by the middle of this decade for light rail car manufacturing.

The number of people employed at the Lincoln plant has grown from just 172 in 1974 to nearly 1,000 today. An additional 400-plus are employed at the Maryville plant, and even more employees are expected to be added when the planned expansion program in Lincoln is completed.

A FULL RANGE OF ENGINEERED PRODUCTS

The range of products produced by Kawasaki's Lincoln plant has expanded dramatically. In 1974, production at the Lincoln facility was limited to motorcycles, including Kawasaki's KZ400, KZ900 LTD, and its Police bike. In 1975, the Jet Ski was added, and in 1980, the company began making ATVs. For a short period, between 1977 and 1981, the plant also produced snowmobiles.

The Lincoln plant began manufacturing utility vehicles in 1987, and in 1995, it produced robots for use in a variety of applications, including welding, painting, bonding, and ergonomics. In 2000, the plant began producing parts for Kawasaki Construction Machinery Corp. of America in Kennesaw, Georgia, and seats for New York City subway cars being built by Kawasaki Rail Car, Inc., in Yonkers, New York.

Today, production at Kawasaki's Lincoln plant includes eight motorcycle models, 10 ATV models, five utility vehicle models, seven Jet Ski models, and three

Mixed model assembly lowers inventory requirements and allows Kawasaki to meet customer demand.

different series of robots. The plant also produces wheel rims, not only for its own products, but also for products manufactured by Honda, Yamaha, and Polaris. Sales of products made by Kawasaki Lincoln total more than $500 million annually, 15 percent of which is from products the plant makes for export.

Through the years, other, more subtle changes also have taken place at Kawasaki's Nebraska facility. The Lincoln plant, which originally was established as a division of Kawasaki Motors Corp., U.S.A., was made a separate entity in 1981 and renamed Kawasaki Motors Manufacturing Corp., U.S.A.

Despite all the changes, one thing has remained constant at Kawasaki—the commitment the company and its Lincoln employees have made to ensuring that the products they manufacture are tops when it comes to quality.

Moreover, the company remains committed to improving its products so that it will always remain a step ahead of its competitors.

Another constant at Kawasaki's manufacturing plant is the company's commitment to its employees, whom it considers its most important asset, and its commitment as an employer to be an active and responsible citizen in the community and state in which it makes its home.

Used in a variety of applications including welding, painting, bonding, and ergonomics, Kawasaki robots are recognized around the world for their high level of technology, reliability, versatility, and ease of use.

Kawasaki Motors Manufacturing Corp., U.S.A.

BEHLEN MFG. CO.

Behlen Mfg. Co., based in Columbus, Nebraska, is a well-established manufacturer of building systems, livestock handling equipment, grain bins and dryers, strip-joining presses, and roto-molded plastic components.

The story of Behlen Mfg. Co. is one of a remarkable business turnaround, of an inspired and inspiring CEO, and a combination of the right group of employees at the right time.

Behlen was founded in 1936 in Walter D. Behlen's garage in Columbus, Nebraska. Its first products were toe caps for work shoes and clamps for wooden egg crates. In 1950, the owners switched the company's focus by expanding their offering with grain bins and dryers, as well as a self-framing building system. Products were directed to drying, handling, and storing grain.

The future of Behlen was cast when A. F. (Tony) Raimondo, destined to become the firm's chairman and CEO, joined Behlen as general manager in 1982. A major change occurred in the grain industry in 1984. Under new government policies, farmers were no longer paid to store excess grain and were instead paid that year not to grow grain at all; Behlen revenues plummeted 50 percent in one year. Behlen was at the time owned by the Wickes Corporation, which was eager to divest itself of the suddenly troubled business—and Raimondo was ready to breathe new life into it.

While others credit Raimondo with the current success of Behlen, Raimondo credits Behlen's remarkable employees: "We believe in people, and that people who are involved, and who are asked for their ideas in a climate of full, two-way communication, will make the company grow." Raimondo's first step was to transform the

Building contractors can apply glass, brick, stone, and other finishing materials to Behlen Building Systems, which are fabricated for nearly any use imaginable.

company culture from one that had been autocratic and hierarchical to one based on an honor system, total communication, and positive recognition. These first steps were painful and slow. But Behlen employees soon chose to decertify their union, and the changes began. Instead of a rigid managerial system, natural leaders among the employees were groomed for leadership positions. "People couldn't believe that we threw out the time clock and started an honor system," says Raimondo. "The new company moved from rules to guidelines."

Recognizing that any sort of transformation required complete commitment from every employee at every level, Raimondo sought help from employees themselves. "We are employee-owned. We share everything in both directions. Employees 'Partners in Progress' can ask or tell me anything," he says. "We have monthly luncheons with employees whose birthdays occur that month. This creates a good mix of employees who do feel comfortable to talk about ideas and concerns." In exchange, Raimondo tells employees all good and all not-so-good financial news.

Behlen also rewards employees financially through creative entrepreneurial tactics. In addition to a base pay, employees receive productivity rewards, profit sharing, and

At company headquarters in Columbus, Nebraska, employees celebrate along with chairman and CEO A. F. (Tony) Raimondo, as Inc. *magazine's 1994 "Turnaround Entrepreneur of the Year" national award winner.*

stock ownership. "This helps involve employees in company productivity and progress," Raimondo says. While initially hesitant with the idea of personal authority, soon employees began presenting improvement ideas, large in both number and scope.

DIVERSIFYING FOR ENHANCED SERVICES & GROWTH

With these changes and several strategic acquisitions, Raimondo recreated Behlen Mfg. Co. into a stable, diversified, growing business, with seven business units:

- **Behlen Livestock Equipment Group**'s four plants, in Nebraska, Indiana, Oregon, and Tennessee, are humming with orders, up nearly 30 percent over 1999.
- **Behlen Building Systems**, in Columbus, Nebraska, produces custom-designed metal building systems that are used in single- or multistory commercial, industrial, institutional, and utility applications. Buildings are shipped worldwide.
- **Inland Buildings** produces custom-made structures designed to withstand heavy snow loads and hurricanes. Its facilities, in Indiana, Wisconsin, and Alabama, serve the eastern half of the United States.
- **Behlen International Ag Systems** is a leading supplier of grain bins and Berico dryers and related handling equipment.
- **Behlen Industrial Products Group** provides custom-designed fabricated metal components and is the largest manufacturer of hydraulic presses used for joining metal coils. Behlen has over 500 presses installed, in over 50 countries worldwide.
- **Behlen Engineered Plastics** specializes in roto-molded polyethylene products which are used extensively across the nation. Products include a proprietary line of agriculture products marketed through the Behlen organization, as well as applications for recreational vehicles, boat seats and gas tanks, and furniture. The company also provides a custom–mold making service and is a

Behlen Mfg. Co. provides a wide variety of products. TOP LEFT: Behlen Livestock Equipment Group welders assemble equipment, such as gates. TOP RIGHT: Behlen Industrial Products Group is a world leader in making strip-joining presses, used to connect coils in continuous line operations. ABOVE LEFT: Behlen Building Systems are designed, fabricated, and shipped worldwide; here, a worker prepares a beam. ABOVE RIGHT: Behlen International Ag Systems fabricates walls and roof panels of grain bins holding up to 670,000 bushels.

national supplier of custom-made parts utilizing metal and poly.

- **BMC Transportation** serves all Behlen businesses with deliveries to 48 states. Its owner-operated tractor-trailers travel more than 7,500,000 miles per year, providing on-time, personal customer services.

Behlen's remarkable turnaround and growth has not gone unnoticed. In 1994, *Inc.* magazine tapped Raimondo as the "Turnaround Entrepreneur of the Year." Other awards include Raimondo's induction into the Nebraska Business Hall of Fame in 1999; and in 2000, he was selected as the Triumph of Agriculture Expo Agri-Award winner. Also in 2000, Behlen was selected for the Nebraska State Edgerton Quality Award of Excellence in Continuous Improvement.

Most significantly, in 1999, Behlen was awarded ISO-9001 certification. Sought by many businesses, this certification indicates that Behlen meets or exceeds a complicated series of internationally accepted quality systems standards.

Behlen's Columbus, Nebraska, facility is the size of 17 football fields. It encompasses a vital business whose bedrock building blocks are strengthening and uplifting people, quality, productivity, and trust and respect.

Behlen's BMC Transportation company makes timely deliveries to customers. Mixed loads are part of the added value Behlen offers.

MIDLANDS PACKAGING CORPORATION

Midlands Packaging Corporation in Lincoln holds a strong regional presence in the container industry, making top quality folding cartons, corrugated containers, and thermoformed plastic packaging for wholesale and retail goods.

Midlands Packaging Corporation was founded in 1972 in an 8,000-square-foot airpark building in Lincoln, Nebraska, by Richard H. Warman and partners Michael Costello and Rodney Imig, who all saw a need for better boxes and service for the wholesale industry. Sales for the first month were about $10,000, and customers were delighted with the company's high quality corrugated boxes and with its commitment to on-time delivery. Within two years, Midlands Packaging had moved into a facility double the size of the original, and has since undergone six expansions, resulting in 210,000 square feet of manufacturing space. Since 1981, the company has been privately owned by Richard Warman and his family.

Today, Midlands Packaging employs 126 at its Lincoln headquarters and production plant. Additional staff members are based in sales offices in Denver, Colorado; Minneapolis, Minnesota; Kansas City, Missouri; and Sioux City, Iowa. While most sales are concentrated in the U.S. Midwest, the company has shipped to customers as far as Venezuela.

Midlands Packaging's monthly sales average in excess of $1.5 million, with annual revenues at $20 million. And, while corrugated boxes are still on the list of products offered, folding cartons with sophisticated printing and laminating and thermoformed plastic packaging have taken over the lion's share of the company's business. Midlands

Offering a broad range of packaging options, Midlands Packaging Corporation, in Lincoln, Nebraska, has 210,000 square feet of manufacturing space with state-of-the-art technologies and processing.

Packaging's customers currently manufacture everything from power tools to pharmaceuticals to popcorn.

President and General Manager Steven Warman, the founder's son, recalls that the company's entry into packaging for retail began in 1981 with the purchase of in-house printing equipment. "This led to a stronger presence for us with national companies," Warman says. Eventually Midlands Packaging gained major clients such as American Tool Companies (hardware); Pfizer, Bayer, and Schering-Plough (animal health products); Novartis Consumer Health (over-the-counter medications); Hollister Incorporated and Mentor Corporation (medical devices); and Abbott Laboratories/HPD (pharmaceuticals).

Midlands Packaging uses sophisticated CAD-CAM (computer-aided design and manufacturing) processes, interchangeable printing and die-cutting setups, and other state-of-the-art tools. But technology alone cannot account for the company's success. Warman says, "Midlands Packaging has succeeded by always doing a little bit better and a little bit more." Quality and service are company hallmarks, as is teamwork. The company works hard to train its employees, involve them in decision making, and recognize their achievements. All these factors work together for Midlands Packaging to maintain its status as a quality leader in the packaging industry.

Midlands Packaging makes packages for goods of all kinds, from pharmaceuticals to consumer foods to tools and more.

MIDLANDS PACKAGING CORPORATION

FACTORIES AMONG THE FIELDS

CHAPTER TEN

MOBILITY AND POWER

TRANSPORTATION AND ENERGY

A traveler in Nebraska might notice that many of its communities are a roughly uniform six to 10 miles apart.

This spacing is by design: As the railroads pushed westward across the state in the late 19th century, they

established a siding with a depot—nucleus of a town or village—at six- to 10-mile intervals, based on how long

it took a farmer to drive a wagon to town and back in one day. There is not a town or village in Nebraska with

a population over 250 that is not, or was not, located on a railroad.

This geographical tidbit is but one symbol of the central role that railroads have played in shaping Nebraska. From the day in 1865 when the first westward rail of the Union Pacific was laid in Omaha until now at the beginning of the 21st century, railroads have been principal arteries of the state's economic lifeblood and tangible influences on its culture.

Today the three main railroads serving Nebraska and its communities are the Union Pacific, the Burlington Northern and Santa Fe, and the Chicago Central and Pacific, totaling nearly 4,000 miles of track.

In sustaining a diverse modern economy and providing hospitable settings for new and expanding businesses, Nebraska in 2000 complements its high-volume rail network with systems across the spectrum of transportation modes—land, air, and water.

NATURAL HUB OF COMMERCE

Its central location makes the state a natural hub for freight shipping of all kinds. Nebraska sits astride cross-country

Interstate 80, which follows the historic Platte River Valley path of explorers and pioneers and is one of the nation's primary long-haul truck routes. Just east across the Missouri River, Interstate 29 provides access to market destinations north and south in the Missouri River basin and beyond. Nebraska's network of more than 15,000 miles of principal state highways still serves its original purpose as a vital farm-to-market connection, while also providing convenient avenues of commerce among other Nebraska businesses.

These advantages and others have helped make trucking a major economic factor in Nebraska, as the success story of Werner Enterprises demonstrates. Starting with one truck in 1956, the company headquartered west of Omaha now ranks third in revenues—over a billion dollars a year—among the nation's truckload carriers, operating a fleet of more than 7,000 tractors and 18,000 trailers with routes and terminals spanning the continental United States.

The convergence of rivers, railroads, and highways has long made Nebraska a crossroads of the nation. Air travel and air freight serve to bring the state even closer to both the Atlantic and Pacific coasts.

The economic benefits of centrality also are reflected in the state's growing air passenger and freight capabilities, spread among 94 public and more than 200 private airports. The largest terminus, Omaha's Eppley Airfield, is served by 12 national and three regional carriers providing more than 180 flights a day. In 1999, more than 3.7 million passengers deplaned at the airport, and it shipped or received more than 172,000 pounds of cargo. Eppley, which recently completed a $70 million expansion and modernization, is one of the fastest growing airports in America.

While steamboats no longer ply Nebraska's bordering waters as carriers of cargo, river traffic still is a significant component of the state's transportation capacity. Omaha's five Missouri River barge lines ship agricultural commodities and raw materials for manufacturing to and from international markets and other major river ports throughout the Missouri and Mississippi River basins.

How will Nebraskans and their goods move about in

The Burlington Northern and Santa Fe , the Union Pacific, and other major railroads continue to play a key role in Nebraska's economy. Two-thirds of the freight originating in the state is farm products.

the new century? With a high-volume, unclogged transportation infrastructure in place, the answer is: easily.

And, as the old millennium closed, Nebraskans were eyeing another new wrinkle in their historic relationship with the iron horse. A state commission was investigating the feasibility of instituting new high-speed rail passenger service from Omaha to Lincoln and perhaps beyond.

POWER TO THE PEOPLE

Given its history of conservative politics and values, Nebraska should not be expected to be the home of a unique statewide socialist enterprise. But it is—and for six decades plus, pragmatic Cornhusker collectivism has produced results the most committed free-enterprise capitalist could envy.

In 1933 the legislature provided for the creation of publicly owned entities to generate and transmit electricity. Today Nebraska is the only state in which the entire electric system, including two nuclear power plants, is owned by the citizens. Utilities such as the Nebraska Public Power District, Omaha Public Power District, and

The first state to complete its segment of the U.S. interstate highway system, Nebraska can continue to take pride in its transportation infrastructure, as this stretch of I-680 through Omaha indicates.

Lincoln Electric System provide most of the state's electricity. In addition, smaller public power districts, 15 rural cooperatives, and 121 municipal systems furnish power.

These operations deliver electricity at rates that statewide are 22 percent below the national average. The utility serving the largest urban market, the Omaha Public Power District, offers rates as much as 21 percent below the national average and has an average system reliability of 99-plus percent with a reserve generating capacity of more than 20 percent.

Public ownership also is a prominent factor in supplying the 132 billion cubic feet of natural gas burned annually in the state. The Metropolitan Utilities District, which provides gas and water to most of the Omaha area, is nonprofit and customer-owned, and its residential natural gas rates are about 35 percent below the national average. Other important natural gas providers in

KIDNAPPED TO NEBRASKA

Seeking settlers to populate their towns and create haulable commerce, railroad companies in the 1870s carried on an avid courtship of émigrés coming from the East. Their salesmen didn't always play fair in this economic development enterprise. One agent wrote: "I met them several times by the trainload, and on one occasion swiped a whole trainload from two Kansas roads. I stole the whole bunch and carried them by special train to Lincoln."

Nebraska include privately owned regional utilities such as Peoples Natural Gas and KN Energy. Northern Natural Gas Co., based in Omaha, manages an interstate pipeline system serving the upper Midwest.

While its most publicized claim to fame in the energy industry is its public power system, Nebraska also has a hand in fossil fuel production. Wells in 19 of

Headed downstream from Omaha, these Missouri River barges will be off-loaded onto seagoing vessels in the Gulf of Mexico. One barge can hold 1,500 tons of soybean meal, the equivalent of 15 railcars.

Responsible maintenance of Nebraska's public power utilities entails upgrading to more efficient transformers and capacitors to enhance system reliability and improve energy conservation.

TOO DRY TO SAIL TOO WET TO PLOW

Although the Platte River Valley ranks as one of the world's great natural transportation corridors, providing a pathway for every kind of conveyance from early handcarts to modern semitrailer trucks, one mode of travel and commerce is absent from its repertoire: waterborne traffic. The Platte is too shallow to be navigable, a reality reflected in Nebraskans' additional description of it as being "a mile wide and an inch deep."

its 93 counties yield about three million barrels of oil and 1.7 billion cubic feet of natural gas a year.

Nebraska's state-owned electric system anticipates substantial sets of challenges and opportunities in the new century. One is maintaining the level of rates and service that has won customers' confidence and is instrumental in economic development. Another is establishing the power districts' degree of participation in the information age; they may be called upon to use their resources to enhance

Roughly two-thirds of Nebraska's electricity is generated by thermal power plants, like the North Omaha Power Station shown here, burning fossil fuels—primarily coal.

delivery of high-speed telecommunications service to rural areas. And the districts already are preparing to preserve for Nebraska the benefits of public ownership in the face of congressional pressure to allow investor-owned utilities to compete in the state.

EASY COME, EASY GO

While the five-county metropolitan Omaha area is spread over about 2,500 square miles and has a population of nearly 700,000, the typical drive to work is only about 18 to 20 minutes. Area radio stations don't broadcast airborne traffic reports after 5:45 p.m. because rush hour is over.

UTILITIES/TRANSPORTATION>>

WERNER ENTERPRISES, INC.

Once a one-man, one-truck operation, Werner Enterprises, Inc., of Omaha has grown and prospered to become one of the nation's five largest truckload carriers, with annual revenues exceeding $1 billion.

Just like the saying "a journey of a thousand miles begins with a single step," the story of a major trucking company, Werner Enterprises, Inc., began with one man and one truck. Today the Omaha-based company is one of the nation's five largest truckload carriers.

When C. L. Werner founded Werner Enterprises in 1956, the company consisted of one employee (himself) and a trucking fleet of one vehicle (his own flatbed truck he used to haul grain and lumber).

Today, nearly a half-century later, Werner is still in the driver's seat, but as chairman and chief executive of Werner Enterprises, a truckload carrier that boasts annual revenues exceeding $1 billion, annual growth averaging 20 percent since 1986, and stock being publicly traded under the symbol WERN on the Nasdaq.

Werner's fleet of trucks, meanwhile, has grown to more than 7,000 tractors and 18,000 trailers, and his pool of employees and independent contractors currently numbers nearly 9,000 people, including his three sons. And while the firm still hauls grain and lumber, it also transports such manufactured goods as irrigation systems, construction equipment, and pipe steel fabrications. It also hauls retail store merchandise, frozen food and paper products, pharmaceuticals, beverages, and building materials, among other things.

SPREADING FAR AND WIDE

The company's base of operations since its founding has spread far beyond Omaha, Nebraska. Today Werner Enterprises provides trucking services throughout the contiguous 48 United States as well as in Canada and Mexico. Full-service terminals are located in Allentown, Pennsylvania; Dallas, Texas; Lithia Springs, Georgia; Fontana, California; Springfield,

Werner Enterprises offers top-of-the-line equipment, such as the 2000, 379 Ultra Cab Peterbilt shown here.

Ohio; Henderson, Colorado; and Phoenix, Arizona, as well as Omaha.

FOUNDING PHILOSOPHY INSPIRES GROWTH

Much of the firm's growth and success is due to Werner's philosophy of providing customers with personal, high quality service that not only meets their expectations, but also exceeds them. It is a philosophy he practiced when he began the company and it is a philosophy that permeates every facet of the firm's operations today.

"Werner Enterprises is uniquely qualified to meet and exceed a shipper's expectations

Werner Enterprises owes much of its success to the personal philosophy of high quality service instilled years ago by chairman, chief executive officer, and founder, C. L. Werner. Those values still hold true today, assuring excellence in service and product details, large and small. In the company conference room, at left, a table with fine inset vitrines holds collections of historic arrowheads.

because we have the best people, the most sophisticated technology, and the best equipment in the industry," Werner says.

In fact, the company is a recognized leader in technology, cited by both *Forbes ASAP* magazine and the U.S. Department of Transportation, as one of the nation's best technology users.

INDUSTRY INNOVATOR

Werner Enterprises was the first trucking company authorized by the Federal Highway Administration to use digital driver logs instead of paper logbooks to keep track of truck movements and drivers' working hours. The digital log system, developed by Werner Enterprises, not only has made life easier for the company's drivers, but also has helped improve highway safety since drivers have more time to concentrate on their driving.

In addition to digital driver logs, the company's Qualcomm™-based satellite system also enables the firm to keep track of the various locations of its familiar blue trucks and their cargo. It also makes possible more accurate estimates of the time customers can expect their shipments to arrive at their destination, and even warns drivers in advance so they can avoid low bridges and other road hazards.

Werner Enterprises offers superior quality fleet maintenance for its drivers at its full-service and small-repair facilities, which are strategically located across the United States.

STATE-OF-THE-ART EQUIPMENT

As for its equipment, Werner Enterprises' truck fleet is among the newest and most technologically advanced in the business. Its tractors average 1.5 years in age while its trailers are, on average, just 2.8 years old. The company remains committed to continually operating a modern fleet to attract and retain qualified drivers and minimize maintenance expenses.

HIGH CALIBER EMPLOYEES

Meanwhile, the company's employees—from its professional drivers to its customer service representatives and administrative staff—are among the most dedicated, knowledgeable, and customer-oriented in the industry. In fact, its people truly set Werner Enterprises apart from other transportation providers.

In short, Werner Enterprises is well positioned to provide the kind of safe, reliable, on-time service at a low cost that is increasingly being demanded of truckload carriers in the 21st century.

"We are not only up to the challenge, we are looking forward to continuing to partner with our customers as their main transportation and people source for many years to come," says Werner.

The knowledge and coordination efforts of employees in its various departments makes Werner Enterprises a national business leader.

LINCOLN ELECTRIC SYSTEM

The mission of the Lincoln, Nebraska, Lincoln Electric System is to provide energy and services of superior value and enhance growth and development of the greater Lincoln area.

Helping customers reduce their energy use and costs is a priority for the nonprofit Lincoln Electric System. It provides many no-fee services to help customers make informed energy choices, including energy audits and evaluation of heating and cooling system needs.

One of the nation's leading utility companies is located in Nebraska's capital city. The customer-owned Lincoln Electric System (LES) is recognized for low costs, financial stability, innovation, and reliable, superior service. In fact, as the new, competitive environment began to develop in the industry, Wall Street analysts identified LES as one of 10 systems in the nation best positioned to successfully compete in a restructured industry.

LOW ENERGY COSTS ATTRACT BUSINESS

An important factor in Lincoln's desirability as a business site is its low electric energy rates, which annual surveys by KPMG LLP have consistently found to be among the *lowest* 10 percent of average rates charged in the United States. This has prompted major businesses and manufacturers to choose Lincoln as a site in which to conduct business and manufacture products. Among the Fortune 500 and Global 500 organizations with operations in Lincoln are State Farm Insurance, Pfizer Animal Health, Archer Daniels Midland, Goodyear Tire & Rubber, Burlington Northern Santa Fe Railway, and Kawasaki Motors Manufacturing Corp, U.S.A.

FINANCIAL STABILITY AND MID-1980S RATE LEVELS

Imagine living and working in a city where the price of electricity is as low today as it was 15 years ago. This is the reality enjoyed by the more than 110,000 customers served by LES. Today, electric rates remain 3 percent lower than in the mid-1980s.

Rates are kept low by controlling costs, particularly those for providing electricity service to customers, which comprise 70 percent of the total expenses incurred by the utility. LES invests in and contracts to provide a balanced mix of resources from some of the nation's most efficient and economical power plants, including Laramie River Station, in Wyoming, and Gerald Gentleman Station, near Sutherland Nebraska, two producers of the lowest cost steam-generated electricity in the nation. LES also maintains strategic alliances with regional utilities to buy, sell, and transmit power when it is economically advantageous.

To ensure the future stability of energy costs, LES established a multimillion-dollar Rate Stabilization Fund in 1998 to cover unanticipated expenditures that could adversely affect electricity rates paid by customers.

Management practices like these have earned Wall Street's respect. Standard and Poor's, for example, cites stable finances, strong business profile, competitive electricity rates, and diverse, low-cost power resources of LES as reasons for assigning its AA rating to the company's Revenue Bond Series 1998A.

Delighted with LES rates, customer Sue Bassler says, "I am so pleased when I open my electric bill and see how low it is month after month, especially as I live in an all-electric home. After paying bills of $300 or more a month in other states, I appreciate the consistently low LES bills."

LES invested $13.9 million in 1999 to ensure that its power delivery system will reliably support loads and growth.

SUPERIOR SERVICE AND RELIABILITY

While changes in the structure of the industry have resulted in tight energy supplies and exorbitant energy costs for many electricity utilities during the past few years, LES has anticipated and planned for the consequences of the industry's new, competitive environment, avoiding adverse impacts. By implementing a combination of strategies—ranging from the execution of short-term contracts to negotiating purchases of electricity from other companies to paying its large business customers that voluntarily reduce energy use during times of high demand—LES has avoided millions of dollars in energy costs.

Plans are in place to deal with the potential impacts of industry deregulation in the future, as well. Chief among them is the acceleration of schedules to build more power-generating facilities in the Lincoln area that will add about 247 megawatts of electricity to the LES power supplies. This additional capacity will also help accommodate the projected growth in peak demand of 2.6 percent annually during the next decade.

Annually, the company invests millions of dollars in capital projects that include the installation, upgrading, or replacement of power lines and substations. These high standards provide LES customers exceptional reliability of electricity service. In 1999, customers experienced an average of just 28.5 minutes without electricity, a reliability level that exceeds 99.99 percent.

THIS UTILITY IS KNOWN FOR ITS INNOVATION

LES has been recognized nationally and internationally for its innovation. For example:

- LES partnered with the University of Nebraska–Lincoln to build a solar-assisted heat pump demonstration home in 1975, resulting in the development of a patented technology to monitor solar performance.
- In 1980, LES became the first utility in the nation to offer home energy audits under the National Energy Conservation Policy Act.
- LES has received the American Public Power Association's Energy Innovator Award twice. The first was in 1983 for developing comprehensive energy management strategies that benefited customers. The second was in 1991 for conceiving a first-of-its-kind technology that increases the summer generating capacity of combustion turbines. This has won LES international acclaim.

LES continues to set the pace for energy innovation, especially in Nebraska. In 1998, it established a program to partner with customers to provide a portion of the energy used in its service area from renewable energy resources. By the end of 1999, two 660-kilowatt wind turbines were funded, built, and put into commercial operation under this program. These wind turbines, combined with 30 percent ownership of two others built under the Nebraska Distributed Wind Energy Project, make LES the largest producer of wind energy in the state.

STRIVING FOR EXCELLENCE IN THE NEW MILLENNIUM

Achievements such as those of LES help the company fulfill its mission to provide energy and services of superior value to its customers, and to enhance the growth and development of the greater Lincoln area. Be assured LES will forge ahead to fulfill this mission in new and better ways in the years to come.

For more information about LES, call 402-475-4211 or visit the company's Web site at www.les.com.

LES sets the pace for Nebraska's energy innovation. It partnered with customers to fund, construct, and maintain two wind turbines under a program to promote the use of renewable resources.

OMAHA PUBLIC POWER DISTRICT

One of the largest publicly owned electric utilities in the nation, the Omaha Public Power District remains firmly

committed to growth and exceptional service at the lowest possible costs.

Committed to growth, customer service, and the lowest possible rates, Omaha Public Power District (OPPD) is a publicly owned, business-managed electric utility that serves nearly 290,000 customers in 13 counties. OPPD's service area covers 5,000 square miles from the banks of the Missouri River in the east, to Burt County in the north, to Richardson County in the south, and to Colfax County in the west.

OPPD generates money for operating expenses strictly from the sale of electricity—without tax revenues. Bond sales provide the funds for major construction projects. In addition, OPPD offers the benefit of operating its own generation, transmission, and distribution facilities. Its total generating capability exceeds two million kilowatts of power.

One of OPPD's coal-fired plants, Nebraska City Station consistently ranks as one of the lowest-cost steam-electric power plants in the nation.

RENOWNED PUBLIC UTILITY

The 11th largest public utility in the United States, OPPD was selected in 1999 as having one of the top 10 utility economic development programs in America by *Site Selection* magazine. OPPD was awarded the honor for its role as a key player in Nebraska's economic development efforts.

Though a familiar name to most people in southeastern Nebraska, OPPD is also a driving force in economic development for the state through job-creating ventures—a fact few may realize. OPPD functions in partnership with the Nebraska Department of Economic Development, the Omaha Chamber of Commerce, and

a myriad of county and community-based development organizations. OPPD helps interested businesses make location decisions by providing assistance with site selection and electric rate information and by offering necessary state and local information.

COMMITTED TO JOB DEVELOPMENT

OPPD's extensive efforts in the area of economic development have been rewarded with successful results over the past few years throughout southeast Nebraska. One prize project is the much-publicized building of the Caterpillar Claas America plant in Sarpy County. This joint venture between Caterpillar and Claas—its German partner—will bring 500 jobs to the Omaha area and will

FROM LEFT: *Sherrye Hutcherson, Roger Christianson, Roberta Pinkerton, and Devin Meisinger of OPPD's Economic Development Department are ready to assist in site-selection searches or other economic development needs.*

be housed in a new $50 million, 500,000-square-foot manufacturing facility.

Another major project for OPPD is the 970-bed correctional facility under construction in Tecumseh that will employ 470 people. After a lengthy location search throughout the state, the Nebraska Department of Corrections chose Tecumseh as the site for the sought-after facility, which will provide much-needed jobs in the rural area. OPPD staff helped the community of Tecumseh to develop the presentations that attracted the Nebraska Department of Corrections to choose Tecumseh.

OPPD account executives regularly work with commercial customers, helping them with their energy-related needs.

average. In fact, OPPD has not had a rate increase since 1992. OPPD has been able to keep its rates low by anticipating the energy needs of the service area and responding to those needs by meeting them in the most economical way possible.

LOW RATES HELP ECONOMIC DEVELOPMENT

Crucial to continued economic development in southeastern Nebraska, and indeed in any area, is availability of low electric rates. OPPD was created in 1946 as a self-supporting political subdivision of the state of Nebraska. An eight-member board of directors elected by service area residents establishes policies and rates. Today, OPPD's rates are well below the national

COST-EFFECTIVE, RELIABLE POWER

OPPD also offers a strong measure of reliability—which is crucial to service areas and to future economic development. Not only does OPPD provide a high level of reliability, but the utility also offers the instant availability of additional power during times of high demand. OPPD designs its systems to ensure an adequate supply of power for its customers, but in the event that additional power is needed, OPPD is a member of the Mid-Continent Area Power Pool (MAPP). MAPP consists of 43 utilities serving 16 million residents in nine upper midwestern states and two Canadian provinces. Through this membership, OPPD can access the pool's operating reserves to maximize economy for customers.

Providing low-cost reliable power, however, is not always enough, particularly for large-use customers who depend on power to boost their efficiency and to keep production time high. Quality of power can vary, depending on voltage fluctuations, equipment malfunctions, and duration of power outages. OPPD constantly monitors the quality of its power for its customers.

For southeastern Nebraska customers—residential, commercial, and industrial—OPPD provides a key resource to the future economic development of the state—high quality, low-cost reliable power.

Energy Plaza in downtown Omaha serves as the location for OPPD's headquarters.

METROPOLITAN UTILITIES DISTRICT

Greater Omaha's Metropolitan Utilities District provides its customer-owners with reliable, economical natural

gas and high quality drinking water, and innovatively plans for the region's future needs.

Omaha's Metropolitan Utilities District has a rich history, rooted in the hopes and dreams of early civic "pioneers" who seemingly foresaw Omaha's growth from a bustling frontier town into the burgeoning hub of business and industry we know today. They knew that for a city to grow and prosper, it needed a reliable source of drinking water and fire protection.

So, in 1879, leaders began planning for a pumping station and water distribution system. A private company built and operated the first plant on the banks of the Missouri River, with reservoirs at Walnut Hill. Before long, however, it was clear that these facilities would not be up to the task, and planning for a larger plant soon began. The Florence Water Treatment Plant was completed and placed in service in 1889.

However, in the ensuing years, frequent ownership and management changes, plus public outcry over high water rates and poor service, spawned a movement for public ownership of the system. After a lengthy legal battle, the city purchased the system in 1912. The next year, the Nebraska Legislature chartered the Metropolitan Water District as a subdivision of the state, and the District as we know it today was born.

During the late 19th and early 20th centuries, gas service also was making inroads in Omaha. In 1868, a private company began selling gas as a fuel for street lights, and later, for ranges. However, when the time came for renewal of the city's franchise to the gas company,

Peakshaving facilities, like the liquefied natural gas plant at 117th and Fort Streets in Omaha, save Metropolitan Utilities District (M.U.D.) customer-owners $6 million per year in pipeline fees that otherwise would be spent to reserve space for transporting additional gas during cold winter months.

citizens, who were now accustomed to the benefits of public utility ownership, voted down the franchise. In 1919, the legislature gave the District control of the gas system. In 1923 the District's name was changed to the Metropolitan Utilities District (M.U.D.).

Since then, M.U.D. has provided reliable, safe natural gas and water service to the Omaha area. The utility now serves more than 167,000 water customers and 176,000 natural gas customers in the Omaha metropolitan area.

As a public utility owned by its customers, the District's mission is to provide customers with safe, reliable service at the lowest possible cost. By comparison, private utilities must maximize returns to shareholders. In effect, the District's customers are its shareholders. Revenues in excess of operating costs are reinvested into the company

In service since 1889, the Florence Water Treatment Plant provides M.U.D. customer-owners with drinking water that surpasses state and federal quality standards.

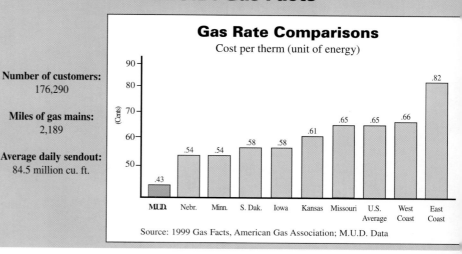

Gas Rate Comparisons
Cost per therm (unit of energy)

Number of customers:
176,290

Miles of gas mains:
2,189

Average daily sendout:
84.5 million cu. ft.

Source: 1999 Gas Facts, American Gas Association; M.U.D. Data

---

In 1999, M.U.D.'s water and gas rates were well below the national average, as seen in these charts.

to improve services, or returned to customer-owners through reduced rates. From 1997 through 1999, the District returned $13.5 million to customer-owners in reduced gas rates.

M.U.D.'s residential natural gas rates are 34 percent below the national average. Water rates also are among the lowest in the Midwest. The annual cost of water for the average residential customer using 110,000 gallons is only $157.41 *(see charts)*.

Public ownership also gives customer-owners a voice in operations. The District is run by an elected, seven-member board of directors, which meets monthly. All meetings are open to the public.

Throughout the coldest winters, M.U.D. ensures an ample supply of natural gas, buying gas from a portfolio of U.S. and Canadian suppliers. By buying large volumes of gas from numerous suppliers and regions, the District ensures reliability while negotiating the most economical prices.

Enhancing the savings are a liquefied natural gas plant and two propane plants which provide "peakshaving" supplies for peak heating days. Annually, these facilities save customer-owners $6 million in pipeline fees which would otherwise be required to reserve pipeline space for transporting additional gas.

M.U.D. also provides a reliable supply of safe, high quality drinking water, pumping an average 90 million gallons per day, with a maximum daily capacity of 234 million gallons from two water treatment plants and several peakshaving wells. Fire protection also is an important service, with more than 20,000 hydrants maintained throughout the M.U.D. service area.

M.U.D.'s treated water has always surpassed state and federal quality standards for drinking water. The District performs at least 300 monthly tests for bacteria alone, plus tests for minerals and other substances. Although not mandated, tests also are conducted for parasites such as cryptosporidium and giardia. Whatever new standards may be

M.U.D. Water Facts

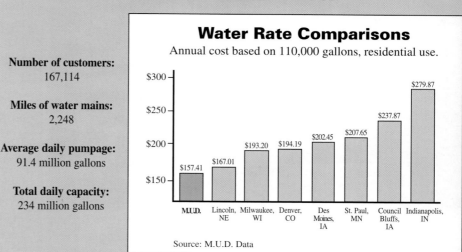

Water Rate Comparisons
Annual cost based on 110,000 gallons, residential use.

Number of customers:
167,114

Miles of water mains:
2,248

Average daily pumpage:
91.4 million gallons

Total daily capacity:
234 million gallons

Source: M.U.D. Data

---

required in the future, M.U.D. is committed to meeting these standards and ensuring the quality customer-owners expect.

The District will continue to meet the water needs of the growing community by planning for the construction of a third treatment plant. The Platte West Project, anticipated to be operating in 2006, will add another 100 million gallons to the District's daily pumping capacity.

Demand for natural gas also will grow as the District explores new uses for it, such as natural gas vehicles and fuel cells for electricity generation. The District supplies gas for fuel cells at First National Bank of Omaha's data processing center, the world's first multicelled, paralleled fuel cell application, generating 800 kilowatts of clean, reliable electrical power.

Through innovation and commitment to quality and service, the Metropolitan Utilities District will continue to meet the changing needs of customer-owners while capitalizing upon the benefits of public utility ownership.

metropolitan
UTILITIES DISTRICT

www.mudomaha.com

ENRON CORP.

Global energy leader Enron Corp.'s Northern Natural Gas Company division and Enron subsidiary Northern Plains

Natural Gas Company, both based in Omaha, deliver natural gas to customers throughout the Midwest and beyond.

Omaha is headquarters for Northern Natural Gas Company and Northern Plains Natural Gas Company.

Enron Corp. is one of the "100 Best Companies to Work for in America," according to *Forbes* magazine, and it is no wonder. It is the leader in its industry as is shown in citations for its innovation and quality management, and it is constantly expanding in response to customer need, and all the while being a good citizen, charitably and environmentally.

Enron is America's largest marketer of electricity and natural gas, according to a May 2000 report by *Gas Daily*, with approximately $34 billion in energy and communication assets. The corporation traces its roots back to 1930, when Northern Natural Gas Company was founded, in Wilmington, Delaware.

Eventually, Northern Natural Gas evolved into many related companies. In 1951, the company moved its headquarters to Omaha, Nebraska. By 1967, it had welcomed the 1,000th community to its gas-delivery network, passed the $1 billion mark in plant investment, and become an international company with facilities in Central and South America and on three Caribbean islands.

In 1978, Northern Natural Gas became InterNorth, and then in 1985, InterNorth and Houston Natural Gas merged and eventually became Enron Corp. Northern Natural Gas is now a division of Enron. While Enron moved its headquarters to Houston, Texas, Northern Natural Gas maintains a strong presence in Omaha. Northern Plains Natural Gas, a stand-alone subsidiary of Enron, is headquartered in Omaha.

NORTHERN NATURAL GAS COMPANY

Northern Natural Gas remains the largest of Enron's six North American pipeline companies, with nearly 200 employees at its Omaha office and 1,100 more operational employees at sites throughout its system. Northern Natural Gas delivers natural gas as the primary source of heat for the upper Midwest, providing natural gas to industrial, commercial, and residential customers in Iowa, Minnesota, Wisconsin, Michigan, South Dakota, and Nebraska.

With nearly 17,000 miles of pipeline from south Texas to Michigan, Northern Natural Gas provides natural gas transportation and storage services to approximately 70 utility customers in the upper Midwest. The company has been aggressive in expanding its pipeline and storage capacity to meet the needs of its customers, implementing a host of new services in 1998 and 1999 alone. It recently completed a five-year expansion program that added about 350 million cubic feet per day of natural gas capacity to its system.

Working with local utility companies, Northern Natural Gas defines peak day needs and develops the capacity to serve them. It can deliver up to 4.3 billion cubic feet of gas on every peak winter day, an increase of 50 percent in the past decade. From schools to hospitals to fertilizer and meat-packing plants, Northern Natural Gas forms partnerships with its customers to serve their unique needs.

CORPORATEWIDE EXCELLENCE AND CONTRIBUTION

Enron has been acknowledged many times for its environmental efforts, including receipt of the EPA's Climate Protection Award and the Corporate Conscience Award, given by the Council on Economic Priorities. *Forbes Global* ranked Enron the top power company in its 1999 inaugural A-list of companies. *Fortune* magazine named Enron "America's Most Innovative Company" and "Most Admired Pipeline Company" an unprecedented five years in a row. In 1999–2000, *Fortune* named Enron number one in "Quality of Management" and chose it as one of the "100 Best Companies to Work for in America." Clearly, Enron and its divisions strive to make a contribution to society.

Each company within Enron also contributes to its community. Northern Natural Gas and Northern Plains Natural Gas enthusiastically participate in Power Hour and Power Blast, programs supporting local sports and after-school tutoring. The companies and their employees support many social and charitable organizations with funding and volunteer work, especially in the areas of youth, education, and literacy.

NORTHERN PLAINS NATURAL GAS COMPANY

The Enron subsidiary Northern Plains Natural Gas Company operates the Northern Border Pipeline system. This is a major transportation link that connects the vast natural gas reserves in the Western Canadian Sedimentary Basin and the United States Williston Basin with markets throughout the United States.

The Northern Border Pipeline serves customers from Chicago, Illinois, north through

All along the thousands of miles of the pipeline route is a microwave system using a series of towers, like this one, and repeater stations to transmit high-frequency radio signals that contain pipeline data.

Iowa, Minnesota, South Dakota, North Dakota, and Montana, to Monchy, Saskatchewan, with its 1,214 miles of pipeline. Approximately 110 employees are housed in the Omaha headquarters of Northern Plains Natural Gas, with another 100 employees located at facilities along the pipeline route.

The Northern Border Pipeline was constructed in 1982 and was expanded and extended during 1991, 1992, and 1998. The expansion in 1998, called "The Chicago Project," extended the pipeline from Harper, Iowa, to Manhattan, Illinois, and expanded the pipeline's delivery capacity to 2.375 billion cubic feet of natural gas per day. In 1999, Northern Border Pipeline estimated that it transports approximately 23 percent of the total amount of natural gas imported from Canada to the United States.

Nearly $1 billion in construction costs was committed to complete The Chicago Project, and another $94 million is allotted for 2001. Clearly, the expansion of Northern Border Pipeline is designed to keep pace with the needs of its customers.

FAR LEFT: *Compressor stations such as this one in North Dakota are needed at a number of locations along a natural gas pipeline to increase pressure lost due to friction between the gas and the pipeline wall. Keeping the gas pressurized is important to maintaining the pipeline's efficiency.* ABOVE: *Inside a compressor station, a gas generator and a power turbine unit together produce approximately 35,000 horsepower and send natural gas down the pipeline at about 21 miles per hour.*

Northern Plains Natural Gas Company
Operator of Northern Border Pipeline Company

NEBRASKA PUBLIC POWER DISTRICT

With the slogan 'Always there when you need us,' Nebraska Public Power District (NPPD) demonstrates its commitment to continued low rates, high reliability, and excellent service for its customer-owners.

Public power: For most Nebraska residents, this is the only type of electric service they have ever known. Since 1933, Nebraska has maintained its status as the only state in the nation whose power companies are completely owned by the people they serve. And Nebraska Public Power District (NPPD) proudly extends this tradition through its slogan, "Always there when you need us."

The creation of public power companies began with hydroelectric projects that brought Nebraska's economy back to life following the Great Depression of 1929. Established as power and irrigation districts, these political subdivisions purchased all private utilities within the state's borders. A 1970 merger between three of the largest public power districts outside of the Omaha area resulted in the formation of NPPD, whose service territory includes parts or all of 91 of Nebraska's 93 counties. NPPD employs approximately 2,200 Nebraskans.

NPPD produces electricity for approximately 395 municipalities and 25 rural power districts and cooperatives. Two coal-fired plants and one nuclear energy–powered station are the utility's primary electricity generators. Additional power supply resources include hydroelectric-power plants, combustion turbines, diesel engines, and wind turbines. The NPPD Transmission Control Center in Doniphan, Nebraska, orchestrates the selling of NPPD electric power and its transmission across a 4,300-mile high-voltage transmission system.

Among the Nebraska Public Power District (NPPD) electricity-generating facilities are Gerald Gentleman Station (shown here), near Sutherland, and Sheldon Station, near Hallam. Both of these plants are powered by low-sulfur coal from Wyoming.

Approximately 85,000 retail customers are supported by a 24-hour, state-of-the-art call center and nine customer service centers located throughout the NPPD service area. An Operation Center in York, a Water Resources Division in North Platte, and the utility's headquarters in Columbus complete the picture of NPPD's major Nebraska facilities.

ENHANCING THE QUALITY OF LIFE

NPPD strives to fulfill its mission of "Enhancing the quality of life in Nebraska" in a multitude of ways.

Communities and Businesses—NPPD partners with communities and wholesale customers to aid and promote their economic development efforts. As a result of the information provided on NPPD's Economic Development Division Web site (sites.nppd.com), two major manufacturers have selected NPPD's service area for the location of their new manufacturing facilities. These projects

For NPPD, groundbreaking ceremonies are a rewarding part of its economic development efforts. Here, Nebraska Governor Mike Johanns helps celebrate the expansion of Longview Fibre Company in Seward, Nebraska.

include a $30 million Valmont expansion in McCook and a Westflex Pipe Manufacturing facility in Beatrice. NPPD's economic development efforts also focus on business expansion and retention opportunities. Innovative programs provided by the utility prompted *Site Selection* magazine to name NPPD one of the top 10 utilities in the nation for economic development.

Residential Customers—Nebraska residents enjoy electricity rates that are 20 percent below the national average and the NPPD commitment to fast, friendly service 24 hours a day. NPPD Internet activities focus on offering customers convenient services, such as the ability to view and pay their bills on-line. As NPPD ventures into E-business, customers will benefit from cost savings derived by the utility's on-line procurement strategy.

New Energy Options—NPPD's geothermal heat pumps, renewable-energy options, surge-protection equipment, and other products and services bring the value of its energy expertise to customers. The NPPD Technical Solutions team assists industrial, commercial, and residential customers with lighting, heating, engineering, and other energy needs. By providing such technical assistance, NPPD maintains strong partnerships with its customer-owners.

The Environment—The NPPD commitment to the natural environment goes beyond the prevention of water and air pollution. The environmental staff protects endangered habitats along the Platte River, and the Water Resources division oversees water rights to ensure proper

Two wind turbines near Springview, Nebraska, help demonstrate the NPPD commitment to use renewable energy resources to generate electricity.

use and safeguards canals that carry water to irrigate 82,000 acres of farmland. NPPD also works with such agencies as the Nebraska Department of Environmental Quality to proactively solve environmental problems and develop a sustainable, healthy environment.

Other Energy Partnerships—NPPD is a member of the Mid-Continent Area Power Pool (MAPP), a voluntary association of electric utilities, and it continually monitors developments regarding regional electricity transmission organizations in order to ensure a safe and continuous supply of electricity for its customers. In partnership with The Energy Authority (TEA), a power-trading alliance based in Jacksonville, Florida, NPPD strives to maximize the value of its power-supply resources and minimize the risks associated with a nationally competitive wholesale market. NPPD works collaboratively with other organizations regarding nuclear energy and federal requirements to improve the equipment used, the products delivered, and the quality of service provided to customers.

THE CUSTOMER'S CHOICE

These efforts are part of NPPD's strategy to be the customer's choice in an increasingly competitive environment. With its continued low rates, high reliability, and excellent customer service, NPPD is confident that it will continue to enhance the quality of life in Nebraska, remaining for its customers, "Always there."

Nebraska governor Mike Johanns and NPPD president and CEO William R. Mayben sign a partnership agreement between NPPD and the Nebraska Department of Environmental Quality. The agreement calls on both partners to share ideas and resources to sustain the environment in Nebraska.

Nebraska Public Power District
Nebraska's Energy Leader

PEOPLES NATURAL GAS

With roots in Nebraska tracing back more than 70 years, Peoples Natural Gas continues to offer innovative energy solutions and cutting-edge technology to customers in 112 communities.

Peoples Natural Gas, a division of UtiliCorp United, an international energy and services company, has been meeting Nebraska's energy needs for more than 70 years.

Founded in Nebraska in 1930, Peoples Natural Gas started out by providing gas service to five communities in the state. In 1985, UtiliCorp United acquired Peoples, enabling the company to offer more varied services, such as LocationOne—a customized economic development service—to its customers. Today, Peoples Natural Gas has grown to serve nearly 180,000 customers in 112 eastern Nebraska communities. Peoples also has operations in Colorado, Iowa, Kansas, and Minnesota.

Within those communities, Peoples maintains a strong tradition of providing educational, economic, and community outreach support. Many of the company's approximately 900 employees are active volunteers in community betterment programs ranging from the United Way to city and chamber of commerce committees.

Peoples offers viable energy solutions, using cutting-edge technology and competitive pricing, to its commercial and industrial customers to help them succeed in the global market. For its residential customers, Peoples offers valuable and reliable support, information, and service as well as reasonable rates.

As a result of its parent company's far-reaching energy operations, services, and expertise, Peoples provides a significant business resource for Nebraska

Peoples Natural Gas employees install a natural gas distribution line to a new industrial customer in Nebraska.

residents and educational and government institutions.

Headquartered in Kansas City, Missouri, UtiliCorp United is a growth-oriented company. UtiliCorp United was formed from Missouri Public Service Company in 1985. (It bought Peoples later that year.) Since that time, the company has grown and prospered through various regulated and nonregulated energy acquisitions in North America. Today, the company provides energy services to more than 4 million customers across the United States and in Australia, Canada, New Zealand, and the United Kingdom. The nation's third largest wholesale marketer of natural gas and the second largest marketer of electricity, according to Financial Times Energy, UtiliCorp serves U.S. customers in Colorado, Iowa, Kansas, Michigan, Minnesota, Missouri, and Nebraska. UtiliCorp United is known throughout the United States as a respected provider of innovative and competitive energy solutions.

UtiliCorp United has been notably recognized for its achievements and innovations. The company was named on *Fortune* magazine's list of America's Most Admired Companies in 1998 and is included on *Forbes* magazine's Platinum 400 listing. UtiliCorp United also ranks 132nd on the Fortune 500 list, based on 1998 sales.

PEOPLES NATURAL GAS

ENERGY ONE ℠

A Division of UtiliCorp United

UtiliCorp United North American Operations

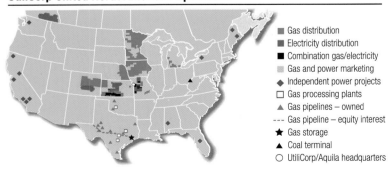

- ■ Gas distribution
- ■ Electricity distribution
- ■ Combination gas/electricity
- ■ Gas and power marketing
- ◆ Independent power projects
- ☐ Gas processing plants
- ▲ Gas pipelines – owned
- --- Gas pipeline – equity interest
- ★ Gas storage
- ▲ Coal terminal
- ○ UtiliCorp/Aquila headquarters

CHAPTER ELEVEN

HEALING IN A NEW CENTURY

MEDICAL TECHNOLOGY AND HEALTH CARE

When Dr. William Bancroft set up his mid-Nebraska practice in 1873, he was the only physician in a 4,600-square-

mile area centered on his office in Lexington. In these early days of statehood, the typical doctor's bag contained

a dozen or so drugs, rarely adequate to effect healing. If Dr. Bancroft was representative of his profession, he

charged one dollar for office visits or house calls in Lexington and 50 cents a mile for appointments in the

country, often being paid in commodities rather than cash.

The isolate prairie physician soon was to have professional company. The state's first medical school, forerunner of the University of Nebraska Medical Center (UNMC), was established in Omaha in 1881, and Creighton University's college of medicine was founded in 1892. By the turn of the century they were educating most of the practitioners who met the health care needs of the burgeoning state's population. Not all fitted the familiar image of the country doctor in his top hat and frock coat; by 1890 there were more than 50 women doctors in Nebraska.

Today more than 3,300 physicians practice in the Cornhusker State, up from about 1,600 just 30 years ago. Their contributions have helped Nebraska vault to a top position in assessments of the quality of health care—10th among the 50 states in the 1999 *Health Care State Rankings*.

Nebraska's health care assets include 108 hospitals with more than 8,400 beds. In the eastern metropolitan area alone there are 16 full-service hospitals, including two university-related teaching hospitals and five schools of nursing.

OLD ST JOSEPHS HOSPITAL
FIRST CREIGHTON MEDICAL COLLEGE

Increasingly, medical resources are being linked, through collaborative processes and high-speed communications networks, to enable institutions and physicians to share information and techniques across Nebraska's 500-mile length and enhance health services in rural areas. The Rural Health Education Network and the Community-Oriented Primary Care Program, led by UNMC and the Creighton University School of Medicine, foster locally based training programs. The state's medical interconnectedness is typified by a 24-hour electrocardiogram interpretation service serving more than 100 rural hospitals and clinics.

COST-SAVING AND LIFESAVING INNOVATIONS

One result of such educational-technological innovation is reflected in the state's record of controlling health care

ABOVE: *Tracing its origins to 1870, Omaha's Saint Joseph Hospital has been affiliated with Creighton University since its medical college was founded in 1892 and remains the primary teaching hospital for Creighton's medical programs.* OPPOSITE: *Memorial Community Hospital and Health System in Blair is a trusted health care provider for every phase of life in the Burt and Washington Counties area.*

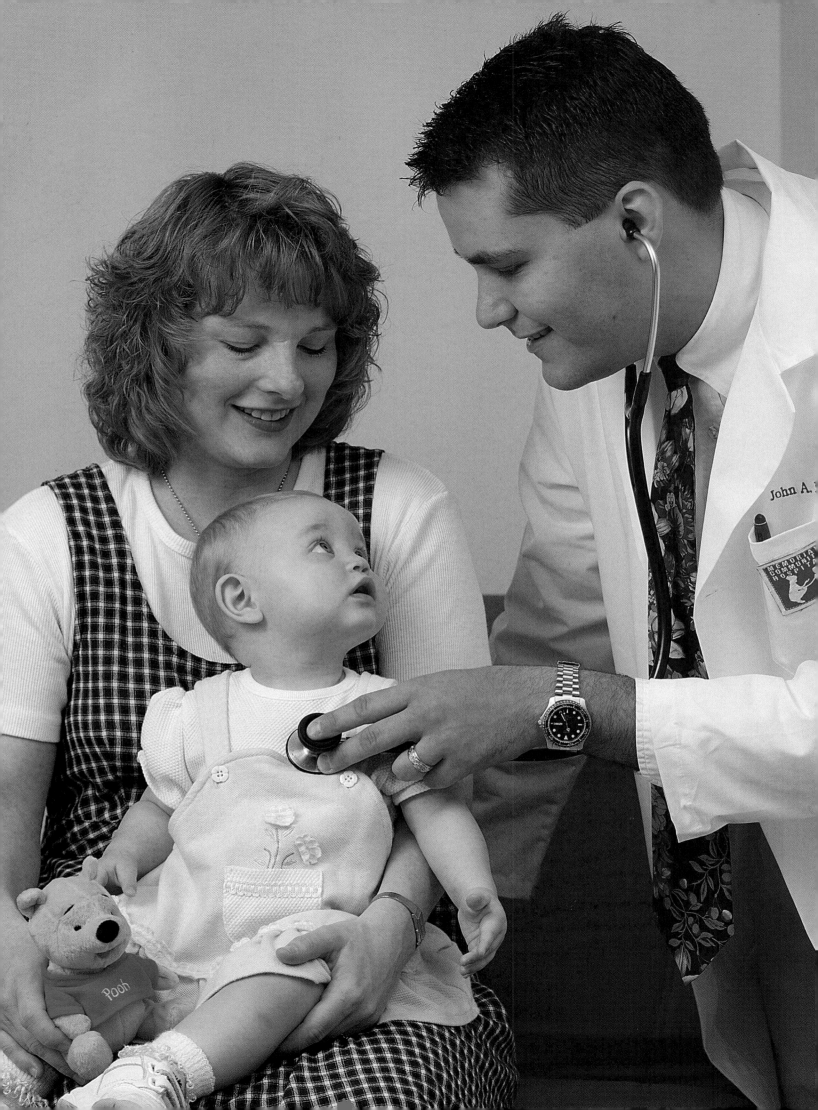

The goal of UneMed Corp., a division of the University of Nebraska Medical Center, is helping medical technology innovations become commercially viable. The corporation serves as an intermediary between the medical center and industry through research collaborations, joint ventures, new company start-ups, and other relationships. Since it was established in 1992, UneMed has assisted researchers in starting five companies, securing licenses, and implementing eight industry-sponsored research agreements.

costs. The American Chamber of Commerce Researchers Association (ACCRA) has reported that costs in the eastern metropolitan area alone are 8 percent lower than the national average.

Besides providing a foundation for effective, economical patient care, Nebraska's major medical institutions are prominent in researching and developing breakthroughs in lifesaving technology. For example, the Lied Transplant Center operated by the Nebraska Health System performed more than 200 solid organ transplants and nearly 200 bone marrow transplants in 1999, with patients

Advanced technology and state-of-the-art medical expertise allow Nebraska's medical establishment to offer patients a comprehensive range of treatment options and surgical procedures.

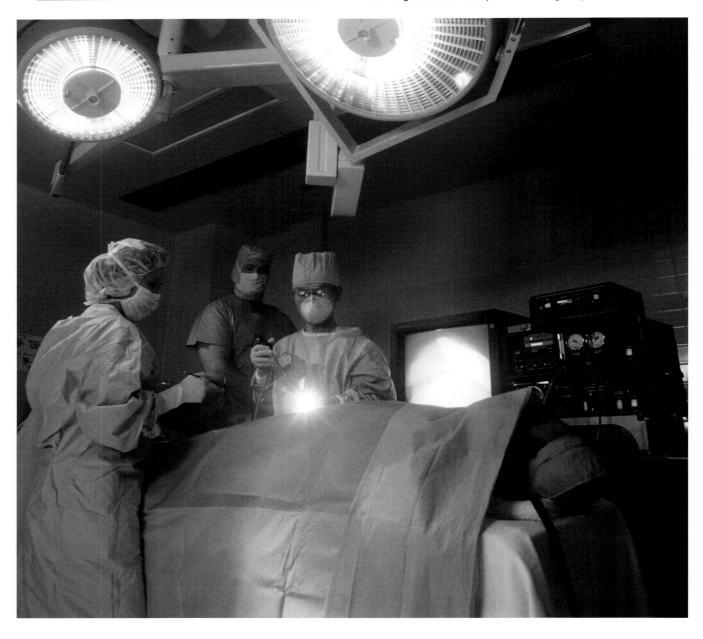

Omaha's Methodist Hospital is renowned for specialties such as cardiac rehabilitation, cancer care, and obstetrics. Adjacent Children's Hospital is Nebraska's only pediatric specialty hospital.

coming from 19 foreign countries and all 50 states. The UNMC Eppley Institute for Research in Cancer and Allied Diseases is one of only 10 laboratory research centers designated by the National Cancer Institute.

The Creighton University Medical Center's osteoporosis research program is one of only three recognized by the National Institutes of Health. And on the downtown Omaha campus of the Creighton-affiliated Saint Joseph Hospital is the Boys Town National Research Hospital, a leading center for the study and treatment of hearing disorders in children.

Nebraskans have learned to diminish distance in building systems that provide an umbrella of health care over the state's geographical expanse. For example, while McCook and other cities and towns in the southern

NEBRASKA'S FIRST PHYSICIANS

The first doctor reported to have practiced in Nebraska was John Gale, an Army surgeon who in 1819 came to Fort Atkinson north of Omaha with troops of the Sixth Infantry. But he was a long way from being the first healer in the territory. The Native American "medicine men," often characterized as voodoo-like performers dancing about and chanting incantations, in reality treated their patients with an efficacy often ignored in frontier lore. They amputated limbs, effected cures with herbs, roots, barks, and animal substances, made effective use of powders and poultices, understood the function of dressings, tourniquets, and splints, and even practiced an early form of psychotherapy.

Prairie Lakes region are served by the 170-member staff of the comprehensive Community Hospital, some 30 medical specialists routinely travel to McCook to provide specialized clinical care. Another example is the Panhandle Mental Health Center in Scottsbluff, which has expanded to serve 11 counties with community mental health services, specializing in the treatment of anger and domestic problems as well as the variety of symptoms children may experience.

ADJUNCTS TO THE HEALING ARTS

Over the years Nebraskans have built an infrastructure of research and technological institutions to complement and support medical practice. One of these is MDS Harris in Lincoln, founded in 1933 as a simple testing center. In 1969 it became one of the nation's first independent labs to provide clinical research and testing for the pharmaceutical industry and today is part of

While farmers the world over associate the name Novartis with seed and crop-protection products, Novartis Consumer Health in Lincoln primarily produces over-the-counter pharmaceuticals for the U.S. market, including Triaminic® cough and cold medicine, Maalox® antacid, and the Tavist® line of allergy remedies.

AT THE FRONT

One of the most renowned medical units of World War I was Base Hospital 49, financed by Nebraskans, organized by the University of Nebraska College of Medicine, and staffed largely by university faculty and alumni. Set up in Allereye, France, on September 12, 1918, it performed an average of 20 surgical operations a day through the armistice and had the best record of saving lives of all the American hospitals in Europe.

NEBRASKA NOBELIST

Dr. George W. Beadle, born on a farm near Wahoo in 1903, was one of the first researchers to suggest that each of the biochemical reactions of a cell is governed by a particular gene. This led to the finding that each gene controls the production of a particular enzyme, and to Beadle's receipt of the Nobel Prize in physiology in 1958. The state's most prominent memorial to the scientist, who died in 1989, is the $31 million George W. Beadle Center for Genetics and Biomaterials Research at the University of Nebraska–Lincoln.

MDS Pharmaceutical Services, one of the world's largest contract research and development organizations.

Streck Laboratories, headquartered in LaVista, manufactures 35 percent of the hematology reference controls used worldwide, with its products sold throughout the United States and in 42 foreign countries. It continues to diversify its services into histology, immunology, and chemicals.

BELOW: *Medical practice and health care in Nebraska are complemented by outstanding research and technological institutions such as MDS Harris, part of MDS Pharmaceutical Services, in Lincoln, and Streck Laboratories, headquartered in LaVista.*

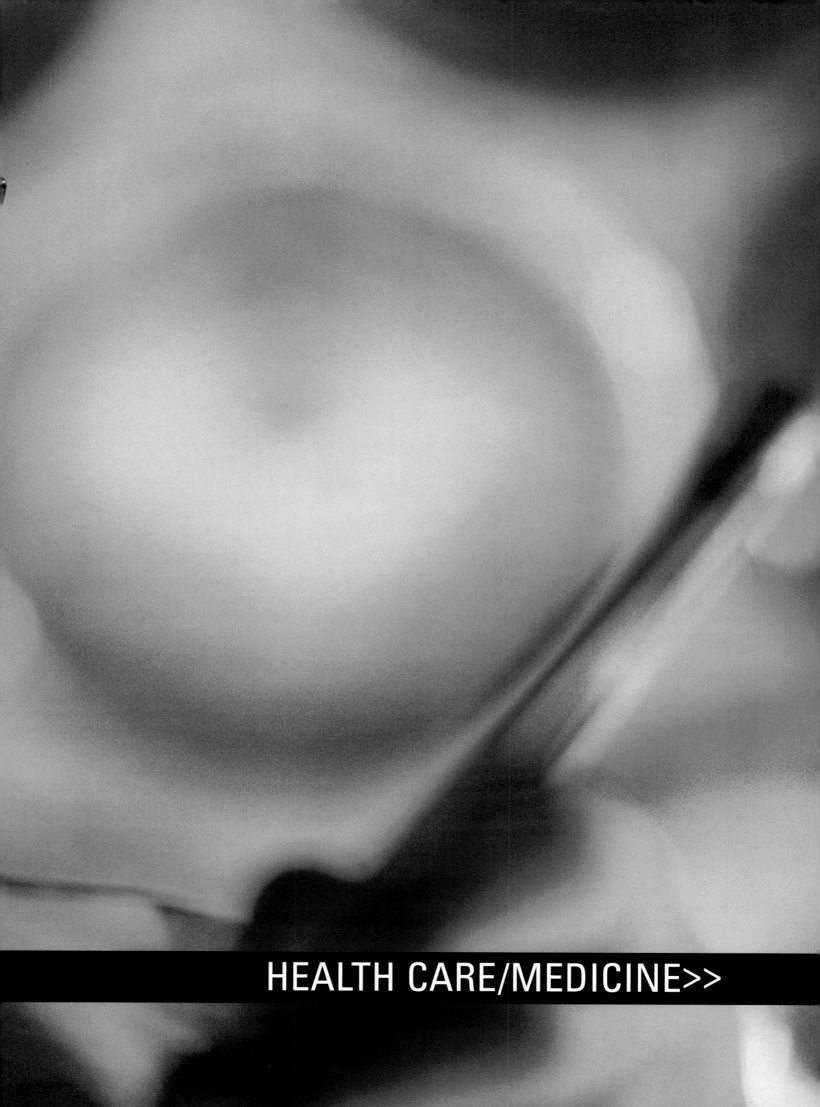

HEALTH CARE/MEDICINE>>

NEBRASKA HEALTH SYSTEM

A partnership of two renowned health care organizations, Nebraska Health System offers comprehensive medical care, a commitment to compassionate patient care, and a dedicated pursuit of innovation.

The merger in October 1997 of two of the area's most prestigious hospitals, Clarkson Hospital and University Hospital, formed a new, vibrant organization—Nebraska Health System.

Nebraska Health System (NHS) has remained "dedicated to excellence and innovation in compassionate, quality health care through teamwork, education, and research"—a mission it takes very seriously. In October 1997, NHS was formed by the merger of University Hospital of the University of Nebraska Medical Center (UNMC) and Clarkson Hospital to provide patients with an encompassing array of health care services not only in the immediate vicinity but throughout the state, the nation, and the world.

A PROUD HISTORY

The history of NHS reflects the history of medical care in the state of Nebraska. Clarkson Hospital, initially named Good Samaritan, was founded as Nebraska's first

hospital in 1869. University Hospital opened in 1917 as the teaching hospital for medical students at the University of Nebraska. Both organizations have earned powerful reputations for their clinical expertise and quality of care, medical specialties and subspecialties, research, and innovative programs. NHS has accumulated an amazing collection of firsts, including the state's first cardiac catheterization in 1955, kidney dialysis treatment in 1957, corneal transplant in 1958, kidney transplant in 1964, peripheral stem cell transplant program in 1984, and heart and liver transplant in 1985—to name a few.

PATIENT FOCUS REDEFINED—EXTRAORDINARY CARE

The entire NHS organization is focused on delivering top quality health care services to the patients it serves. This focus is apparent in the breadth and depth of its services in the following specialty areas: cardiology, transplantation, oncology, rheumatology, wound care, burn center, geriatrics, pediatrics, women's health, renal, and ancillary care centers.

In partnership with UNMC, Nebraska Health System transplantation and oncology programs for adults and children are nationally and internationally recognized. In addition to medical and radiation oncology, patients benefit from leading-edge cancer treatment and care, research, investigational drugs, and clinical trials through the UNMC Eppley Cancer Center. The only National

The Lied Transplant Center, a state-of-the-art facility that can accommodate all phases of organ transplantation, opened to patients in 1999.

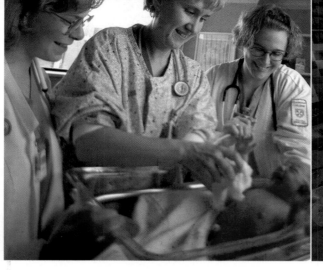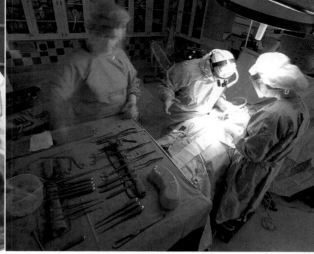

Cancer Institute–designated cancer center in the six-state region, Eppley serves patients from all 50 states and 19 foreign countries.

Patients with cancer and other diseases come to NHS for many types of transplantation, including stem cell, bone marrow, liver, small bowel, kidney, and pancreas. At the Lied Transplant Center, opened in 1999, patients receive chemotherapy, aphaeresis, and other treatments.

PATIENT-FRIENDLY LOCATIONS

In addition to the main campus in central Omaha, NHS provides convenient patient care in several locations throughout the region. NHS physicians conduct more than 300 outpatient clinics in four states. The system operates six dialysis clinics in Nebraska and southwest Iowa and five mammography facilities. A comprehensive ambulatory care center with complete surgical suites, lab and X-ray facilities, CT scan, ultrasound, EKG, and cardiac monitoring is located in west Omaha at NHS Clarkson West. This facility also houses Emergicare, a 24-hour emergency department staffed by professionals trained in advanced life support for minor and major illnesses and injuries. NHS also has an affiliation agreement with Shenandoah Memorial Hospital in Shenandoah, Iowa.

NHS is also proud to be a sponsor of Mid-America Hospital Alliance (MAHA), comprised of 29 health care providers who have come together to create a consortium of rural and urban hospitals to enhance the quality, availability, and coordination of the state's health care services.

With nearly 1,000 primary and specialty care physicians in private practice, and with the University Medical Associates consisting of UNMC physicians who represent every medical specialty, as well as 1,200 registered nurses, NHS has grown to meet the demanding needs of its marketplace.

The system also has expanded its collaboration with other institutions. NHS and Methodist Health System

The combined talent and expertise of NHS clinical and administrative staff deliver not just excellent but extraordinary care to the patients they serve.

have combined mental health programs and formed a new joint venture—Richard Young Center.

MEETING FUTURE CHALLENGES

Today, Nebraska Health System is one of Omaha's largest employers with approximately 5,000 employees. NHS is also the primary teaching site for UNMC, a leading academic medical center that trains 2,500 students in medicine, nursing, pharmacy, and allied health. In addition, nearly 400 residents and fellows are trained each year at the facility. NHS enjoys a proud history as two distinct organizations and a very bright future as one unified system.

Recent national recognition has been bestowed on the health care system. In 1999, Nebraska Health System, in partnership with UNMC, was named Best Hospital for cancer and rheumatology care by *U.S. News & World Report* magazine. The hospital system also received the Marriott Sodexho Award for its Cooperative Care Program at the Lied Transplant Center and was given the Consumer Choice Award by National Research Corporation (NRC), a Lincoln, Nebraska–based company.

Increased market share, critical to the health and existence of hospitals in the 21st century, is proof that Nebraska Health System is more than meeting patient expectations and the merger of the two hospitals is succeeding. While challenges await, NHS looks forward to the future with strong, impressive support from the community and its exceptional staff.

Extraordinary Care

NHS NEBRASKA HEALTH SYSTEM

CLARKSON HOSPITAL • UNIVERSITY HOSPITAL

A Partner with University of Nebraska Medical Center

METHODIST HEALTH SYSTEM

Methodist Health System, a network of three renowned medical facilities, meets the health care needs of the communities it serves by being true to its simple commitment of caring for people.

The hospitals of the Methodist Health System—Jennie Edmundson, Methodist, and Richard Young Center—began shaping the Omaha, Nebraska–Council Bluffs, Iowa, health care community more than 116 years ago. Today the hospitals continue to make a difference in countless lives.

The oldest health care system in the area, the organization was created in 1982 by Methodist Hospital leaders who realized the progressive direction in which health care was heading and decided to create a network to better meet the needs of the area's residents.

A SIMPLE MISSION

The mission of the network is simple: "Methodist Health System is committed to caring for people. We do this by being the heart of health care." The network is dedicated to improving people's quality of life by supporting excellence in health care and health care education.

Jennie Edmundson Hospital, the oldest organization in the system, was founded in 1886 by a group of church women who were known as the "Faith Band." These pioneering women opened the hospital as a five-room cottage in Council Bluffs, Iowa, in order to provide medical care to anyone who needed it. This mission of service to all continues yet today. Named in memory of Jennie Way Hart Edmundson, wife of the hospital's prime benefactor in its early years, "Jennie Ed" remains in the same location it has occupied

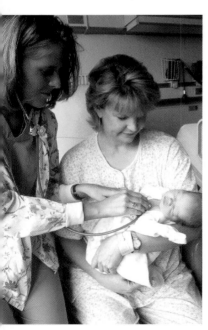

Methodist Hospital in Omaha, Nebraska, one of Methodist Health System's hospitals, has been named winner of a Consumer Choice Award (given by National Research Associates) every year since the award was implemented, in 1996. Methodist Hospital is known for specialties that include cardiology, high-risk obstetrics, oncology, orthopaedics, neurology, and urology.

More babies are born each year at Methodist Hospital than at any other hospital in the Omaha area.

near downtown Council Bluffs since 1907. Nearly a century later, after decades of steady growth, Jennie has the only cancer care program in Southwest Iowa that is accredited by the American College of Surgeon's Commission on Cancer, is the area's top provider of maternal/child care, and also is the location of an expanded cardiac center that offers cardiac catheterization and rehabilitation services. Headed by David Holcomb, Jennie is southwest Iowa's largest hospital, offering 230 beds and more than 130 physicians.

Methodist Hospital, located across the river in Omaha, was founded in 1891 in order to provide physical care in a spiritual setting. Continued growth of the hospital paralleled the westward expansion of Omaha, hastening a move to the current location at 84th and West Dodge Road in 1968. Today there are 430 beds at Methodist Hospital, an acute care medical facility that is regarded as one of the best full-service hospitals in the area. Headed by John M. Fraser, Methodist Hospital is a leader in such disciplines as cancer care, cardiac rehabilitation, and obstetrical services. The hospital delivers approximately 3,000 babies a year—more than any other hospital in the region.

The Richard Young Center, located in Omaha, is the third component of the Methodist Health System. Richard Young has been providing innovative behavioral health care since 1931 and is part of a joint effort with Nebraska Health System and the University of Nebraska Medical Center. The unique behavioral health center houses 305 beds, offers a medical campus dedicated to mental health, and provides 24-hour information and referral services as well as residential and outpatient treatment programs. Sandy Carson, president, oversees Richard Young, steering it into the 21st century as a model for behavioral health services.

A PROUD TRADITION

The proud tradition of Methodist Health System is continued by the Physicians Clinic, which is the largest multispecialty group practice in eastern Nebraska and western Iowa. After joining the system in 1991, Physicians Clinic grew from 36 physicians to its current status, employing more than 180 physicians representing 17 specialties in more than 30 clinics in Nebraska and Iowa. Physicians Clinic provides quality patient care to more than 615,000 patients annually.

In addition to traditional hospital-based care, Methodist Health System reaches far into each community with a wide variety of services. Health Touch

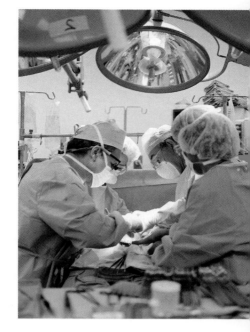

Methodist Health System physicians offer their patients fine care, setting standards for high quality health care in Nebraska and Iowa. In addition, Methodist Health System physicians are leaders in the use of the newest medical technology and treatments and the latest advances in surgery.

One is a 24-hour toll-free hotline that provides callers with a complete source of information, including physician referral, help for new parents, community health services, and educational classes.

Methodist Health System is also a pioneer in service to the elderly. Senior services offered at Methodist, Jennie Edmundson, and The Richard Young Center promote wellness and help maintain a high quality of life for persons aged 55 and older. Methodist Hospital's Geriatric Evaluation Clinic helps families assess the challenges facing an elderly member.

Stephen Long, Methodist Health System's president and CEO, and the leaders of the affiliated entities are eagerly preparing for the future. With a proven track record of correctly assessing future areas of growth—and responding to those needs—the system's leaders will continue to develop the most appropriate health care services for their highly valued patients and families.

METHODIST HEALTH SYSTEM

The Best Care Comes from the Heart®

Jennie Edmundson Hospital in Council Bluffs, Iowa, part of Methodist Health System, is the only hospital in southwest Iowa with a cancer care program accredited by the American College of Surgeon's Commission on Cancer. Other specialties of the hospital include obstetrics, cardiology, and physical rehabilitation.

SAINT JOSEPH HOSPITAL

A devoted leader in medical research, technology, prevention, and treatment, and the primary teaching hospital for

Creighton University medical programs, Saint Joseph Hospital serves the greater Omaha region.

Healing Mind, Body, and Spirit. It is a commitment that reflects Saint Joseph Hospital's rich tradition, founded solidly in Judeo-Christian beliefs and nurtured through time. This commitment rose from humble beginnings. In 1870, when the hospital's first building was constructed, the City of Omaha itself was only 14 years old and little more than an outpost on the western march of civilization.

Great dedication and devotion to healing had led the Sisters of Mercy to reach out to the community and ultimately raise $12,000 to fund what became Saint Joseph Mercy Hospital.

The tradition of healing continued when the Sisters of Saint Francis purchased the hospital 10 years later. That tradition grew, as did the hospital, until on June 13, 1892, a new facility was opened, at Creighton University Medical Center. It was named Creighton Memorial Saint Joseph Hospital to honor its primary benefactors, John A. and Sarah Emily Creighton.

At Saint Joseph Hospital today, the tradition of teaching is as strong as ever. It continues to serve as the

Omaha's Saint Joseph Hospital is based on a commitment to healing mind, body, and spirit.

primary teaching hospital for the physicians and allied health care professionals of Creighton University's various medical programs. Within the hospital, students grow to understand that healing extends beyond the physical, to the mind and spirit.

Working side by side with leading health care professionals, students at the hospital prosper in an environment that features the latest medical innovations in medical technology and treatment.

Saint Joseph Hospital is on the leading edge of medical research, technology, prevention, and treatment. It has attracted authorities in many specialty areas, such as cardiology, hereditary cancer, osteoporosis, trauma, women's health, neonatology, orthopaedics, and primary care.

The compassionate work of the Sisters of Mercy and the Sisters of Saint Francis for Saint Joseph

Together, Saint Joseph Hospital and Creighton University form a partnership that attracts and educates some of the brightest minds in the nation.

The programs at Saint Joseph Hospital facilitate a healing environment founded on a dedication to the preservation and enhancement of life.

HEALING MIND, BODY, AND SPIRIT
The Commitment of Saint Joseph Hospital

"Saint Joseph Hospital is committed to the prevention of illness, the restoration and improvement of health, and the compassionate care of the suffering.

"We are dedicated to the preservation and enhancement of life by providing leadership in patient care, education, and research responsive to the health needs of our community.

"We will pursue our vision with Judeo-Catholic heritage as our foundation and the hospital values as our guide."

SAINT JOSEPH HOSPITAL
AT CREIGHTON UNIVERSITY MEDICAL CENTER
Tenet HealthSystem

Hospital and their dedication to healing the sick have long been revered in the Omaha community. One newspaper editorial has been preserved that dates all the way back to March 21, 1882. In describing the hospital, it pays a tribute that now bridges three centuries:

> "Saint Joseph Hospital has been among us for years as the home of the sick. Rich and poor alike, all creeds and all conditions, have shared in its blessings and benefactions during this time. Within its humble walls the devout and devoted women, who have consecrated their lives to the care of the sick and suffering, have been ministering to thousands of men and women whose only claim upon them was founded in human brotherhood."
>
> —*The Omaha World-Herald*

Saint Joseph Hospital is a pioneer of air ambulance services for Omaha. A helicopter transport serving the area within a 150-mile radius of Omaha makes access to the hospital's services available to people in rural Nebraska and Iowa.

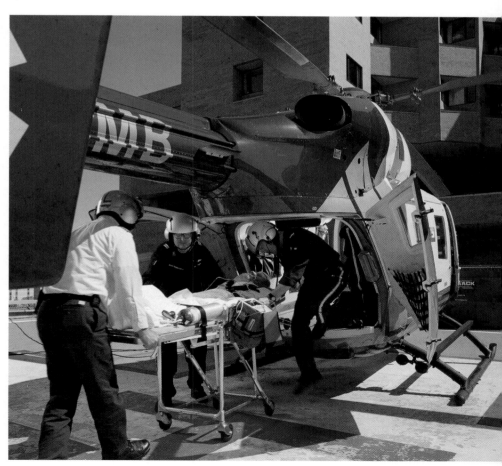

OMNI BEHAVIORAL HEALTH

With a vision for helping Nebraska's most vulnerable children, OMNI Behavioral Health strives to give personal, community-based therapeutic care to children with behavioral and emotional disturbances.

Until 1993, a child with emotional disturbance living in eastern Nebraska often faced psychiatric hospitalization, usually in a town far from home. While the existing psychiatric hospitals provided such children with medically approved treatments, separation from parents and family often exacerbated the child's behavioral and emotional difficulties.

In 1993, William Reay, Ph.D., Morgan Kelly, J.D., M.A., C.P.H.Q. (Certified Professional in Healthcare Quality), and Kendal Osbahr, M.H.S. (Masters in Human Services), who were working together in government-based mental health programs, sought a better way to help these children and their parents. The three believed these children would be served better through community-based services delivered to children in and near their homes where their parents could assist with service planning and delivery. Later that year, Reay, Kelly, and Osbahr founded OMNI Behavioral Health on a small, prepaid contract of $150,000 from the state of Nebraska. The contract called for the development of alternative services to psychiatric hospitalization in eastern Nebraska.

HELPING CHILDREN GET HEALTHY

Just 23 children from the targeted regions (northeast and southeast Nebraska) were receiving state care in 1993. These children had behavioral or emotional problems. In 1992, the state paid $292,000 per child for such hospitalized care. After the development and implementation

OMNI Behavioral Health was founded in 1993 by (from left) Morgan Kelly, William Reay, and Kendal Osbahr.

of OMNI's economically efficient, community-based services, the state of Nebraska saved $2 million in the first 18 months alone. In 1999, more than 200 children ages six to 19 were served.

Consistent with its legal and professional obligations to provide services in the least restrictive setting available, OMNI's philosophy is to serve children at home with their parents if at all possible. OMNI's community-based therapeutic services are provided to children who live in one of four group homes or 120 foster homes, or are connected with home-based therapists and family support workers. A cadre of more than 100 employees delivers the much-needed services through offices in Beatrice, Columbus, Lincoln, North Platte, and Omaha. The offices serve not only these cities and Seward, but also the outlying rural areas.

With the foundation of successful community-based services firmly in place, Reay, Kelly, and

OMNI foster parents are shown here with their children.

Osbahr have sought to take their plan—to improve services for children with emotional and behavioral disturbances while creating cost savings—to other communities. OMNI Behavioral Health has expanded the traditional concept of legal advocacy to include community advocacy, in order to serve the needs of those whose voices can't be heard.

OMNI Behavioral Health challenges the common misconception that many people have about children with emotional disturbances—that they are dangerous to themselves and others and must be kept separate from a community while receiving treatment. Part of the emphasis of advocacy is to promote understanding and to encourage communities to balance doing the right thing with doing the efficient thing.

Initially working through the growing family movement, Reay developed contracts with Georgetown University to promote the idea of encouraging communities in all parts of the country to change the way they serve emotionally disturbed children. OMNI Behavioral Health is particularly interested in promoting advocacy within minority communities, historically an underserved population in the field of mental health. OMNI's ethnically diverse professional staff excels in advocating for, coordinating, and delivering culturally competent community-based services in any of Nebraska's patchwork quilt of neighborhoods.

EXPANDING OFFERINGS AND SERVICE AREAS

In the future, Dr. Reay anticipates that OMNI Behavioral Health will continue providing community-based behavioral health services in Nebraska as well as encouraging advocacy throughout the United States. "We will undoubtedly continue to build on our depth

OMNI Behavioral Health's foster care and administrative staff includes (back row, from left) Susan Feyen, T. J. Seward, Nicole DeLoa, Reay, Colleen Roth, Tish Mosher, Kelly, Osbahr, Mickey Laufenberg, and Shari Lecci; and (front row, from left) Colleen Evans, Erin Wimpey, Rhonda Rollerson, and April Anderson.

and talent in Nebraska. Because we are a nonprofit organization, generating profit is not our main mission. Our main motive is to encourage communities to integrate children within their own communities, not only because it is the more economical and efficient thing, but also the right thing to do," says Reay.

A key challenge for OMNI Behavioral Health is to continue developing services in a wide variety of ethnic and cultural communities. "In the past, services were developed and provided to these diverse groups by white men, then the majority population. It just doesn't work that way. Different cultures raise children in different ways. We need to encourage the spectrum of America's ethnic groups to advocate for themselves," Reay says.

Reay, Kelly, and Osbahr had a vision for Nebraska's most vulnerable children—those who have emotional and behavioral disorders. After years of working within the system, other key professionals have joined the efforts to improve service delivery as well as cost efficiency. A few of these professionals include Deb Reay, M.S.W., M.A.; Jeanette Gearhart; Deb Monfelt; Colleen Roth; Susan Feyen; Mark Ward; Rachel Luchsinger; and Dr. Lee Zlomke. Because of OMNI's cutting-edge programs, other areas of the United States can now look forward to such innovative programs through community-based advocacy and service.

Pictured at left are staff and youths from the Seward Family Support Center.

BRYANLGH MEDICAL CENTER

Nonprofit, locally owned BryanLGH Medical Center is a regional, tertiary health care facility that offers

nationally ranked heart and orthopaedic programs.

As health care continues to change in the nation and in Nebraska, so has BryanLGH Medical Center adapted to meet the need for low cost, high quality care. In fact, BryanLGH has played a major role in the development of Lincoln as a major regional health care center. As part of the Heartland Health Alliance, a statewide network of 32 hospitals, BryanLGH has forged strong partnerships with other hospitals, physicians, and communities. That collaboration has helped to make high quality, cost-effective health care services available throughout Nebraska, as well as in northern Kansas and southern South Dakota.

BryanLGH Medical Center offers comprehensive services including a nationally recognized, premier heart program. The BryanLGH cardiovascular services program was ranked for two consecutive years in the 100 Top Hospitals™ national study conducted by HCIA-Sachs. In 1999, BryanLGH orthopaedic services achieved the 100 Top Hospitals ranking for its orthopaedic services and hip- and knee-joint replacement surgery.

In addition, BryanLGH has the only Gamma Knife Center in Nebraska, a Level II trauma center, and comprehensive mental health services. The medical center offers a full range of other specialties that include oncology;

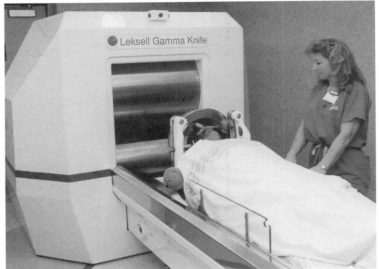

BryanLGH is the only Nebraska hospital offering Gamma Knife treatment. The Nebraska Gamma Knife Center at BryanLGH serves patients throughout the region, and Lincoln is among only 38 American cities with this technology.

women's health; inpatient, outpatient, and emergency services; air ambulance; rehabilitation; transitional care; home health care; and education for health professionals as well as community members.

EVOLVING HEALTH CARE, NEW PARTNERSHIPS

BryanLGH Medical Center is the result of a 1997 merger between Lincoln General Hospital and Bryan Memorial Hospital.

The BryanLGH story began more than 90 years ago with the incorporation in 1910 of the Lincoln Hospital Association. This association established Lincoln General Hospital in 1925.

BryanLGH offers a nationally recognized premier heart program serving thousands of patients and using the latest technology, surgical and catheterization procedures, artificial heart assist devices, automatic implantable defibrillators, and medications. The comprehensive program spans Nebraska, bringing mobile diagnostic and treatment technology to more than 40 communities.

BryanLGH
MEDICAL CENTER

The history of Bryan Memorial Hospital dates back to 1920, when local ministers and laymen created a board to establish what was to become Bryan Memorial Hospital. The hospital opened in 1926.

Today, as one combined organization, BryanLGH Medical Center is Lincoln's largest health care facility, a 583-bed nonprofit, locally owned health care organization. The hospital has two acute care facilities, at BryanLGH Medical Center West and BryanLGH Medical Center East, and operates several outpatient centers.

A VISION FOR THE FUTURE

To continue its role as a regional health care leader, BryanLGH is in the process of a multimillion-dollar construction project. Renovation of BryanLGH West is under way, and when finished will include a state-of-the-art trauma center/emergency department, new space for mental health services, inpatient and outpatient surgical services, a new Independence Center for chemical dependency services, medical office buildings, and parking facilities.

At BryanLGH East, new construction will expand cardiovascular services, and create a state-of-the-art women's health center.

The construction project, plus redesigned care delivery systems, will allow the people of BryanLGH to raise the level of care and services provided and create operating efficiencies with no duplication of specialty services at either location.

More than 3,600 employees at BryanLGH Medical Center work in partnership with patients, physicians, family members, and guests to provide the most comprehensive range of health care services using the latest technology and treatments available.

ADVANCED TRAINING, TECHNOLOGY, AND TREATMENT

With a focus on patient-centered care, BryanLGH staff members hold core beliefs related to integrity, teamwork, service, leadership, and value. When visitors walk through the doors of BryanLGH they can see these beliefs in action—through the comprehensive range of health care services and resources, state-of-the-art facilities, and most of all, in the people of BryanLGH. The organization is home to more than 3,600 well-trained staff members and 500 physicians who are committed to providing the most comprehensive range of health care services using the latest technology and treatments available. Augmenting their professional expertise and dedication to service, the people of BryanLGH place the patient at the center of all they do, providing care that is holistic, healing, and compassionate.

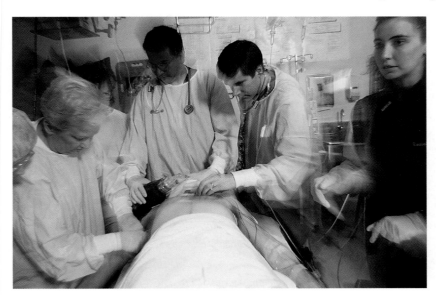

BryanLGH offers many specialty services, including emergency/trauma, and is designated a Level II Trauma Center. BryanLGH was nationally ranked for two consecutive years in the 100 Top Hospitals™ study by HCIA-Sachs for its cardiovascular program and for orthopaedic services, including hip- and knee-joint replacement surgeries.

BLAIR MEMORIAL COMMUNITY HOSPITAL AND HEALTH SYSTEM

With a mission 'To heal, nurture, and promote health,' Memorial Community Hospital and Health System strives to ensure that superior medical services and personal care for its clients are always available and close to home.

Built in 1956, Memorial Community Hospital in Blair, Nebraska, has a proud tradition of providing superior quality medical services with a personal, caring touch.

COMMUNITY COMMITMENT

The commitment to have a community hospital began in 1956 when 80 community groups united to undertake a door-to-door campaign in the rural townships of Washington and Burt Counties. Through vision and unbridled spirit, the people of these two areas worked to make Memorial Community Hospital and Health System (MCH) in Blair, Nebraska, a reality. MCH, in turn, has responded with equal commitment, vision, and energy, providing superior health care services for more than 40 years.

CONTINUING THE COMMITMENT

The people of the two counties who founded MCH knew how important local health care is to a rural community's quality of life. Similarly, a local family practice physician who has been in Blair for 35 years, Dr. K. C. Bagby, has always known that Memorial Community Hospital is a vital asset to the area it serves. However, when Dr. Bagby's wife, Carole Bagby, suffered a stroke early one morning, he experienced firsthand just how much MCH is needed.

"Luckily, Carole recognized what was happening and we sought immediate attention at MCH," Dr. Bagby says. The hospital staff responded quickly and the physician on call ordered a spiral CT scan. In minutes, accurate information was available that allowed the providers to administer tissue plasminogen activator (TPA), the blood clot–buster drug. MCH's technology played a major role in this time-critical process, enabling Mrs. Bagby to make a full recovery.

Since the beginning, MCH has been guided by its mission, "To heal, nurture, and promote health." Enhanced services, technology, programs, and facilities have been the hospital's main focus in serving diverse health care needs. As a result, MCH has grown to become a broader health system that includes access to specialty care, operation of a home health and hospice agency, and the formation of a primary care clinic network with 12 health care providers serving in Blair, Tekamah, and Fort Calhoun.

MCH continues to look toward the future with a commitment and mission to efficiently provide the best health care services possible. As part of its long-range strategic plan, MCH has focused on improving the way health care is delivered, through a scheduled program of new construction, renovation, new equipment, and system upgrades.

As MCH moves forward in the 21st century, plans are under way to build a new primary care clinic in Blair as well as to renovate surgery suites, laboratory, emergency room, and in-patient rooms. "Continuing the Commitment" is MCH Health System's quest to ensure that high quality medical services and personal care for its clients are always available and close to home.

As part of its commitment to the community, MCH Health System offers expectant families excellent maternity services ranging from prenatal health care and childbirth education to a positive, supportive birth experience for both mother and coach.

ALEGENT HEALTH

The health care providers of Alegent Health hospitals, long-term care facilities, and other treatment sites in Nebraska and western Iowa strive to blend the art and science of medicine with the power of hope.

Alegent Health is a community-based health care system. Its integrated and comprehensive organization of health services focuses on care of the sick while emphasizing prevention, wellness, and education. The hospitals and clinics of Alegent Health provide leadership in primary care, pediatrics, maternity, inpatient/outpatient surgery, cardiology, oncology, orthopaedics, home care, rehabilitation, behavioral services, family counseling, and other services designed to meet the region's health care needs. *Alegent* is derived from the word *allegiance*, intended to connote strength, stability, and comfort. It reflects a long-standing tradition dedicated to serving all people of the region.

Alegent Health consists of seven acute care hospitals (1,433 beds, with plans to expand Lakeside HealthPark into a hospital by 2005); two long-term care facilities (456 beds); a primary care physician network of 40 sites, with more than 150 staff physician associates; and a Physician Hospital Organization with a membership of approximately 900 physicians. Alegent Health encompasses more than 100 service locations in Nebraska and western Iowa and a staff of 7,500 employees. An additional 42 hospitals and more than 200 physician clinics also are affiliated with Alegent Health through the

Members discover a whole new approach to good health at Alegent Health, which includes fitness workouts, as shown at this facility.

Alegent–Nebraska Purchasing Group.

Alegent Health's goal is to be the region's preferred network and employer of choice for those working in health care because of its values-based, mission-driven orientation; high quality, cost-effective services; and commitment to care for the body, mind, and spirit of each person served. To achieve this expectation, Alegent Health strives to:

- be the region's preferred health network that employers and employees will have access to;
- be nationally recognized for helping people through all of life's stages;
- be valued by the communities it serves for its emphasis on good health and health improvement. Alegent Health collaborates with churches, businesses, and community service organizations;
- distinguish itself by its employees and physicians, who are fully engaged in its mission of maintaining a faith-based environment in which to work and practice medicine, and who live the organization's values, blending the art and science of medicine with the power of hope and miracles;
- be universally identified with healing and known regionwide for its lifetime personal relationships.

Alegent Health, formed on January 1, 1996, is a nonprofit corporation responsible for the leadership, management, and direction of all operations of Bergan Mercy Health System, sponsored by Catholic Health Initiatives, and Immanuel Health Systems, affiliated with ELCA (Evangelical Lutheran Church in America), Nebraska Synod.

ALEGENT HEALTH

HEALTH CARE FACILITIES IN NEBRASKA
- Alegent Health Bergan Mercy Medical Center, Omaha
- Alegent Health Immanuel Medical Center, Omaha
- Alegent Health Midlands Community Hospital, Papillion
- Alegent Health Memorial Hospital, Schuyler
- Alegent Health Lakeside HealthPark, Omaha

HEALTH CARE FACILITIES IN IOWA
- Alegent Health Southwest Iowa Medical Center, Mercy Hospital, Council Bluffs
- Alegent Health Mercy Hospital, Corning
- Alegent Health Community Memorial Hospital, Missouri Valley

LONG-TERM CARE FACILITIES
- Alegent Health Immanuel Fontenelle Home, Omaha
- Alegent Health Mercy Care Center, Omaha

CLARKSON COLLEGE

Practicing core values of learning, caring, commitment, integrity, and excellence, Clarkson College serves as a leader in educating health care providers, offering a broad range of health science degree programs.

Clarkson College's history began in 1870, with the founding of The Ladies' Hospital by a group of charitable women representing many religious faiths. Seven months later, the founders transferred the hospital to Nebraska's first Episcopal bishop, Robert H. Clarkson. It was Bishop Clarkson and his wife, Meliora Clarkson, who developed the hospital as one of the first charitable hospitals in Omaha. After Bishop Clarkson died, in 1884, Mrs. Clarkson continued the couple's charitable work, leading a tireless effort to advance the hospital. Because the women working there needed to be trained, in 1888 the hospital opened a school of nursing—the first in Nebraska. The facility and its many health-related activities eventually became Clarkson Regional Health Services Inc., and the school of nursing became Clarkson College, a private, Episcopal-affiliated, coeducational school.

Today Clarkson College continues to serve as a leader in health care education, offering a broad range of health-science degree programs including nursing, health-related business, medical imaging, occupational therapy assistant, physical therapist assistant, and radiologic technology. Always maintaining a fundamental "Tradition of Excellence," Clarkson College's mission is to educate professionals who will provide high quality health care for patients and their families. Clarkson graduates, prepared in a state-of-the-art environment, also are ready to meet the technical challenges of a world in which health care and information technology are increasingly integrated.

Clarkson College is proud of its low student-faculty ratio; its teachers, who are national and local leaders in their fields; and its fine skills-training laboratories, equipped to simulate actual health care environments. Programs at Clarkson College also are enriched by affiliation with the Nebraska Health System—one of the

Students at Clarkson College are offered numerous health science degree programs, including graduate and undergraduate nursing, radiologic technology and medical imaging, and health-related business. Programs are also offered to help students become physical therapist and occupational therapy assistants.

nation's premier health care systems—which gives access to comprehensive, quality clinical resources. The college's Success Center offers students counseling, academic skills development, and career planning. These benefits combine to give Clarkson graduates a competitive advantage in their chosen careers.

For more than 110 years, Clarkson College has been preparing graduates who excel as health care professionals. "We are committed to build on our 'tradition of excellence' as we continue to educate leaders in the ever-changing health care field," says Dr. J. W. Upright, president of Clarkson. "It is our students' enthusiasm and dedication that fuels our commitment to maintain Clarkson as a leading health sciences college."

Learning, caring, commitment, integrity, and excellence—these are Clarkson College's core values. For additional information, visit the college's Web site at www.clarksoncollege.edu.

J. W. Upright, Ed.D., is president of Clarkson College.

CHAPTER TWELVE

SUSTAINING A GROWING ECONOMY

FINANCIAL AND PROFESSIONAL SERVICES

Like so many enterprises that started on a shoestring and grew with Nebraska into business landmarks, the

insurance industry has roots in the stick-together spirit of the 19th-century pioneers. The Cornhusker State's long-

standing prominence as one of the nation's premier insurance centers had its beginnings in the fraternal benefit

organizations formed to help immigrants deal with matters of life and death in their new homeland. Some began

as simple burial societies established by different nationality groups dedicated to taking care of their own.

Most notable among these is the Woodmen of the World Life Insurance Society, the world's largest non-religious fraternal organization, with almost 3,000 lodges across the United States. Founded in 1890, it now serves nearly a million members from its Omaha office in the imposing Woodmen Tower and has more than $30 billion of life insurance in force.

In all, more than 30 life, health, accident, and property insurance firms are headquartered in Nebraska, including one of the most famous in the industry, the Mutual of Omaha Companies.

Mutual of Omaha's first claim to prominence is its standing as the largest provider of individual and family health policies in the United States. Recently it also has become a national power in group insurance and has expanded into the financial services field with its acquisition of Kirkpatrick Pettis, one of the Midwest's leading brokerage and investment firms.

Also based here are industry leaders such as Acceptance Insurance Companies, the nation's third largest crop insurer, covering everything from corn to canola for 150,000 farmer-policyholders; Physician's Mutual, which employs more than 1,000 and is one of Nebraska's largest businesses; Guarantee Life, which before its recent conversion to a stock company was one of America's largest mutual insurance firms; Blue Cross and Blue Shield of Nebraska, which has posted continued annual growth in the face of uncertain health care trends; and Ameritas Life, headquartered in Lincoln, which boasts more than $4 billion in assets with $11 billion of insurance in force and is a national leader in group dental coverage.

Insurance companies based in the Cornhusker State have a total of more than $310 billion of policies in effect—a graphic demonstration of how far the industry has come since those immigrant burial societies paid a $100 monument benefit.

ASSET BUILDING

On the face of it, Herman and Augustus Kountze couldn't have chosen a worse time to make their move. They

Nebraska pioneered the use of bank-issued credit cards in the 1950s. Half a century later, its financial institutions continue to offer innovative products and professional service with a personal touch.

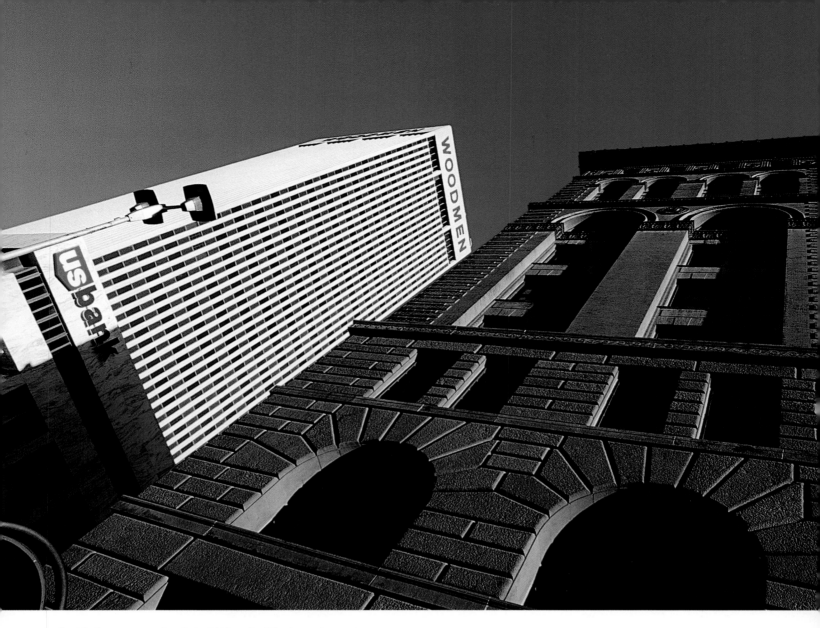

decided to open a bank in Nebraska Territory in 1857, a year in which a nationwide financial panic caused the failure of virtually every bank in the territory, made money so scarce as to be almost nonexistent, and drove interest rates to as high as 10 percent a month.

But the Kountze Bros. Bank not only survived, it prospered. In 1863 the brothers received a federal charter, and their one-room institution became First National Bank of Omaha, the first national bank west of the Missouri River. The operation that once dealt with trappers for their beaver pelts and served such depositors as Buffalo Bill Cody has grown into a regional and national financial power. The bank and its parent company, First National of Nebraska, run nearly 50 locations in the Midwest and West, with more than $9 billion in assets and over 6.6 million customers. It's one of the nation's largest issuers and processors of VISA and MasterCards and has averaged more than 14 percent compounded growth since 1972.

Woodmen of the World Life Insurance Society and US Bank share space in the Woodmen Tower, shown looming over the Omaha Building, Omaha's first 10-story structure. Built in 1889–90, the landmark edifice is now home to the law firm of Kutak Rock.

Perhaps in 1857 the Kountze brothers saw something in Nebraska's future beyond the financial doldrums of the year. If so, they had company, for the record of banking in the state is studded with stories of successful institutions that persevered and flourished through the 20th century.

These include Norwest Bank Nebraska, formerly U.S. National Bank, which began a year earlier even than the Kountzes' bank and has become one of the state's largest banking institutions, with 28 community offices statewide. To round out the 20th century, Norwest was completing a merger with another storied name in Western finance, Wells Fargo. US Bank, another of Nebraska's venerable institutions, debuted as Omaha National Bank and grew to nearly $4 billion in assets as it evolved successfully into

In the financial panic of 1857 it was discovered that most of the wildcat banks in Nebraska Territory had been founded on no more than the strength of irresponsible legislative charters and the proprietors' urge to make a quick buck by issuing worthless paper currency. A sheriff's writ against one of these failed institutions listed these assets: "Thirteen sacks of flour, one large iron safe, one counter, one desk, one stove drum and pipe, three arm chairs, and one map of Douglas County."

FirsTier Bank and then became part of the Minneapolis-headquartered US Bancorp in 1996.

Although Omaha-based banks are the Cornhusker State's largest because of the metropolitan area's population concentration and economic activity, Nebraska's agricultural, industrial, commercial, and consumer banking needs are met by some 525 FDIC-insured and state-chartered banks totaling more than $31 billion in assets. The capital alone is served by 15 banks, including

Founded in 1909, Mutual of Omaha is one of the largest insurance providers in the United States. Its corporate symbol, an Indian chief in headdress, graces the home office in downtown Omaha.

Founded in 1899, the Nebraska State Bar Association has 8,400 members dedicated to improving the administration of justice.

one of Nebraska's largest, Lincoln's billion-dollar National Bank of Commerce, which is also being merged with Wells Fargo. Reflecting the importance of the state's leading industry, more than one dollar in five of Nebraska bank loans in 1998 was in the agricultural sector.

More than $14 billion of Cornhusker assets is invested in the state's savings and loan institutions. Among the

KEEPING FIT CORNHUSKER STYLE

The Wellness Councils of America (WELCOA), headquartered in Omaha, directs efforts in nearly two-thirds of the nation's workplaces that have employee fitness programs. WELCOA was the idea of William M. Kizer, chief executive officer of Central States Health and Life Co. of Omaha.

most prominent is Commercial Federal Bank, founded over a century ago with less than $10,000 in assets to help residents of South Omaha—a separate municipality in those days—buy their own homes. Today Commercial Federal serves more than 700,000 households with a wide range of financial services.

LIVING UP TO THE MOTTO

One of the most famous legal cases in Western history played out in a frontier courtroom at Fort Omaha in 1879: the trial of the Ponca chief Standing Bear, arrested for refusing to stay on a reservation in Oklahoma and trying to return with his people to their homeland in northeast Nebraska. Standing Bear was vindicated when the judge ruled that he was being illegally held and that Native Americans were entitled to the protections of the Bill of Rights. Standing Bear was defended as a public service by two of Nebraska's most prominent attorneys, Andrew J. Poppleton and John L. Webster—an early indication that Nebraskans would stand by their new state motto, "Equality Before the Law."

In the 21st century, Nebraskans and their enterprises are represented by law firms old enough to trace their heritage to the Poppleton-Webster era and new enough to have had their beginnings in computer-linked offices. One of the most prominent national firms based here is Kutak Rock, which numbers more than 250 attorneys in Omaha and 12 other cities and has served several Fortune 500 companies and every major investment banking firm in the United States.

Private communications firms complement the efforts of state agencies and commodities associations to promote and market Nebraska goods and services domestically and abroad.

GETTING THE MESSAGE OUT

From pioneer pamphleteers promoting land speculations and patent medicines to 21st-century specialists in creating commercial Web sites, Nebraskans have had a flair for making their products and services known to wide audiences.

State agencies, commodity associations, and private organizations cooperate in global efforts to increase the export of Nebraska goods, especially grains and livestock. And Nebraska is the birthplace of one of the largest international advertising and marketing communications firms, Bozell Worldwide. Founded in 1923 by two Omaha newspapermen working out of a one-room office with no telephone, it now bills more than $3 billion annually and has 115 offices in more than 50 countries.

Nebraska's 525 state-chartered and FDIC-insured banks hold more than $31 billion in assets. Savings and loan institutions account for another $14 billion in Cornhusker assets.

A WILDERNESS TRADITION

Mutual of Omaha's Wild Kingdom, for a generation one of America's best-loved nature shows, is now seen less often on television, but the insurance company that sponsored it continues to maintain the conservationist and environmental ideas it espoused. Mutual of Omaha's Wildlife Heritage Center provides cash grants to zoos and nature centers and awards scholarships to 30 colleges and universities across the nation.

PROFESSIONAL SERVICES>>

WEST TELESERVICES CORPORATION

West TeleServices Corporation is a leading provider of innovative, full-service customer care solutions that help Fortune 500 and E-100 companies acquire, retain, and grow profitable customer relationships.

Omaha, Nebraska–based West TeleServices Corporation (NASDAQ:WSTC) is one of the nation's leading providers of outsourced customer relationship management services using the telephone and the Internet. "West acts as an 'extended enterprise' that manages large premium-brand companies' customer contact programs as well or better than they can internally," said Thomas B. Barker, West president and chief executive officer.

West TeleServices was founded in 1986 by Mary and Gary West with the vision to always provide high-end, large-scale transaction processing.

West's strategic approach began immediately with the launch of the company's Operator Teleservices division, which quickly became a leading national provider of inbound teleservices. Inbound media-driven campaigns generating large call volumes are the most difficult applications to manage, because supplying the appropriate number of agents requires real-time adjustments to complex call-projection models. West has perfected this skill thanks to more than a decade of experience managing large-volume programs.

The corporate headquarters of West TeleServices Corporation is located in Omaha, Nebraska, where the company was founded in 1986.

In 1989, West added the Interactive Teleservices division, which provides interactive voice response (IVR) services for applications as diverse as bank card activation, utility outage reporting, and prepaid calling cards. Again, the company applied its significant technology to create what has become the largest provider of interactive voice processing services in North America.

West's Direct Teleservices division, launched in 1990 to

West TeleServices employees are committed to providing complete customer care. The company's team of approximately 24,000 employees, including over 750 IT professionals, operate out of 27 state-of-the-art contact centers and seven interactive voice and data processing centers across North America.

meet the growing demand for outbound services, is widely used by companies seeking to enhance customer relationships through cross-selling and other outreach services.

Increasingly, West's clients use a blend of all three services.

In 1996, West TeleServices reorganized and initiated a public stock offering. Today, the company employs more than 24,000 people who provide customer care from 27 contact centers and seven automated voice and data processing centers in 13 states and Canada. More than 3,500 people are employed in Omaha.

West stands alone in the scope and quality of services it provides in each of these service arenas. The company processed more than four *billion* minutes of telephony-related transactions in 1999, placing it at the top of its industry. In the 1999 *Call Center CRM Solutions* magazine ranking of teleservices providers, West was rated number one nationally for both interactive and outbound services, and number three for inbound services.

West offers much more than these three services, formidable as they are. In keeping with a tradition of deploying leading-edge technology on its clients' behalf, in 1997 West added Web-enabled customer care workstations. And in early 2000, after thorough design and testing, the company launched West *icare*. This innovative real-time service lets clients use the Web to initiate

West iCare supports a suite of Internet-based, real-time interaction tools fully integrated into West's customer care platform.

communications including chat, Voice over Internet Protocol (VoIP), call-back, E-mail, or fax. West *icare* is fully integrated into West's existing customer care platform, which is supported by more than 750 technology professionals.

It's this continual reinvention of the company that has allowed West to enjoy annual revenue growth in excess of 20 percent. West anticipates continued growth at this rate throughout 2002, with revenue estimated to be approximately $700 million in 2000.

West has attained this steady, profitable growth without the aid of mergers or acquisitions. "West has grown because we take care of our customers and play an integral role in the growth plans for some of the best brands in the world," Barker said.

West owes its success to its unique commitment to quality technology and the extraordinary efforts of its people, who share a dedication to operational excellence. West has helped a number of clients win the prestigious Malcolm Baldridge National Quality Award, presented by the President of the United States in recognition of performance excellence in overall management systems.

As the new century progresses, the technology platforms will continue to change. The industry will continue to evolve. And West will continue to lead the way by expanding services based on its clients' needs. The one constant is West's employees, who constantly demonstrate their willingness to go the extra mile, according to Barker. "We take great pride in the bright, energetic people who make West what it is today and what it will be tomorrow."

Client services . . . West's key to providing proactive and creative solutions to meet clients' needs.

DLR GROUP

One of the nation's leading architectural and engineering firms, DLR Group takes pride in its ability to serve its clients through design excellence, total facility service, and employee ownership.

"From the beginning, project diversification and midwestern work values significantly influenced our company's growth," says Dale Hallock, AIA, managing principal of DLR Group. "So did our founding partners' dedication to extending company ownership to employees." Today DLR Group is a team of nearly 600 employee-owners, located in 19 U.S. cities. Recognized among the nation's top architectural and engineering firms, DLR Group's growth is reflected in commercial, educational, justice, health care, sports, and recreational buildings across the country.

In the beginning, DLR Group employed traditional design capabilities, which quickly expanded into associated services, including technology planning, sustainable design, urban planning, and public/private partnerships to facilitate alternative development and construction methods. "There remains a constant desire to expand markets, services, and geographic reach to ensure the most responsive service to our clients," says Hallock.

DLR Group clients include Ameritrade, Valmont Industries, Blue Cross Blue Shield, Alegent Health, Amazon.com, and The Boeing Company. Award-winning projects for all branches of the U.S. Department of Defense and ongoing consultation for the U.S. Department of Housing and Urban Development affirm their commitment to government service.

From schools to universities nationwide, more than 2000 projects demonstrate DLR Group's focus on educational facility innovation. The Peter Kiewit Institute of Information Science, Technology and Engineering at the

DLR Group provides master planning and design for Fortune 500 clients, including the Omaha, Nebraska, Valmont Industries facility, shown here.

DLR Group

University of Nebraska at Omaha campus was designed by DLR Group to enable the university to help remedy the region's shortage of high-tech workers. This innovative "building as a lab" has placed the university in the national spotlight.

Nebraska's newest state correctional institution, in Tecumseh, and the new Roman L. Hruska Courthouse, in Omaha, represent more than 200 justice facilities in the firm's nationwide portfolio. Consistently ranked among the leading justice design firms, DLR Group embarked on its first international project in 1999—a correctional center in New Zealand.

With clients such as the New York Yankees, the International Speedway Corporation, the University of Nebraska, and the University of Florida, the DLR Group's reputation as a preeminent sports and entertainment designer is gaining momentum. Other notable projects include renovation of the 1.5 million-square-foot Ala Moana Center in Hawaii and new convention centers, hotels, and arenas planned for Omaha, Nebraska, and Overland Park, Kansas.

"Our mission remains the same," says Hallock. "DLR Group will continue to serve the nation through design excellence, total facility service, and employee ownership."

The distinctive Peter Kiewit Institute, designed by DLR Group, seeks to merge the cultures of higher education and business to create an ideal learning environment for future engineering professionals, and for research and teaching.

NEBRASKA DEPARTMENT OF ECONOMIC DEVELOPMENT

A one-stop source for all-inclusive information about the state, the Nebraska Department of Economic

Development is on a mission to promote the 'good life' of Nebraska.

The Department's logo refers to the genuine characteristics, values, and opportunities that form the basis for the good life in Nebraska.

GENUINE.
Nebraska

Created in 1967, the Nebraska Department of Economic Development has, for many years, shared information on Nebraska with people looking for a great place to live, work, and conduct business. That information is easily accessible through the department's Web site at www.neded.org or by calling 800-426-6505.

WORKING TOGETHER TO BUILD SUCCESS

The combined mission of the various divisions of the department is to provide quality leadership and services that enable Nebraska communities, businesses, and people to succeed in a global economy. The Community and Rural Development Division provides affordable community infrastructure and housing development finance around the state, using a variety of resources. The Business Development Division helps both new and existing employers in the state with financing, job training, and accessing new markets and technologies. The Travel and Tourism Division provides a wealth of information for visitors to the state, bolstering a travel industry that is now Nebraska's third largest source of revenue from outside the state, following agriculture and manufacturing.

A GENUINELY GREAT STATE

Through extensive effort, all aspects of the Nebraska Department of Economic Development are aimed at demonstrating one key point: Nebraska is a genuinely great place. It is a great place in which to grow up, form lasting friendships, start a career or business, raise a family, and otherwise develop and prosper. In short, Nebraska provides a social and physical environment that has historically nurtured, and amply rewarded, both individual initiative and group cooperation. It offers a high quality of life that Nebraskans are increasingly proud of and willing to share with others.

THE CITY OF OMAHA

With a tradition of economic vibrancy, community spirit, and traditional midwestern values, the progressive city

of Omaha, Nebraska, continually develops and revitalizes its business, cultural, and recreational resources.

Rapidly becoming recognized as one of the most progressive cities in the United States, Omaha, Nebraska, the 43rd largest city in the nation, is experiencing unheralded growth and prosperity.

Omaha is home to five Fortune 500 companies and more than 18,000 businesses. In 1999, *Forbes* cited Omaha as the 13th best city in the nation in its "Best Places for Business and Careers." And Omaha was labeled a "boom town" by *U.S. News & World Report,* among many other accolades.

Shown in this rendering, the City of Omaha's convention center and arena being planned for completion in 2003 is an example of Omaha's vigorous support of progressive economic development.

Omaha's robust economy continues to support a tradition of high quality of life, complete with affordable housing, a low crime rate, and unparalleled education and health care, as well as first class historical and recreational attractions, such as the world-renowned Omaha Henry Doorly Zoo, Rosenblatt Stadium, the historic Old Market district, the Omaha Community Playhouse, the Orpheum Theater, and the Joslyn Art Museum.

According to Indian legend, Omaha means "above all others upon a stream." This title couldn't be more prophetic, as the Missouri River corridor continues to be the anchor for economic development and revitalization within the city, especially downtown.

Most notably, a brand new $281 million convention center and sports arena, the largest

One of the City of Omaha's many treasures, the Henry Doorly Zoo has lions and tigers and penguins and the Lied Jungle, shown here, the world's largest indoor tropical rain forest, which has its own apes.

public works facility ever undertaken in the state of Nebraska, is replacing the rail yards of the Union Pacific Railroad as the primary link between the downtown business district, the riverfront, and Omaha Eppley Airfield.

While the convention center and arena will serve as a tremendous catalyst for economic and recreational growth, Omaha continues to reinvigorate a city of growing cosmopolitan class and is engaged in several additional large-scale development projects. According to John Lehning, director of construction and leasing, First National Bank's new 40-story office tower will be the tallest structure in the Midwest and will take center stage in the fast-changing Omaha skyline. The city also recently completed construction of the new Roman Hruska Federal Courthouse and is engaged in projects to expand the Omaha World-Herald and ConAgra.

On all fronts, the city of Omaha can be defined in one word—*progress.* It is no secret that Omaha's vision, community spirit, economic vibrancy, and traditional midwestern values truly make it one of the biggest gems in the heart of the nation.

FINANCIAL SERVICES>>

COMMERCIAL FEDERAL BANK

Committed to customer service and future growth, Commercial Federal Bank continues to build on its long

tradition of providing innovative and diversified products and services to America's Heartland.

Commercial Federal Bank has been an integral part of the banking industry in Omaha and in the Midwest since it was founded, more than 100 years ago.

Now in its second century, Commercial Federal Bank is light years away from the little business that began in 1887, when a group of South Omaha leaders pooled their resources to form the South Omaha Loan and Building Association. With assets totaling $10,000, the group created the small company in order to provide opportunities for home ownership and financial security. In 1893, the little company had prospered enough to hire its first full-time employee, James J. Fitzgerald, a 24-year-old Irish immigrant who would serve the company for 64 years.

Spurred by much growth, the company changed its name in 1910 to Commercial Savings and Loan to reflect the broader range of services provided by the company. Commercial Savings and Loan survived the Great Depression when many of its counterparts could not, and began to grow again at the beginning of the war. By the end of the war, the company was thriving with new services and features. Commercial was among the pioneers in developing financial advertising on television in 1952

T. J. O'Neil, left, and James J. "J. J." Fitzgerald pose in front of the early South Omaha office. The 24-year-old Fitzgerald joined the South Omaha Loan and Building Association in 1893, launching a 64-year career with the company that is known today as Commercial Federal Bank. William A. Fitzgerald, the company's current chairman and chief executive officer, is his grandson.

The Commercial Savings & Loan Association's three-story office building at 4824 South 24th Street served as Commercial Federal Bank's home office from the 1920s until 1962, when the company relocated to 45th and Dodge.

and, in 1953, it was the first financial institution in the state to open a bank office with a drive-up window. In 1955, William F. Fitzgerald took over for his father as president of the company.

In 1972, the company acquired a federal charter and as a result changed its name to Commercial Federal Savings and Loan. Over the next decade, Commercial Federal continued to build its network of retail banks throughout the state and, in 1990, amended its charter in order to become a federal savings bank. A new name emerged—Commercial Federal Bank.

CHANGES BRING BENEFITS TO CUSTOMERS

Along with name changes have come changes in size and scope. Through its expansion efforts, the institution now offers more services to commercial customers. The bank currently employs a total of 3,400 people, including over

1,300 employees in Nebraska, and offers more than 230 locations in Nebraska, Arizona, Colorado, Iowa, Kansas, Minnesota, Missouri, and Oklahoma.

At the end of 1999, assets of Commercial Federal Corporation, the parent company of Commercial Federal Bank, totaled $13.3 billion.

In recent years the bank has focused on acquisitions. Since 1995, Commercial Federal Bank has expanded continually, and today the company has more than 230 branch offices in Nebraska, Iowa, Colorado, Kansas, Oklahoma, Missouri, Minnesota, and Arizona. William A. Fitzgerald, chairman of the board and chief executive officer as well as the third generation of the family to run the business says, "Commercial Federal Bank continues to grow in the demographically desirable and dynamic Midwest, particularly in urban and rural markets. With the integration of more than 230 branches, we are ready to maximize our customer base of approximately 700,000 households by cross-selling our diversified product mix. We are confident that the combination of this strategy and significantly strengthened systems and products will produce sustainable growth and enhanced shareholder value."

DIVERSIFIED PRODUCTS AND SERVICES

Commercial Federal Bank's "diversified product mix" represents an impressive array of innovative services. One of the most innovative is the new Internet banking program, Access*Online*. This new product recognizes the time constraints now faced by busy people as well as an increasing comfort with and reliance on the Internet. Access*Online*, an extension of the computerized home banking program pioneered by the bank in 1996, is an Internet browser–based transactional and

William A. Fitzgerald joined Commercial Federal Bank in 1952, and was named president in 1974, chief executive officer in 1983, and chairman of the board in 1994.

In 1953, Commercial opened the first bank in Nebraska with a drive-up window, in Omaha. Contrary to the opinions of a number of critics who predicted that customers would never use the facility, the office was an instant success. During the grand opening, cars lined up for two blocks as their occupants waited to open savings accounts and collect their gifts of pen and pencil sets and cigarette lighters.

informational banking service (www.comfedbank.com), featuring local weather, headline news, and stock market reports, in addition to information about bank services and locations.

In addition to its many products and services, Commercial Federal Bank has long been known for its community involvement. Every summer for the past 10 years, the bank has sponsored a family concert at Memorial Park in the heart of Omaha. Featuring local and national music groups and a spectacular fireworks display, "Commercial Federal Celebrates America" is attended each year by more than 40,000 people.

Commercial Federal Bank is wholeheartedly embracing the challenges of the new century. Fitzgerald believes strongly that the key to future growth is focusing on customer service. With such a diverse mix of bank products, customers already loyal to the bank can be served by more than just one product. "Bank personnel are trained to build on customer relationships through cross-selling opportunities to the 700,000 Commercial Federal Bank households. Commercial Federal is committed to its customers in the Heartland."

FIRST NATIONAL BANK OF OMAHA

A solid financial leader with a reputation for success, First National Bank of Omaha has been meeting the needs of communities throughout Nebraska for nearly 150 years.

At 40 stories and 633 feet high, the new First National Tower will permanently redefine the Omaha skyline when completed in 2002. It will be the key feature of First National's new office and technology district in downtown Omaha. Photo © Mike Kleveter

In an industry characterized by megamergers and ever-changing marquees, First National Bank of Omaha is proud to have a history that dates back nearly 150 years. Built upon humble beginnings in 1857, First National Bank of Omaha has risen to prominence just as Omaha has grown from a tiny village housing a few hardy pioneers to a thriving metropolitan city.

First National's story is also the saga of three industrious families—the Kountzes, Davises, and Lauritzens—who built the company from a small operation in a little wood frame building near the edge of the Missouri River into a nationwide multi-billion-dollar success story. The bank's well-established culture of providing personalized customer service and innovative quality products has garnered it a reputation as the leading banking institution in the region.

The First National Bank of Omaha began in 1857—during a period known as the "wildcat banking" era—when two young brothers from Ohio, Augustus and Herman Kountze, established the bank by trading gold dust and buffalo hides.

Noted Omahan and investor Edward Creighton served as the bank's first president. During the 19th century, under the Kountze and Creighton leadership, the bank worked hard to enhance the city's business and cultural growth by supporting such projects as the Omaha Stockyards, the Trans-Mississippi Exposition of 1898, and Creighton University. Community involvement continues to be a guiding principle of the bank's business philosophy.

STEADY GROWTH

In 1914, Herman Kountze's brother-in-law, F. H. Davis, assumed the presidency. In 1916, First National Bank of Omaha constructed its new headquarters—a skyscraper of 14 stories located at 16th and Farnam Streets. His son and successor, T. L. Davis, who took over in 1934, demonstrated the innovation and foresight typical of the bank's leadership when he established a consumer credit corporation in the 1930s. While other banks at that time specialized in lending to commercial clients, First National Bank of Omaha built a thriving business handling auto, coal, home repair, and other installment loans for a large number of middle-income consumers, thus creating a lasting retail lending culture.

In the 1940s, John Lauritzen joined his brother-in-law John Davis, son of T. L., at the company. Lauritzen was anxious to build a national business—one that would stretch far beyond Omaha. His greatest contribution to First National was his pioneering and promotion of the bank credit card business. Starting in 1953, this innovative product was John's "baby," which grew up to become

First National Bank of Omaha was a pioneer in the credit card industry. John R. Lauritzen laid the foundation for the bank's success as a leading credit card issuer and merchant processing organization when he introduced First Charge credit card in 1953.

two nationwide businesses (card issuing and merchant processing) and the largest operating divisions of the company.

In 1953, John Davis became the third generation of the Davis family to serve as president. Bruce Lauritzen, the bank's current president since 1987, is the fifth generation of his family to serve the First National Bank of Omaha. He carries on a tradition of providing superior quality products with innovative technology and superior customer service.

first national bank of omaha
MEMBER FDIC

A COMPANY WITH RICH ASSETS

First National Bank of Omaha's holding company, First National of Nebraska, is the third largest bank holding company headquartered west of Omaha.

Organized in 1968, First National of Nebraska's assets grew more than fourfold during the 1990s, extending its banking operations to communities across Nebraska and into Colorado and Kansas.

Today, First National of Nebraska and its affiliates offer more than $9 billion in assets and employ more than 6,000 associates who are located in every state. Primary banking offices are found in Colorado, Kansas, Nebraska, and South Dakota. First National is also the nation's largest in-house bank processor of merchant credit card transactions, one of the 15 largest bank issuers of Visa and Mastercard, a top 20 processor of automated clearing house transactions, and one of the 15 largest providers of cash management services in the nation.

As the new century begins, the bank continues to serve as a catalyst for the growth and development of the state. In the late 1990s, the company constructed impressive new buildings for the First National Bank of North Platte, the Platte Valley Bank in Kearney, and the First Bankcard Service Center in Wayne.

The strength of First National Bank of Omaha's commitment to Nebraska is further demonstrated by its $300 million redevelopment project in downtown Omaha. The bank's Technology Center, a 194,000-square-foot facility that processes more than $6 million in credit card transactions per hour, utilizes an independent power system that is the largest application of fuel cell technology in the world. Fuel cell technology allows First National to operate independently of the public utility grid, ensuring that the center will have uninterrupted computer-grade power 24 hours a day, seven days a week.

There is no doubt that First National Bank of Omaha will continue to be "The bank Omaha calls first."

First National of Nebraska is the leading banking organization across the state. Its commitment to Nebraska is emphasized by the new headquarters building for Platte Valley State Bank in Kearney. Photo © Jeffrey Bebee

FIRST DATA CORPORATION

First Data Corporation, with numerous business units and nearly 8,000 employees in Nebraska, is a worldwide leader in payment services and electronic commerce, moving more than $1 trillion in transactions annually.

Every year, First Data Corporation helps financial institutions, merchants, and consumers electronically move more than $1 trillion. Whether helping businesses sell their products at stores or over the Internet or processing a consumer's credit card transaction, First Data's more than 30,000 employees around the globe work together to make it easy for businesses to operate and for consumers to buy the things they need.

Although First Data is not a household name, it touches many consumers' lives. People can efficiently transfer money to friends or relatives worldwide through Western Union® and can safely write checks that are approved within seconds thanks to First Data's TeleCheck system. Every day, First Data is making it easier, faster, and more secure for people and businesses to buy goods and services.

GLOBAL EXPANSION

The origins of this electronic commerce leader can be traced back to Omaha in 1971, when a small company was created to provide card-processing services to an association of seven Midwest banks. First Data Resources, as the start-up company was called, led to

The First Data Technology Campus, at 72nd and Pacific Streets in Omaha, plays an integral role in the company's global transaction card-processing operations.

the creation of Atlanta, Georgia–based First Data Corporation, and made a name for itself as the world's leading credit card transaction processor.

In 1976, First Data Resources became the first company to process both Visa (then BankAmericard) and MasterCard (then Master Charge) transactions. By 1980, First Data Resources had increased its Omaha employee base to 2,000 and achieved annual revenues of $50 million.

Today, First Data Resources, with more than 12,000 employees worldwide, including nearly 8,000 in Nebraska, is a business unit of First Data Corporation. First Data Resources has become a major player in the world of electronic commerce, serving more than 1,400 banks and other card issuers representing more than 260 million card accounts around the world.

Several other business units of First Data Corporation (NYSE: FDC) also have operations in Nebraska. Along

The First Data Technology Campus in Omaha is located next to the University of Nebraska's Peter Kiewit Institute of Information Science, Technology and Engineering.

with First Data Resources are First Data Merchant Services, Teleservices, First Data Solutions, and Call Interactive.

These businesses serve some of the largest corporate names in the world—GE Capital, Chase Manhattan Bank, First U.S.A./Bank One, Sears, AT&T, and American Express—with card-processing services, leading-edge interactive voice response systems, and voice center services. In addition, First Data Resources partners with international financial services companies through its offices in the United Kingdom, Australia, Spain, Germany, and Mexico.

THE ELECTRONIC COMMERCE EDGE

To serve leading companies in the financial industry, First Data's Omaha operations feature the latest in advanced technology. Its world-class Data Center, which operates 24 hours a day, seven days a week, handles credit and debit card transactions from around the globe. Omaha also is home to First Data's Powerhouse, a power supply with one of the nation's highest levels of system redundancy, for back-up that ensures continuous uninterrupted processing. Financial institutions also rely on First Data to print and mail millions of card statements every day from its award-winning operations in Omaha.

In support of the advancement of technology statewide, First Data works with Nebraska's K–12 educators, high schools, colleges, and universities to promote technology education. And in 1996, First Data purchased more than 140 acres of land in Omaha and donated 70 acres of the property to the University of Nebraska for The Peter Kiewit Institute of Information Science, Technology and Engineering. This technology institute, along with First Data's partnerships with educational institutions, helps to develop, attract, and retain a talented technology workforce in Nebraska.

As a new century begins, the future at First Data looks bright. Strong partnerships, technology capabilities, and strategic direction provide First Data with unlimited possibilities to expand its electronic

Operating 24 hours a day, seven days a week, the First Data Resources Data Center handles millions of credit and debit card transactions from around the world.

commerce offerings. As real-time buying and selling on the Internet continue at an accelerating pace, the need for processing and safeguarding transactions, as well as collecting and maintaining purchasing information, will, too. First Data intends to be a dominant force in Internet expansion, offering the ability to make purchasing easier and more convenient for businesses and consumers.

Moving toward achieving its mission—to process every electronic payment worldwide from the point of sale to the point of settlement—First Data and its subsidiaries have been expanding the capabilities of electronic commerce. Thanks to one of the latest innovations of First Data Resources, consumers now can apply for and receive credit in less than 60 seconds to make purchases on the Internet—whether for books or theater tickets or other goods and services. First Data will continue to be at the forefront of the shift from paper to electronic transactions, driving new developments and applications that make buying and paying on-line more convenient.

From its humble beginnings in 1971 to its worldwide presence as a transaction-processing leader, First Data's success, and that of its clients, is permanently linked to the resources of Nebraska.

INSURANCE SERVICES>>

WOODMEN OF THE WORLD
OMAHA WOODMEN LIFE INSURANCE SOCIETY

Proudly known as "The FAMILY Fraternity®," Woodmen of the World/Omaha Woodmen Life Insurance Society

remains true to its mission of offering insurance protection and fraternal benefits to members and their families.

Providing insurance protection and fraternal benefits to its members for more than 110 years, Woodmen of the World Life Insurance Society is one of the largest fraternal benefit societies in the United States. Headquartered in Omaha, Nebraska, Woodmen has more than 840,000 members nationwide who hold nearly one million life insurance, hospital supplement, and annuity certificates.

As "The FAMILY Fraternity®," Woodmen provides its members with much more than just insurance protection. Through 2,600 lodges nationwide, members receive many fraternal benefits and have the opportunity to take part in Woodmen-sponsored fraternal, social, and civic activities designed to strengthen families and improve the communities in which they live.

These activities include conducting educational and social programs for Woodmen youth and senior members; promoting patriotism through the presentation of U.S. flags; donating equipment to police, fire, and rescue units; recognizing individuals with awards for conservation and outstanding citizenship; and providing disaster relief services through a partnership with the American Red Cross.

Woodmen's fraternal benefits include financial support for members diagnosed with catastrophic illnesses; assistance for members' orphaned children; and insurance protection for members' newborn babies.

Woodmen is one of the nation's oldest fraternal benefit societies and has been a proud member of the Nebraska business community since its founding in Omaha on June 6, 1890, by Joseph Cullen Root.

Executive officers of Woodmen of the World/ Omaha Woodmen Life Insurance Society include, from left, Wayne Graham, executive vice president; James Bridges, national treasurer; John G. Bookout, national president; and James Mounce, national secretary.

Root's idea for the name "Woodmen" is believed to have come from a speech he heard about woodsmen clearing forests in order to provide shelter for their families. His intention was to create an organization dedicated to protecting its members while also promoting service to others in the spirit of fraternalism.

Throughout its 110-year history, Woodmen has promoted fraternalism in a wide variety of ways. These include establishing a national fraternal service fund to assist lodges with civic and charitable activities and creating a patriotic program that includes giving U.S. flags to schools, churches, and other civic and nonprofit organizations; providing copies of the *American Patriot's Handbook* to schools and newly naturalized citizens; and awarding students for proficiency in American history. Today, in fact, Woodmen is one of the nation's largest presenters of U.S. flags.

Woodmen has a long history of providing activities for its youth members with the first Woodmen youth program

organized in 1903. During the 1940s, the youth program emphasized camping and other outdoor activities. Today, Woodmen youth, known as Rangers, take part in many enjoyable and educational activities, including attending summer camps located across the nation.

SUPPORTING AND STRENGTHENING FAMILIES

In 1958, Woodmen's commitment to supporting and strengthening families was formalized as the society adopted the phrase "The FAMILY Fraternity" as its official slogan.

In 1969, Woodmen completed construction of the 30-story Woodmen Tower, which at the time was the tallest structure between Chicago and the Pacific Ocean, and today remains the tallest building in Omaha. The construction of the Woodmen Tower was lauded as a major step in the revival of downtown Omaha as a business and civic center.

Woodmen experienced phenomenal growth throughout the 1970s and 1980s as new life insurance products and fraternal benefits were added. In 1990, Woodmen observed its 100th anniversary with centennial celebrations in Omaha and throughout the nation.

In 1998, Woodmen formed a partnership with the American Red Cross to provide a caring force of disaster relief volunteers. In communities across the nation, Woodmen lodges work with American Red Cross chapters to create disaster action teams that respond to a variety of disaster situations. Today, more than 750 Woodmen members are certified in disaster relief and belong to 68 Woodmen/ Red Cross disaster action teams nationwide. In addition, Woodmen supports the efforts of the American Red Cross with equipment, supplies, and the use of Woodmen lodge halls and summer camps as disaster relief sites.

A dominant feature of the Omaha skyline, the 30-story Woodmen Tower serves as Woodmen's home office.

Woodmen offers life insurance and annuity products designed to meet the needs of America's families.

MEETING MEMBERS' NEEDS

Woodmen offers its members a full range of life insurance, annuity, and hospital supplement products designed to meet the changing needs of families, as well as a comprehensive package of fraternal benefits and activities. In addition, the society's 550 home office associates and 1,700 field associates work together to serve the insurance needs of its members throughout the nation.

This combination of innovative insurance products, caring fraternal programs, and exceptional service has enabled Woodmen to become one of the nation's leading fraternal benefit societies, with life insurance in force exceeding $30 billion and assets of more than $5 billion.

While much has changed over Woodmen's 110-year history, the principles that guided its founding have remained constant: meeting the needs of its members and their families through insurance protection and fraternal benefits while providing service to others. It is this commitment that truly makes Woodmen "The FAMILY Fraternity."

FARMERS MUTUAL INSURANCE COMPANY OF NEBRASKA

Farmers Mutual Insurance Company of Nebraska, headquartered in Lincoln, insures homes, farms, and automobiles for policyholders across Nebraska and South Dakota.

Farmers Mutual Insurance Company of Nebraska has woven a rich tapestry of history since its humble beginnings in 1891. And, those strong threads of vision and value first presented in the dreams of the early farmers more than a century ago have carried through to the new millennium with the company's enduring commitment to providing reliable insurance protection at a reasonable cost.

"It was the founders' intention that those providing the insurance stay in close touch with the requirements of those who needed and purchased it," says Byron L. Boslau, chairman, president, and chief executive officer of Farmers Mutual. "Over the years this close relationship between the company and its market has produced a unique and responsive company. It has been a long time since 1891, but the original reasons for the creation of Farmers Mutual are as valid today as they were then."

Currently holding 40 percent of the farm-insurance market, Farmers Mutual is the largest domiciled personal lines property and casualty insurer in Nebraska. The company plays a dominant role as a leading writer of personal insurance lines in Nebraska and in South Dakota and has maintained a strong belief in the concept of "mutual" insurance.

A LEGACY OF SUPPORT FOR POLICYHOLDERS

That concept was hard won by the company's founding fathers. As farmers they had little to combat the prohibitive costs set by established insurance companies located in the

Since 1962, the home of Farmers Mutual has been at 1220 Lincoln Mall, in the shadow of the state capitol.

eastern part of the United States. Because farming was considered an undesirable risk at that time, insurance—when it was available—was well beyond the economic reach of the average farmer. So, farmers all over the Midwest united and lobbied for legislation that would allow them to form their own mutual-assessment companies and insure themselves at a reasonable cost. This effort became a reality in the Nebraska legislature of 1891, with the passage of legislation allowing the formation of farm mutuals. That same year, 22 farmers living near Lincoln met and signed the articles of incorporation forming a new statewide mutual to be known as Farmers Mutual Insurance Company of Nebraska.

For 59 years beginning in 1903, the Lincoln headquarters of Farmers Mutual was at 1220 P Street.

Over the many years that followed, the company supported its policyholders through war, the Great Depression, inflationary cycles, drought, and seasons of consecutive record-breaking storms, to grow into its position today as the leading Nebraska-based insurer of homes, farms, and automobiles. As one of the 100 largest mutual insurance companies in the United States, Farmers Mutual is proud of its historic contribution in fire prevention and in education programs for rural areas. The company was instrumental in developing much-needed fire districts throughout Nebraska's farmlands, enabling quicker response times to the more-isolated areas. Today Farmers Mutual remains committed to supporting fire districts in Nebraska and South Dakota by donating funds to purchase fire-fighting equipment. Farmers Mutual also continues its long legacy of working on industry-related legislative matters and is considered an industry leader for its lobbying efforts.

"Our company is owned by its policyholders, so we take very seriously our responsibility as stewards of their money," says Boslau.

FINANCIAL STRENGTH

Headquartered in Lincoln, Farmers Mutual employs 208 people throughout Nebraska and has eight claims offices, with locations in Omaha, Norfolk, Grand Island, Columbus, North Platte, Kearney, and Scottsbluff. More than 1,500 independent agents represent the company in Nebraska and South Dakota.

The strong financial position of Farmers Mutual is imperative for it to protect its policyholders in the aftermath of volatile weather.

FARMERS MUTUAL *INSURANCE COMPANY* OF NEBRASKA

"We only sell our products through independent agents, and they are very loyal to us," Boslau says. "Our motto is to provide the best service at the most reasonable cost, which in turn creates a very stable marketplace."

Stability within the ranks of Farmers Mutual also is apparent. Only six company presidents have preceded Boslau, who points to the recent celebration of 13 employees reaching their 25th anniversary year with the company as another example of continuity.

The financial position of Farmers Mutual is one of the strongest in the industry, putting the company in the top 150 of the more than 3,200 insurance companies in the United States. This strength protects its more than 180,000 Nebraska and South Dakota policyholders. Its consistently high surplus, more than $110 million in 1999, means policyholders can depend on more than good weather for guaranteed protection of their life investments. During 1999, Farmers Mutual also established new company records with more than $200 million in assets and more than $100 million in written premiums.

"Security from financial loss has never been more important to society than it is today," says Boslau. "When our policyholders purchase insurance, we promise we will be there if a loss occurs, to help them return their lives to normal. Our financial strength assures that we can keep that promise."

A highly trained Farmers Mutual adjuster, one of 65 located throughout Nebraska, inspects a vehicle. The company is dedicated to providing prompt, fair, quality claim service to its agents and policyholders.

MUTUAL OF OMAHA COMPANIES

The Mutual of Omaha Companies offer businesses and individuals not only comprehensive life, health, and property insurance packages, but also annuities, mutual funds, and brokerage and public finance services.

Located on more than 30 acres of land in midtown Omaha, the Mutual of Omaha campus is a recognized landmark in the community.

Over the past 90 years, Mutual of Omaha has earned a reputation as a solid family-oriented company that is reliable, knowledgeable, and customer driven. These attributes have made Mutual of Omaha one of the top providers of individual and group health insurance in the nation, as well as a respected financial services organization. Mutual of Omaha offers a comprehensive line of products and services to individuals, small businesses, and large employers. These include life, health, dental, disability, long-term care, Medicare Supplement, and property casualty coverage, along with annuities, mutual funds, and full-service brokerage and public finance services.

SOLID FOUNDATION, UNLIMITED POSSIBILITIES

The strong performance by Mutual of Omaha is a direct result of not only its products, but also its unwavering commitment to customer service. This is a tradition that began with the founding of the company in 1909 by a young medical student named C. C. Criss and his wife, Mabel Criss, who was the first female officer at Mutual of Omaha.

Mutual of Omaha's ability to diversify product offerings and provide top-notch customer service has enabled it to grow into an organization with total assets of nearly $15 billion, placed it in the Fortune 500, and earned it strong ratings from the four major rating services for overall financial strength.

EMPLOYER OF CHOICE

Mutual of Omaha's 5,500 associates benefit by working for a company that values quality of life, offering an in-house wellness center, credit union, and dry cleaning service, tuition reimbursement, and referrals for the care of family members. Such benefits have earned Mutual of Omaha the Gold Well Workplace award, a place on *Working Mother* magazine's list of the "100 Best Companies for Working Mothers," and the title Nebraska Employer of the Year.

CARING ABOUT THE WORLD

This concern for quality of life also extends to strong support for the community. Mutual of Omaha contributes to a variety of educational, cultural, and civic programs, including United Way/CHAD, Camp Fire Boys and Girls, Fontenelle Forest Association, NCAA College World Series, YWCA, and St. Augustine Indian Mission.

A history of caring for the community is also seen in Mutual of Omaha's sponsorship of family television programming, such as *Wild Kingdom*, which helped bring Mutual of Omaha into the national spotlight and demonstrated its belief in conservation of animals and all the earth's natural resources.

In the ever-changing business world, one thing remains constant—Mutual of Omaha's focus on serving the needs of its customers.

NOURISHMENT FOR A GROWING ECONOMY

CHAPTER THIRTEEN

HOME AND WORK IN A NEW CENTURY

RESIDENTIAL AND COMMERCIAL DEVELOPMENT

In 1803 the United States bought the land that is now Nebraska from France for about four cents an acre. Fifty-four years after the Louisiana Purchase, a single building lot in a Missouri River community was offered by speculators at as much as $10,000. Those who invest in Cornhusker State home or business property today can be thankful that that rate of land inflation didn't continue. In fact, the affordability of residential and commercial real

estate is one of Nebraska's most attractive and often-cited amenities—a main factor in its ranking as one of the most livable states in the nation.

Even in the state's eastern urban areas, where land and construction costs are comparatively higher, Nebraska residents and newcomers find housing economical. In Omaha, factoring in apartment rents, new home prices, mortgage rates, and monthly house payments, the American Chamber of Commerce Researchers Association (ACCRA) found housing costs at the end of 1999 to be 9 percent below the U.S. average. And statewide, about 70 percent of the occupied housing units are owner occupied, giving Nebraska a rate of home ownership significantly higher than the national average.

The vigorous growth in Cornhusker State commercial real estate development is best illustrated by the current renaissance of the downtown areas of Omaha and Lincoln. Both cities are seeing major core growth in office space, hotel rooms, entertainment complexes, specialty retailing, and of course, associated parking space. In the closing year of the 20th century, about 90

percent of Omaha's office space was occupied, and the occupancy rate in five million square feet of industrial lease space had reached 81 percent.

Though it may fall short of the epic land rush of 19th-century homesteaders, the healthy demand for both commercial and residential space has also contributed to the success and growth of Nebraska's real estate professionals. Offering a comprehensive array of services, from property management to international relocation, prominent firms in this sector include CBSHOME Real Estate, Grubb & Ellis/Pacific Realty Group, and NP Dodge Real Estate.

BUILDING A HERITAGE

Creating a modern, prosperous society on the once-forbidding prairie has included the design and construction of landmarks that have helped secure Nebraska's place in the

ABOVE: *Nebraska's pool of architectural and engineering talent is capable of tackling projects of any size.* OPPOSITE: *Completed in 1991, the $90 million Landmark Center houses the Omaha offices of Qwest Communications (formerly US West), MFS Network Technologies, and other prominent companies.*

The breathtaking atrium at the Strategic Air Command Museum in Ashland consists of 525 glass panels—one of many award-winning designs by the Omaha architectural firm of Leo A Daly.

nation's architectural showcase. Probably the most notable is the state capitol, designed by Bertram G. Goodhue and generally recognized as one of the most significant public buildings in America. Other treasures include the Joslyn Art Museum in Omaha, by John and Alan MacDonald; Philip Johnson's Sheldon Memorial Art Gallery in Lincoln; and Edward Durrell Stone's Stuhr Museum of the Prairie Pioneer in Grand Island.

Nebraska claims some of the nation's outstanding architectural and engineering firms. One is Leo A Daly, which was founded in Omaha by the late Leo A Daly and has grown into a global enterprise. Recent projects include a $110 million office tower in Hong Kong, two $50 million office complexes in the United Arab Emirates, and an airport terminal in the Philippines. Leo A Daly first established its overseas presence more than 30 years ago with a facility in Hong Kong and since has

A milking shed takes shape at a dairy farm in Seward. Construction for the agricultural industry has become a specialty of Nebraska building contractors.

become one of the leading architectural firms in Asia. At home, the company has designed many of Omaha's most prominent business and civic structures, complementing in tangible form the founder's personal contributions as a leader in the city's philanthropic activities.

HDR, Inc., has its headquarters and one of three major design centers in Omaha. It has completed large-scale projects in 30 foreign countries and all 50 states, including the Boston Central Artery, the largest civil works project in the United States. In cooperation with a

FROM SHOESTRING TO NATIONAL PROMINENCE

One of Nebraska's home-grown success stories is the Campos Construction Co. of Omaha. Started by Robert Campos on $500 capital, it has become general contractor on multimillion-dollar projects locally and nationally and has been instrumental in renovating such national landmarks as the homes of Presidents Truman, Hoover, and Lincoln. The firm also built the Gerald R. Ford Conservation Center in Omaha.

Shortly after the Kansas-Nebraska Act of 1854 officially opened Nebraska Territory to settlement, the *Nebraska Palladium*—published at Bellevue, the state's oldest town—set a municipal goal of becoming "the center of commerce, and the half-way house between the Atlantic and Pacific Ocean." The community still is inching toward that objective, becoming in 1999 the third largest city in Nebraska.

London firm, HDR designed the recent addition of a striking $45 million pavilion at the Joslyn Art Museum. Elsewhere, Omaha is dotted with educational, cultural, and civic facilities donated to the community by retired chairman Charles W. Durham and his late wife, Marge.

Two other firms, both established in the 1960s, have managed in just over 30 years to diversify across a wide spectrum of design and construction: The DLR Group

From downtown to the suburbs, Nebraska's metropolitan areas have experienced steady development thanks to strong business-government partnerships and Cornhuskers' entrepreneurial spirit.

New home construction in Nebraska communities like southeast Lincoln continues to provide economical housing in one of the fastest growing areas in the midwestern United States.

(Dana Larson Roubal and Associates) is an employee-owned firm with headquarters in Omaha and offices in 18 other U.S. cities and Mexico; and Bahr Vermeer Haecker Architects, founded in Lincoln, now also has offices in Omaha and Pasadena, California.

Nebraska's first private residences were tepees and sod houses. Its first business structure was a log cabin trading post. That today's comfortable and progressive environment of home and work has grown from such crude beginnings in a comparatively short span of history offers bright promise for the growth of the Cornhusker State in a new century.

TRUTH IN ADVERTISING?

Early land speculators were imaginative if not accurate. Most new town plats in Nebraska were described as "located adjacent to the very finest groves of timber, surrounded by a very rich agricultural country, in prospective, abundantly supplied with building rock of the finest description, beautifully watered, and possessing very fine indications of lead, iron, coal, and salt in great abundance." Such extravagance led Nebraska City editor J. Sterling Morton to observe: "In my opinion we felt richer, better, and more millionairish than any other poor deluded mortals ever did on the same amount of moonshine and pluck."

DEVELOPMENT>>

LEO A DALY

Committed to the global promotion of design excellence, Leo A Daly has become one of the world's leading planning, architectural, engineering, and interior design firms.

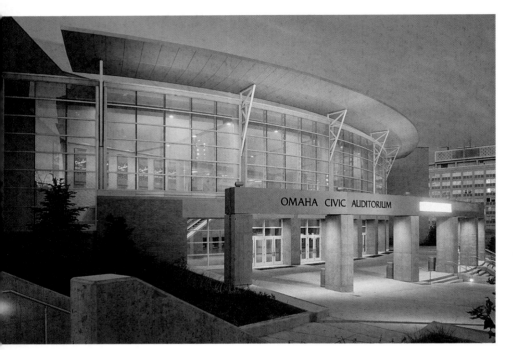

The Omaha Civic Auditorium was designed by Leo A Daly in 1994. © Paul Brokering/Leo A Daly

airline terminals, zoos, high-rise office buildings, schools, universities, computer centers, hospitals, and day care centers.

Its clients represent nations as well as local government agencies, entire industries as well as individual corporations, and for-profit as well as nonprofit institutions.

WORLDWIDE DESIGN SERVICE

As testimony to its expansive reach, the company today maintains offices in 12 U.S. cities in addition to its Omaha headquarters, as well as offices in Hong Kong, Dubai, Madrid, and Berlin. Its success is evident by national and international design and engineering awards and citations it has received during its remarkable history.

Much of the success of the Leo A Daly firm can be attributed to the company's unwavering devotion to design excellence, regardless of the size of the assigned project.

Leo A Daly utilizes its unique "team concept" approach in each of its projects, bringing together architects, planners, engineers, and interior designers to collaborate, thus assuring that even the largest and most challenging of its assignments is not only aesthetically pleasing but also completely functional, comfortable, durable, environmentally sound, and efficient.

In fact, the "team concept" approach, developed by Leo A Daly

Founded in Omaha by Leo A. Daly Sr. in 1915, Leo A Daly has long been recognized as one of the world's premier planning, architectural, engineering, and interior design firms.

For 85 years the firm has been designing not only many of Nebraska's most significant landmarks, but also numerous structures throughout the United States and in more than 50 countries around the world.

First under the leadership of Leo A. Daly Sr., then Leo A. Daly Jr., and currently Leo A. Daly III, the firm has grown to include a staff of more than 800 design and engineering professionals within the United States and abroad.

Beginning with the historic Boys Town campus in Omaha in the 1930s, the company's projects have included entire communities,

Leo A Daly designed the Creighton University administration building in 1929.

LEO A DALY

PLANNING

ARCHITECTURE

ENGINEERING

INTERIORS

EST.1915

as a result of the company's extensive wartime work during the 1940s, has become one of the firm's most enduring contributions to the design field.

A VARIETY OF PROJECTS

The company's design expertise crosses several fields. Its expertise in designing high-tech facilities, for example, is unmatched. As a result of its design work involving U.S. defense facilities during the 1950s and 1960s, including the Strategic Air Command's Worldwide Command Center at Nebraska's Offutt Air Force Base, the firm practiced high-technology facility design long before "high-tech" became common terminology.

In recent years, the company has successfully completed the design of such technologically demanding facilities as the Union Pacific Railroad's Harriman Dispatch Center in Omaha, which monitors and controls more than 700 trains over 23,000 miles of track around the clock; and the First Data Resources Center at the University of Nebraska's Information Technology Campus.

Facilities at the University of Nebraska in Lincoln and Omaha, and at Omaha's Creighton University are among the many educational and health facilities the firm has designed.

The Tower at First National Center in Omaha, Nebraska, was designed by Leo A Daly in the years 1997–99. © Jack Pottle Esto/Leo A Daly

In the aviation industry, the company's credits include The Boeing Corporation's first jet air-start fueling facilities, which were built in the 1960s, and more recently such notable airport facilities as the air-traffic control tower at John F. Kennedy International Airport in New York City and the North Terminal at Ronald Reagan National Airport in Washington, D.C. In recent years the firm has designed more than $1 billion in new airport facilities around the world.

LANDMARK DESIGNS

Nebraska has been the major beneficiary of the company's design efforts, insuring the firm a place in the state's history and part of its heritage in the 21st century. In addition to Boys Town, numerous office towers, hotels, and other projects, Leo A Daly is responsible for the design of popular state landmarks such as Omaha's Henry Doorly Zoo; the city's Memorial Park, including its World War II Memorial; the Ak-Sar-Ben Racing facilities; Rosenblatt Stadium, home of the NCAA's annual collegiate baseball national championship tournament; Omaha's Eppley Airfield; Omaha Civic Auditorium; and the award-winning Strategic Air Command Museum, one of Nebraska's newest tourist attractions.

As for the future, the company has set its sights on continued growth within Nebraska, the United States, and abroad while maintaining its nearly century-long commitment to the simple principle of design excellence.

Leo A Daly designed the Strategic Air Command Museum in Ashland, Nebraska, in 1995. © Paul Brokering/Leo A Daly

MILLARD LUMBER INC.

A family-owned business for more than half a century, Millard Lumber Inc. sells basic and leading-edge building materials and products to meet the needs of both professional contractors and do-it-yourself homeowners.

In 1952, Millard Lumber and Grain catered to the rural farming community, and also began its entry into the housing market with a more complete selection of building materials.

The story of the growth and success of Millard Lumber Inc. is essentially a story of the growth and success of the community of Millard, Nebraska. Less than a half century ago, Millard was an outpost of civilization alongside the Union Pacific Railroad tracks. The region was dominated by the city of Omaha, about a half-hour drive northeast by Model T.

Around the 1950s, all of this was to change. One of the local companies, Millard Lumber and Grain, was a lumber, coal, and grain business that had changed little since its founding in 1883 by William von Dohren. Then, in 1947, the firm was purchased by George F. Russell and his partner, Raymond M. Watson. Russell soon recognized that the area was becoming less agriculture based and that gas and electric heating were replacing coal heating. Russell got out of grain and coal and began focusing on building materials and products, which he supplied both for professional contractors and do-it-yourself homeowners.

RECOGNIZING OPPORTUNITY

In 1956, Western Electric announced a huge new plant that was to be built on Millard's doorstep. For the next two decades, the village of Millard experienced the greatest percentage increase in population of all communities in Nebraska. All these people needed homes, and all these homes required building materials. Both Millard and Millard Lumber grew. During his more than four decades in the business, Russell also worked extensively for his local, state, and national communities. After his death, in 1990, the Millard School Board of Education named the George F. Russell Middle School in honor of his many contributions to the community.

Today, G. Richard (Rick) Russell, George Russell's son, runs the business. The Russell family remains central not only to Millard Lumber, but also to the community as a whole. Rick and Carol Russell and many Millard Lumber employees are active in local organizations, assuming leadership positions in the United Way, Children's Hospital, Prevent Blindness, the Emmy Gifford Children's Theater, Omaha Children's Museum, Millard Lions Club, YMCA, and many others.

The latest in delivery equipment assures the Millard Lumber customer of proper material placement on the job site.

The professional sales staff consults with builders on the job site to ensure a quality finished product.

For half a century, the mission of Millard Lumber has not changed. All staff members work together as a team to provide quality building materials that consistently exceed customers' expectations. "We have always tried to provide basic building materials and have continually added product lines that augment the basics. We also strive to have quality jobs for employees while being a good corporate citizen in the community," says Russell. The company employs more than 200 people at its three locations, in Omaha and Lincoln, Nebraska, and in Des Moines, Iowa. Millard Lumber has won many human resource awards, including the Award of Honor with Distinction from the Safety and Health Council for nine of the past 10 years.

NEW MATERIALS, NEW EFFICIENCIES

While do-it-yourself homeowners are enthralled by the myriad products available at Millard Lumber, the focus of the business is on the needs of professional contractors. Today's contractors work in a much-changed building industry. In general construction, gone are the days when a highly skilled carpenter could work with the variations in natural materials and make a piece of lumber to fit a space. Selling manufactured pre-built wall sections has become a strength for Millard Lumber. "These pre-built sections shorten home-construction time. This efficiency means lower costs and consistent quality to pass on to the homeowner," says Russell. "We can now provide a uniform product to our customers, one that can be quickly assembled with a high level of quality." Another change in the building industry has

been the development of all-wood I-shaped joists. "These have taken the place of solid-sawn lumber joists," Russell says. "These I-joists are essentially engineered lumber, which makes them uniform in size and better for conservation."

Along with building-industry changes, houses themselves have changed. "While homes may look the same on the outside, the house inside is really a different structure," says Russell. "People are now expecting energy-efficient glass, to cut heating costs, and metal-clad windows, for easy maintenance. Houses also are much tighter, through air-infiltration barriers." Millard Lumber has been on the leading edge in supplying products that reflect such changes.

Millard Lumber's Web site (www.millardlumber.com) provides product information for its customers. "Customers are more educated now about building materials," Russell says. "Our customers also look more at the quality of products and our Web site can help answer their questions."

The presence at Millard Lumber of the Russell family will continue well into the 21st century. Rick and Carol Russell's oldest son, Joel, has joined the family business. Joel Russell will undoubtedly walk in his father and his grandfather's footsteps in both the business and in the community.

The Design Center allows contractors and their customers an opportunity for hands-on selection of quality building materials.

HDR, INC.

One of the industry's leading architectural, engineering, and consulting firms, HDR remains committed to

helping clients around the world find solutions and achieve success.

An employee-owned, worldwide architectural, engineering, and consulting firm, HDR, Inc., continues to follow its mission of "Shaping the Future Through Creative Solutions and Visionary Leadership."

With headquarters in Omaha, Nebraska, HDR has been helping clients meet their design and consulting needs since the firm was started in 1917. HDR's success with services from multimillion-dollar projects to those of smaller scope demonstrates the range of talent and experience the company brings to its clients. From leadership in research to award-winning designs to one-of-a-kind solutions, HDR focuses on improving people's lives and communities.

AN INDUSTRY AWARD WINNER

HDR provides services in transportation, water, environmental and resource management, health care, justice, and science and technology. It also offers project development, planning, design-build services, alternative delivery services, and management and competitiveness consulting.

A stellar reputation precedes the company, and professional publications consistently rank it among the leading consulting and design firms. HDR was ranked by *Engineering News-Record* magazine in 2000 as number 28 of the top 500 design firms and has been ranked among the survey's top 50 U.S. firms since 1967.

When showcasing its clients and their projects, HDR is annually among top industry award winners for

Situated midway between Omaha and Lincoln, the AirePlex Entertainment Park, being developed by HDR, Inc., will protect the natural environment at a former quarry on a scenic Platte River bluff. The project includes a 17,000-seat amphitheater, theme restaurant, concessions, and a children's music camp.

planning, consulting, and design. In 1999 alone, the company won more than a dozen national awards and numerous state and regional awards.

HDR employees have been instrumental in the growth and development of communities and infrastructure across the United States and abroad. Challenging projects allow employees to use their talents and develop a wide range of skills, from technical to managerial to interpersonal. All HDR offices partner with their communities for projects such as Habitat for Humanity and local cleanup days.

FOUNDED IN OMAHA TO SERVE COMMUNITIES

HDR was founded as the Henningson Engineering Company in Omaha by H. H. Henningson, who recognized the city's need for roads, water and sewer systems, municipal buildings, public utilities, and electrical plants.

HDR created Omaha's beautiful Heartland of America Park from a previously contaminated site along the Missouri River, saving the community over $10 million in remediation costs. The park now serves as an anchor for "Back to the River Redevelopment" in Omaha and is a community recreation park and gathering spot. The project was awarded the Engineering Excellence Grand Award by the Nebraska chapter of the American Consulting Engineers Council (ACEC).

Charles W. Durham joined HDR while still a student, in 1938, and after his graduation the following year, he was hired full-time. Durham became a partner in 1946 as did Willard Richardson, who had joined the company in 1936. With the naming of the new partners, the name of the company was changed to Henningson, Durham & Richardson.

In the next few years, as the company known today as HDR took on more projects, its staff more than doubled. By the end of the 1950s, HDR added an architecture department to its growing list of services. As a result of its growing customer base, HDR opened offices throughout the nation to provide expanded services.

In the 1960s, HDR signaled its entry into the health care field with such projects as St. Mary's Hospital in Scottsbluff, Nebraska, and the University of Nebraska Medical Center in Omaha. The firm's first major medical-facility project—the Nebraska Methodist Hospital in Omaha—was built in 1962. By 1976, design projects for more than 100 major medical facilities were under way in 34 states and in Saudi Arabia.

HDR's specialization in justice facilities began in 1976. In the same year, HDR acquired a Minneapolis firm noted for its power and energy facilities engineering. HDR design of commercial and institutional facilities began with the Federal Building and the United States Post Office in Omaha in 1956, and led to the development of HDR's science and technology program that today serves leading firms in the high-tech field.

HDR is one of the few large employee-owned firms in its industry. "HDR's vision, mission, and values continue to fortify its solid foundation, which is strengthened by employee ownership," says Richard R. Bell, chairman and CEO.

HDR designed this new complex for Omaha Children's Hospital, which previously shared space with another tertiary hospital and had no place for expansion. The hospital's new site, across the street from its former site, is adjacent to the building that houses its outpatient functions. The new 240,000-square-foot site enabled the hospital to consolidate functions, expand essential services, and create new services.

GROWING THROUGH EXPANSION AND MERGERS

Since 1995, HDR has grown significantly, with new offices and mergers and acquisitions. It maintains more than 60 offices worldwide, with over 3,000 employees, and projects completed or under way in all 50 states and 40 countries.

Firms recently joining HDR have specializations in transportation planning and surveying, architectural design, microelectronics, biopharmaceuticals, corporate office buildings, interiors, land development, geographic information systems (GIS), program management, and civil, environmental, forensic, and structural engineering.

HDR's recent work abroad includes a multimillion-dollar hydropower project in Gursugut, Turkey; the Autostrada, a major highway in Poland; health care consulting and facilities in the United Kingdom, Mexico, and Malaysia; and projects in Puerto Rico and the Far East.

Its ability to draw upon company resources and expertise enables HDR to help clients achieve goals—whether the development of a state-of-the-art water treatment plant, compliance with new industry regulations, or the determination of a new model for project development.

"HDR's greatest strength remains in its ability to share expertise and resources across the company and, through local project teams, to meet or exceed client expectations. In 2000 and beyond, this unique ability will be the cornerstone of our capacity to serve our clients more effectively than our competitors," Bell says.

Located on a downtown urban site, the Omaha World-Herald Freedom Center complex will house a new printing press and other equipment for the Omaha World-Herald. The design by HDR provides a campuslike setting that ties together new and existing buildings.

GRUBB & ELLIS/PACIFIC REALTY

An industry-leading commercial real estate firm, Grubb & Ellis/Pacific Realty of Omaha provides its long list of clients a full range of services, from property and facilities management to retail leasing and sales.

Developed by Grubb & Ellis/ Pacific Realty, the office building at 1200 Landmark Center in Omaha is home to such companies as Qwest Communications, MFS Network Technologies, and PricewaterhouseCoopers.

Establishing the leading commercial real estate brokerage and property management firm in Omaha takes a lot of key ingredients. It requires name recognition, a strong focus on customer needs, and most importantly, it takes a team of top real estate professionals striving to achieve common goals. Grubb & Ellis/Pacific Realty of Omaha has all these ingredients in place. Consequently, the company is an ongoing success story, continually building a record of outstanding growth and achievement.

HUMBLE BEGINNINGS

Like many firms, Grubb & Ellis/Pacific Realty sprang from humble beginnings. When Jay Noddle, its founder, president, and driving force, moved to Omaha from Denver and started Pacific Realty Group in 1987, his automobile served as his office. However, as a result of his determination and success in putting together a first-rate team of real estate professionals, it didn't take long for his firm to rise to the top of Omaha's real estate industry.

By 1996, Pacific Realty Group's portfolio of management properties had surpassed five million square feet, and its brokerage division had generated $170 million in leases and sales from 320 transactions.

In 1997, the firm established an affiliation with Illinois-based Grubb & Ellis, one of the largest commercial real estate brokerage and property management firms in the world. As a result, a new entity, Grubb & Ellis/Pacific Realty, promising "Property Solutions Worldwide," was created with the ability to handle all types of commercial real estate transactions throughout the world from Omaha.

REAL ESTATE LEADER

As Omaha's top real estate adviser, property manager, and one of its major real estate developers, Grubb & Ellis/Pacific Realty is also contributing mightily to Omaha's economy. Through its real estate services, the firm is helping to reinforce the city's position as one of the nation's preeminent agribusiness and insurance centers and is playing a key role in Omaha's emergence as a telecommunications and computing hub.

Today, the company is not just the top real estate firm in Omaha but one of the largest real estate advisory service providers in the Midwest. It boasts a staff of more than 100 full-time employees, several part-time associates,

Grubb & Ellis/Pacific Realty was instrumental in the development of Omaha's ConAgra/Heartland of America Park, a 104-acre mixed-use project consisting of offices, hospitality facilities, public park land, and a lake. Shown here is the ConAgra Campus.

The 13710 Building is located within the prestigious First National Business Park, a Grubb & Ellis/Pacific Realty project.

and a network of offices in Omaha and Lincoln, Nebraska, as well as in Iowa and Nevada.

A list of Grubb & Ellis/Pacific Realty's corporate clients, in fact, reads like a who's who of firms across Nebraska, and includes such well-known companies as Prudential Insurance Company of America, Mutual of Omaha, and Union Pacific Railroad.

In addition, Grubb & Ellis/Pacific Realty is providing real estate management services for such prominent firms as Prudential Realty Group, Procter & Gamble Company, State Farm Insurance, John Hancock Mutual Life Insurance Company, Hyatt Corporation, and G. E. Capital Realty Group.

Others benefiting from the company's real estate services include Berkshire Hathaway, the product of Omaha superstar investor Warren Buffett; Campbell Soup; the City of Omaha; ConAgra, Inc.; DHL Airways, Inc.; Drake University; Lucent Technologies; MCI; Sun Oil; and the state of Nebraska.

PLAYING A KEY ROLE IN DEVELOPMENT

As for development, Pacific Realty has played a key role in bringing about the construction of such Omaha real estate landmarks as One Pacific Place, 1200 Landmark Center, ConAgra/Heartland of America Park, Papillion Business & Technology Park, and the First National Business Park. And currently it is actively involved in the redevelopment of a 33-block section of Omaha's central business district.

It's not surprising then, to hear Omaha insiders proclaim that Pacific Realty in many ways, *is* Omaha.

As for the scope of its activities, the company now oversees the management of approximately 4.6 million square feet of properties, generating over $16 million in management receipts annually. In addition, it generates over $2 million a year from its construction administration services; leases approximately 3.5 million square feet of office, retail, and industrial space annually; and assists in sales transactions totaling $90 million to $100 million each year.

A FULL SPECTRUM OF SERVICES

Grubb & Ellis/Pacific Realty offers its clients the entire spectrum of commercial real estate services: brokerage; lease administration; tenant representation; office, industrial, and retail leasing and sales; asset management; property management; comprehensive development services; advisory and consulting services; real estate tax consulting; tenant finish construction supervision; and construction and permanent financing services.

Many of these services are not unique in the real estate business. But what is unique about Grubb & Ellis/Pacific Realty is that it is the best in the business at performing these functions. Just ask any of the many companies, institutions, and government agencies on its long list of clients.

Grubb & Ellis/Pacific Realty's One Pacific Place has long been considered one of Omaha's most desirable business addresses.

CHAPTER FOURTEEN

FROM SODDIE TO CYBERSPACE

EDUCATION

Educational technology in Nebraska's first schools consisted—if the school district was flush—of crude writing slates and scratchy markers. The schoolhouse typically was a "soddie," constructed of chunks of turf pried off the prairie. The school "year" could be as short as three months, because of the hardships involved and the need for children to help out at home. Small wonder that although the territorial legislature passed a free

public school act in 1855, four years later only about one school-age child in four attended school.

Some 140 years later, the old writing slate has gone digital, year-round school is a reality in some areas, and Nebraska's educational attainments regularly rank among the best in the nation.

Technologically speaking, the state has the second lowest number in America of pupils per instructional computer, second highest number of teachers who use the Internet for instruction, and is third in the number of Internet-connected computers per student. About 85 percent of Nebraskans over age 25 have graduated from high school, and about one in five have college degrees. Nebraska students routinely score well above average on ACT and SAT college-entrance exams. Complementing the public educational system is a variety of church-related and other private schools across the state, enrolling about 8 percent of the elementary- and secondary-age population.

Overall, the quality of education in Nebraska and students' demonstrated eagerness to take advantage of it are significant factors in maintaining a growing economy. Nebraska's businesses depend on a highly educated,

strongly motivated homegrown workforce, and the availability of such a valuable employee pool is a powerful magnet in attracting new employers to the state.

It has not come without a price. Overcoming problems of geographical distance and variations in population density always have been a challenge to educators. As early as 1883, state law provided that no school district could be smaller than four square miles or have fewer than 15 children of school age. In a state of more than 77,000 square miles, this insistence on localization resulted in a proliferation of school districts—more than 7,000 by 1920. Through transportation improvements that produced a more mobile population, and by gradual progress toward consolidation, this number had been reduced to 624 districts by the 1997–98 school year.

ABOVE: *In addition to this dairy store, facilities at the University of Nebraska–Lincoln include pilot plants and laboratory services that assist the food industry with product and process development.* OPPOSITE: *Omaha's oldest secondary school, Central High School was founded in 1859 and stands on the site of the original state capitol. The cornerstone of the present school building was laid in 1900.*

The Great Plains Blizzard of 1888 is remembered in Nebraska as the "Schoolchildren's Blizzard." It blew in suddenly on January 9, just as schools were letting out and pupils were starting home, most of them on foot. Many were among the 100 to 200 persons estimated to have died in the storm; many more were saved by teachers who kept them in their one-room schoolhouses overnight.

Students at the University of Nebraska at Kearney (UNK) relax at Cope Memorial Fountain. Founded in 1903, the former state college became part of the University of Nebraska system in 1991. Enrollment at UNK reached 6,780 in fall 1999.

Even at that, Nebraska still maintains more school districts than any but five much more populous states. A challenge to educators in the new century is to strive for the appropriate balance between the advantages of small, local schools and the opportunities offered in larger districts. Another challenge is represented by Nebraska's continuing effort to distribute the costs of education fairly among population groups, geographical areas, and modes of taxation while maintaining the level of support that has moved the state's children from the sod schoolhouse to the galaxies of cyberspace.

HIGHER EDUCATION: EXCELLENCE AND DIVERSITY

Probably unwittingly, the first legislature to meet after Nebraska became a state in 1867 made a decision that was to ensure the permanent centrality of the University

Creighton University education students get hands-on experience at the school's modern child-care development center.

of Nebraska (UN) in the state's system of higher education. Lawmakers decreed that it would be "united as one educational institution." This meant that there would be no Nebraska State, Nebraska Tech, or Nebraska A&M to compete for funds, prestige, and loyalty.

It did not mean that public postsecondary education would be available only in one location. Today, operating under the aegis of the statewide system and the governance of one elected board of regents, UN includes the main campus in Lincoln, the University of Nebraska at Omaha (UNO), the University of Nebraska at Kearney, and the University of Nebraska College of Medicine in Omaha.

The state also operates three colleges focusing mainly on teacher training at Wayne, Chadron, and Peru. (Peru is the only survivor of the 23 colleges chartered by ambitious territorial legislatures before 1867.) And six community colleges offer technologically oriented

'HELP, HEALING, HOPE'

Child development authorities around the world have studied and emulated approaches used in an educational-humanitarian institution that has become a Nebraska landmark: Boys Town. The nonsectarian home west of Omaha, which has taken in girls since 1979, includes a middle school, high school, vocational school, and a number of off-campus programs such as the Boys Town National Research Hospital in Omaha, specializing in childhood communications disorders. (The more inclusive name Girls and Boys Town was adopted in 2000 by the organization's national programs and locations.)

In 1998 Nebraska began an initiative that is changing classroom instruction and moving students to higher levels of learning. Called STARS (School-based Teacher-led Assessment and Reporting System), the initiative involves setting learning standards for all students; pulling together teachers from across the state to focus on helping students to meet or exceed those standards; and reporting student progress to local communities, parents, and policy makers.

education along with traditional curricular elements on 14 geographically dispersed campuses.

The newest jewel in Nebraska's crown of university-level teaching and research facilities is the Peter Kiewit Institute of Science, Technology and Engineering at UNO, the product of an imaginative business-academic partnership. First Data Corporation, Omaha's largest employer, donated the land and is completing an adjacent $40 million technology center. Other private

In 1999 and again in 2000, Creighton University, a Jesuit school founded in Omaha in 1878, topped U.S. News & World Report's *rankings of regional universities in the midwestern United States.*

companies, foundations, and the state have provided $70 million to build and endow the institute and provide scholarships.

Private universities and colleges also are geared up for a technological era. Bellevue University in Sarpy County opened its Center for Information Technology five years ago, and enrollment since then has quadrupled. The Creighton University Institute of Technology offers accelerated programs in computer programming and other skills to help accommodate the employment needs of the area's rapidly growing number of technology-driven companies.

Creighton, frequently cited in surveys as one of the nation's finest universities, also operates a medical school, making Omaha the smallest city in the nation to have two medical colleges.

Nebraska's smaller private or church-connected colleges and universities generally offer a traditional liberal arts education, complemented by specialized disciplines. Some also are proud to maintain the ethnic

Though often overshadowed by the University of Nebraska–Lincoln Cornhuskers, the University of Nebraska at Omaha Mavericks field their own intercollegiate teams, vying in the NCAA North Central Conference in everything from football to women's volleyball.

or national heritage transplanted to Nebraska by their European founders.

In all, Nebraska is home to more than two dozen institutions of higher learning, sharing a common goal of educational excellence while pursuing their diverse individual destinies.

AS GOOD AS IT GETS

In 1994 Walter Mientka of the University of Nebraska faculty coached the U.S. team to the first perfect score ever attained in the International Mathematics Olympiad, an annual competition among talented high school students from nearly 100 countries.

HIGHER EDUCATION>>

UNIVERSITY OF NEBRASKA

At each of its four campuses, the University of Nebraska seeks the highest quality in all its educational and

research endeavors and continually pursues change to ensure growth and keep pace with the future.

 The state of Nebraska was founded by a small group of hardy pioneers in 1867. Less than two years later, in 1869, these farsighted new Nebraskans founded the University of Nebraska.

The new land-grant university adopted a goal that remains timely even today: "To afford the inhabitants of this state with the means of acquiring a thorough knowledge of the various branches of literature, science, and the arts." Today, more than 130 years later, that goal is still pursued at the four campuses of the University of Nebraska.

The success of the state of Nebraska is linked to the success of the university. University president L. Dennis Smith speaks to this connection: "The University of Nebraska has historically been an integral part of the success of the state of Nebraska and the well-being of its people. This relationship between the state and the university seems bound to grow even stronger in the future."

In 1902, the Omaha Medical College became part of the university. In 1903, the University of Nebraska became the first institution west of the Mississippi to

Quality teaching is a defining element of students' experience at the University of Nebraska–Lincoln.

offer graduate education. The year 1968 brought dramatic change to the university. The former University of Omaha joined the state university system, becoming the University of Nebraska at Omaha; and the University of Nebraska Medical Center was made a separate campus. In 1991, the fourth and westernmost campus was added to the system with the inclusion of the University of Nebraska at Kearney, previously a state college.

With its four campuses, the university enrolls more than 46,000 students, and each year, nearly 8,500 students earn their undergraduate, graduate, or professional degrees.

The University of Nebraska has shaped itself to answer the needs of students who take a nontraditional route to higher learning. It works closely with Nebraska Educational Telecommunications, which uses technologies such as closed-circuit television, fiber optics, and multiple-channel satellites to give students who are off campus or in remote locations opportunities for full degree programs or nondegree classes. For a state with many far-flung rural communities, education is remarkably accessible to virtually all residents and amenable to the various paths its students might take.

Cope Fountain is an appealing landmark on the campus of the University of Nebraska at Kearney.

UNIVERSITY OF NEBRASKA–LINCOLN

The Lincoln campus of the University of Nebraska (UNL) is the primary research and doctoral degree–granting facility of the system. UNL is a member of the prestigious Association of American Universities. In 1999 UNL was rated by *U.S. News & World Report* in the second tier of the publication's "America's Best Colleges" list. The magazine also placed UNL in the "Best Value" category of 50 schools. UNL is proud of its 22 Rhodes scholars and welcomed 29 National Merit scholars in its 1999 freshman class.

The largest of the four university campuses, UNL is home to more than 22,500 students, including some 18,000 undergraduate students and 4,500 graduate and professional students. Research is particularly emphasized at this campus. The university's Technology Development Center in Lincoln was created to pair the university and the private sector in technological research endeavors. Typically, fledgling businesses form such partnerships and are able to make good use of the center's supportive services. Ultimately this brings increased business to all quadrants of the state.

UNL also is home to biotechnology research projects. At the George W. Beadle Center for Genetics and Biomaterials Research, recent projects of particular importance to agriculture-rich Nebraska involve developing genetic plant materials to create plants with high resistance to predators such as insects, viruses, and herbicides.

Innovative research is essential to high quality clinical practice and education at the University of Nebraska Medical Center.

At UNL's Institute of Agriculture and Natural Resources (IANR), scientists in its major research arm, the Agricultural Research Division, are developing methods to make farming and ranching more productive, profitable, and environmentally sound. An allied component of UNL's IANR is the Nebraska College of Technical Agriculture (NCTA), in Curtis, Nebraska. NCTA offers a hands-on, experiential learning environment. For its one-year course, it awards a certificate and for its two-year curricula, an Associate Degree of Applied Science.

UNIVERSITY OF NEBRASKA MEDICAL CENTER

The mission of the university's health sciences campus, University of Nebraska Medical Center (UNMC), is to improve the health of Nebraskans through innovative education, cutting-edge technology, and superior patient care. Many of Nebraska's future health care providers—physicians, dentists, nurses, pharmacists, and allied health professionals—will be trained at UNMC.

UNMC includes the colleges of Dentistry, Medicine, Nursing, and Pharmacy; the School of Allied Health Professionals; the Munroe-Meyer Institute for Genetics and Rehabilitation; and the Eppley Institute

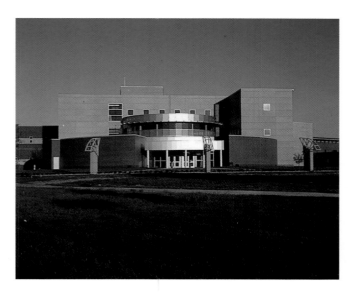

The Peter Kiewit Institute on the south campus of the University of Nebraska at Omaha defines state-of-the-art teaching and research in information science, technology, and engineering.

Nearly 4,000 students earn their degrees from the University of Nebraska–Lincoln each year.

for Research in Cancer and Allied Diseases. UNMC is home to more than 2,000 undergraduate, graduate, and professional students.

High quality education is emphasized in all health sciences disciplines. In recognition of evolving medical priorities, UNMC particularly highlights education in primary care. In April 2000, *U.S. News & World Report* ranked six UNMC programs among the best in the nation: Primary Care, Physician's Assistant, Physical Therapy, Doctor of Pharmacy, Rural Health Medicine, and Master's in Nursing.

Research is a driving factor at UNMC. In recent years, research grants and contracts have reached $34 million annually. Key research areas include treatment of rheumatoid arthritis, prevention and treatment of cancer, and the transplantation of peripheral stem cells.

Memorial Bell Tower symbolizes the strength and lasting value of the educational experience at the University of Nebraska at Kearney.

The Lied Transplant Center opened in 1999 and was immediately heralded for its innovative concept for patient care. Transplant patients arrive with their caregivers, and both stay in hotel-like suites and are trained in aftercare procedures. Patients come from around the world for this unique program.

UNIVERSITY OF NEBRASKA AT OMAHA

Because of its distinctly metropolitan emphasis, the University of Nebraska at Omaha (UNO) is unique within the university system. This is a natural outgrowth of the school's early days as a municipal commuter college. Enrollment of more than 12,500 includes numerous part-time students who are following non-traditional paths to higher education and who help shape the nature of the school. Graduate and professional students include nearly 3,000 people who are continuing their education immediately after college or returning after a number of years to enhance their careers. UNO's first residence halls opened in 1999, changing the campus community by making it home to several hundred students.

Responding to national trends, local strengths, and the technology needs of industry throughout Nebraska, UNO is home to The Peter Kiewit Institute of Information Science, Technology and Engineering (IST&E). IST&E offers undergraduate and graduate programs in computer science, information systems and quantitative analysis, and telecommunications, as well as a broad array of engineering curricula in cooperation with UNL. The institute's new buildings and residence hall are on the new south campus, a few blocks from the main campus.

Students from across the nation are interested in this new high-tech education and those selected will benefit from specialized academic programs and

training conducted in collaboration with industry. The program is designed to shape students' skills for careers as information technology specialists. The state as a whole will benefit from the highly trained graduates of the institute and its distance-education capabilities.

UNIVERSITY OF NEBRASKA AT KEARNEY

The University of Nebraska at Kearney (UNK), in central Nebraska, serves students from throughout Nebraska and from many other states and nations. UNK offers liberal arts, business, technology, and education programs. Nearly 7,000 students are enrolled, including 1,000 graduate students.

The relatively smaller size of this campus affords close relationships between faculty and students, with careful academic advising and support. In addition to high quality classroom teaching, UNK conducts noteworthy research. In one project, students investigated Nebraska's Platte River watershed, focusing on the impact and ecological effects of water flow regulations. In another research project, participants studied the notion of privatizing Social Security and the potential ripple effects of such an action on the nation's economy.

ADDRESSING THE FUTURE

President Dennis Smith is strongly committed to high quality education for Nebraska. "For this state to prosper, and for her citizens to enjoy productive and rewarding lives, the University of Nebraska must offer the finest education available anywhere, build on its strength as a major research institution, and put its expertise at the disposal of the public in innovative ways."

For UNL, this means an emphasis on becoming a major research and teaching institute and bringing in highly qualified teachers and researchers. For UNO, this means even closer ties to the local community. Omaha has become such a hub for information technology that some people feel the information science field itself will witness gains because of UNO's focus. The UNMC campus is well on its way to becoming a world-class innovator in teaching, research, and health care. New research towers are planned that will increase research space and capability. At UNK, the future means enhancing its already high quality classroom teaching, with a special emphasis on undergraduate students and research initiatives.

President Smith recognizes the changing nature of the future for the university: "The University of Nebraska has embarked on a number of broad-scale efforts destined to cause profound changes across all four of its campuses." These campuses are eager for the future.

The future for each campus is one of growth and of quality.

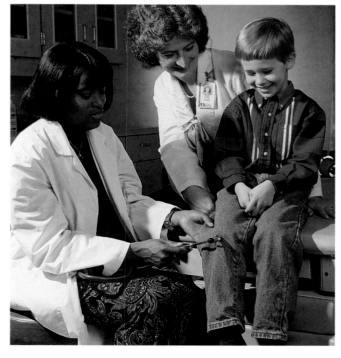

Nearly half of Nebraska's health care professionals are educated at the University of Nebraska Medical Center.

CREIGHTON UNIVERSITY

Ranked as one of the Midwest's top universities, Creighton University offers comprehensive, technologically advanced curricula, academic and professional degrees, and a nurturing environment.

The 94-acre Creighton University campus near downtown Omaha is home to undergraduate, graduate, and professional schools.

Creighton University, an internationally recognized comprehensive university in Omaha, is a primary resource for research and leadership for business, industry, and health care. Founded in 1878 in memory of Omaha pioneer entrepreneur Edward Creighton, a builder of the first transcontinental telegraph, Creighton offers undergraduate, graduate, and professional degrees and information technology training. It has been ranked as one of the Midwest's top universities by *U.S. News & World Report* and as a top value by other major national publications.

Students are attracted from across the nation and 60 other countries to this Jesuit Catholic school, which has an enrollment of 6,300. The 94-acre downtown Omaha campus has been rated one of the best technologically "wired" in the nation by *Yahoo! Internet Life* magazine, and several programs are offered for distance learners. Creighton students learn in a friendly, nurturing environment that is guided by the Jesuit ideal of educating the whole person: mind, body, and spirit. Students are part of a thriving campus community that offers opportunities for personal growth and service and the chance to work for social justice. Students also may take advantage of the many cultural and entertainment venues available in the metropolitan area.

BUSINESS, SCIENCE, AND THE ARTS

Creighton University's College of Business Administration, through its Joe Ricketts Center in Electronic Commerce and Database Marketing, offers one of the nation's few master of science degrees in electronic commerce. Through Beijing University, in China, the college also offers, in partnership with other Jesuit schools, an international M.B.A. degree. Within the college is the MacAllister Chair in Regional Economics; the university tracks the economy of a region of nine Midwest and three Mountain states through the MacAllister Chair. In addition to offering an undergraduate degree in business, the college offers master's degrees, including the M.B.A. and the M.S.–I.T.M. (Information Technology Management). It also offers joint master's degrees, including M.B.A./M.S.–ITM; M.S.–ITM–Master of Computer Science; M.B.A./Master of International Relations; M.B.A./J.D.; M.B.A./Pharm.D.; and a J.D./E-commerce dual-degree program.

The Creighton Institute for Information Technology and Management, located in west Omaha, provides accelerated, nondegree education in existing and emerging information technologies, to meet the specific needs of area businesses.

The Creighton College of Arts & Sciences offers strong liberal arts curricula anchored in ethics and critical

Students come to Creighton University from throughout the United States and more than 60 other countries.

Widely recognized for its computer facilities for students, Creighton University offers high-tech classrooms. The downtown Omaha campus has been ranked as one of the best technologically "wired" in the nation.

thinking, with opportunities for service and foreign study. Some 40 majors are offered. Outstanding fine arts and performing arts programs are housed in the multifaceted, modern Lied Education Center for the Arts, a home to Creighton's nationally known playwrights, authors, photojournalists, sculptors, artists, and performers.

At University College, students on nontraditional tracks may enter noncredit workshops and training programs or programs leading to certificates, associate degrees, or bachelor's degrees. There are preprofessional programs for physicians, dentists, pharmacists, and allied health professionals. University College offers a number of accelerated courses and is known for its programs in Christian spirituality, ministry, and priestly formation.

Creighton University School of Law graduates have prominent roles in courtrooms and boardrooms, in legislative and judicial chambers. The Creighton law school faculty are leaders in shaping and defining the evolving aspects of the law, from the relationship of religion, science, and law to instructions for jurors. Law students learn from hands-on experience at the Milton R. Abrahams Legal Clinic. Students and the entire surrounding legal community benefit from the Klutznick Law Library/McGrath, North, Mullin & Kratz Legal Research Center.

THE HEALTH CARE PROFESSIONS

The Creighton name is synonymous with outstanding health care. Creighton University's School of Nursing offers both traditional and accelerated nursing programs, as well as an RN to BSN (Registered Nurse to Bachelor of Science in Nursing) program. At the graduate level, students earn master's degrees in family and adult nurse practitioner. The school has the only dual-track cardiac health master's program in the nation.

Researchers in the Creighton University School of Medicine are world-renowned for their findings in hereditary cancer and osteoporosis research, and the school also has one of the region's best cardiac care centers. Saint Joseph Hospital, a state-of-the-art health care facility, is the primary teaching hospital for the School of Medicine; the school also is affiliated with metropolitan Omaha family health care clinics operated by Creighton Medical Associates. In addition, the school gives much-needed care to many underserved patients.

Dentists graduate from the Creighton University School of Dentistry with one of the best available clinical educations, reflected in consistently high scores on qualifying exams. Research in restorative as well as preventive dental care has resulted in worldwide acclaim in such areas as dental laser procedures.

The Creighton University School of Pharmacy and Allied Health Professions offers entry-level doctoral programs in pharmacy, physical therapy, and occupational therapy. Known internationally for its outstanding curricula, innovative teaching, and distance learning, the school also offers a bachelor's degree in emergency medical services.

Creighton's Graduate School offers doctoral degrees in biomedical sciences and a wide array of master's programs, including the interdisciplinary master's degree in health services administration, which it now offers on the World Wide Web for distance learners.

The Lied Education Center for the Arts provides state-of-the-art facilities for students in the performing and visual arts.

METROPOLITAN COMMUNITY COLLEGE

Offering affordable, accessible, and superior quality education, Metropolitan Community College continues to grow in both scope and stature as the third largest post-secondary institution in Nebraska.

Metropolitan Community College trains today's workforce for the jobs of today and tomorrow by providing superior quality, affordable education that is available to all citizens of its service area—Dodge, Douglas, Sarpy, and Washington Counties.

Since Metro opened in 1974 in a renovated warehouse in Omaha, the college has grown in scope and stature. Today, the college has three main campuses: Elkhorn Valley, Fort Omaha, and South Omaha; and two centers: Fremont Center in Fremont and Sarpy Center in LaVista. Classes are also held at many other sites.

All campuses offer well-equipped microcomputer laboratories, learning centers, and libraries. Students can choose from more than 100 programs, from industrial trades to health care to computer technologies to academic transfer. Students find Metro affordable and accessible, with easy registration by telephone or the Internet, convenient class times and locations, free parking, opportunities for distance learning, and counseling and other services. For less than $3,000, students can earn a two-year degree and begin work in their field of choice or transfer to a four-year college.

With more than 46,000 credit and noncredit students, Metro is the third largest post-secondary institution

On Metropolitan Community College's Fort Omaha campus, in Omaha, many classes are held in Building 10 (above), which also is the site of the food service area and other administrative functions.

in Nebraska. Yet Metro has many of the advantages of a much smaller college. Class sizes are small, typically 20 to 30 students, to allow for more personal attention. Metro also offers the community a Continuing Education program, with classes to fit just about every student's interest.

Since 1980, Metro has pioneered efforts to build an inclusive community truly dedicated to human equality. Metro leads all Nebraska colleges and universities with the percentage of students who are members of minority groups—almost 18 percent, or one in five students. About 55 percent of students are women. In the student body, the average age is approximately 31.

The Workforce Development Institute™ (WDI) offers custom-designed training for business and industry; conducts skills assessment and job profiling; and offers licensure and certification exams, training for Microsoft certification, and occupation-specific courses in Spanish. WDI provides expert trainers to companies to conduct sessions for busy employees at convenient times and suitable locations. Metro's goal is to help businesses improve productivity in an increasingly competitive world.

Graduates of Metropolitan Community College excel at finding success in the workplace. Seventy-one percent of graduates gain employment in their field of training, and 96 percent remain in Nebraska to work. Fifty-three percent of Metro graduates go on to further education.

At Metropolitan Community College, courses that include computer learning are the most popular. Here, a student works in an architectural drafting and design class. Metro has more than 50 technology classrooms and 1,200 computers available for student use.

SOUTHEAST COMMUNITY COLLEGE

Southeast Community College serves over 30,000 students each year at its Lincoln, Beatrice, and Milford campuses

through community courses, broadcast telecourses, live transmissions to high schools, and Internet classes.

Southeast Community College (SCC) serves students at its Lincoln, Beatrice, and Milford campuses. It provides Continuing Education classes on the campuses and throughout southeast Nebraska, and custom-designed training seminars for business and industry in 15 southeast Nebraska counties. SCC also offers education via telecourses and satellite and other distance education to high school and college students. Each year SCC opens the door to education to more than 30,000 full-time and part-time students who enroll in credit and noncredit courses.

SCC was created in 1973 as one of six Nebraska community colleges. It is accredited by the North Central Association of Colleges and Schools. SCC students can earn an associate's degree in two years in one of the 49 vocational and technical programs or in the Academic Transfer program. SCC offers academic advising, financial aid, tutoring, and job placement services, as well as campus amenities such as libraries, computer laboratories, and wellness centers. The Beatrice and Milford campuses provide residence halls. College life at SCC includes a variety of extracurricular programs and activities, including music, theater, intercollegiate and intramural sports, and student government.

Academic instructors hold at least a master's degree in their teaching field, while technical instructors have both formal and vocational education. Classroom instruction is just part of the SCC education experience. Well-equipped vocational and technical laboratories enable students to practice the skills they have learned in the classroom. Students also can gain hands-on training at businesses and institutions that serve as SCC partners in preparing students for careers. In 1999, 96 percent of SCC vocational and technical program graduates were placed in jobs or continued their education.

The Academic Transfer program allows students to complete the first two years of a four-year degree, studying

Above is the Lincoln campus of Southeast Community College (SCC).

the basics, such as history, natural sciences, the humanities, mathematics, and speech. In 1999, 98 percent of SCC Academic Transfer students continued their education or were placed in jobs. According to reports from senior institutions, SCC students achieve the same grade averages and earn bachelor's degrees at the same rate as students who begin their education in four-year colleges.

SCC is entering the 21st century with increasing distance-education opportunities. Via fiber-optic connections between SCC and many southeast Nebraska high schools, high school students receive live audio and video instruction in academic college courses. SCC also provides Internet classes in psychology, sociology, mathematics, and other academic college courses, and a complete on-line associate's degree in Business Administration. Each of these efforts is aimed at making education more accessible for SCC students now and in the future.

At left is SCC's Milford campus and below, the Beatrice campus.

CHAPTER FIFTEEN

PLEASURABLE PURSUITS

HOSPITALITY, TOURISM, AND RETAIL

In the 19th century Nebraska's most compelling tourist attraction—if wagon trains of pioneers can be called tourists—was Chimney Rock, an imposing spire towering over the plains near Scottsbluff. It was mentioned in travelers' diaries and journals more often than any other aspect of the Oregon Trail. Today the venerable monument occupies a humbler place on Nebraska's list of must-sees and must-dos for visitors and home folks.

Though still an awe-inspiring sight, it doesn't even rank in the top 10 of the state's most popular natural and man-made attractions.

Top honors as a visitor magnet go to Omaha's Henry Doorly Zoo, whose features include a walk-through aquarium in which humans can get up close and personal with sharks, the world's largest indoor rain forest, an IMAX theater, and animal life from around the world, housed in a flowered, peaceful setting next to the city's Rosenblatt Stadium. In a typical year the zoo draws well over a million visitors.

Other favorite destinations range from the recreational to the historical to the artistic—from Mahoney State Park near Ashland in the east to the Hastings Museum/Lied IMAX Theater in the center to Fort Robinson State Park in the far northwest.

THE VALUE OF A DOLLAR

Travel and tourism represent Nebraska's third largest industry after agriculture and manufacturing, totaling $3 billion a year in traveler expenditures and employing some 37,000. The "multiplier" is 2.7, meaning that every dollar a visitor spends in the state is respent until it's worth $2.70.

The dollar has another added value: Whether it's spent photographing bighorns in the Pine Ridge, hunting or fishing in virtually every part of the state, or browsing the art treasures in Omaha's Joslyn Museum, it also buys a large ration of the traditional friendliness with which Nebraskans treat each other and their guests. Visitors are greeted with a warmth and openness born in the settlers' need for kinship on the lonely plains and developed over a century and a half of the neighborliness that sustains rural life. The availability of a workforce with this kind of friendly, helpful attitude is part of what drew Hyatt, Marriott, Omni, and Westin to locate international hotel and resort reservations centers in Omaha.

Linked with travel and tourism is Nebraska's robust retail trade. Cash registers typically ring up about $11 billion a year in establishments ranging from the

ABOVE: *The Lied Jungle at Omaha's popular Henry Doorly Zoo is reputed to be the largest indoor rain forest in the world.* OPPOSITE: *At Scotts Bluff National Monument, a pair of covered wagons mark the historic Oregon Trail below this soaring eminence of sandstone, siltstone, and volcanic ash.*

Rock Creek Station, near Fairbury in southeast Nebraska, was a stop on the Overland Stage route. It's also where James Butler "Wild Bill" Hickok killed his first man, in 1861. The victim was David C. McCanles, who operated the station. Today Rock Creek Station State Historical Park features a picnic area, campground, visitors center, and re-created buildings, including the cabin where Wild Bill pulled the trigger.

smallest bait-and-tackle shop on Lake McConaughy to Borsheim's in Omaha, the nation's largest single-store seller of jewelry and gifts. And as befits a state whose early commerce depended heavily on its role as an outfitter for the opening of the West, Nebraska continues to be a regional wholesale center, recording more than $32 billion in annual trade.

Once home to a congregation organized in 1891 by German immigrants, Trinity Lutheran Church at the Lincoln County Historical Museum, near North Platte, has been completely restored, right down to its 1902 reed pump organ.

When the University of Nebraska–Lincoln football team plays at home, a sizable portion of the state's population can be found rooting for their beloved Cornhuskers at Memorial Stadium.

THAT BIG RED SPIRIT

A special word is in order about one of the favorite home-state destinations of tens of thousands of Nebraskans: Memorial Stadium in Lincoln, home of the five-time national champion Cornhusker football team. On home-game Saturdays, the 77,000-some red-clad population of the stadium makes it the third largest community in the state; the last time even a single seat

BIRD-WATCHING, NEBRASKA-STYLE

In late winter and early spring, the Platte River and adjoining wetlands in central Nebraska host one of the largest masses of migratory birds in the world—more than half a million sandhill cranes and nearly 10 million ducks and geese. Clay County alone has 13 different waterfowl-production areas, lagoons, and wildlife management areas offering breathtaking views of the massive flocks.

Eastern and western species and several different ecosystems meet in the Nature Conservancy's Niobrara Valley Preserve, known as "the crossroads of the Great Plains," in north-central Nebraska.

HISTORY CAN BE FUN

That Nebraskans and their guests are mindful of the state's colorful past is underlined by the continued success of one of the Cornhuskers' many historical observances, the annual John C. Fremont Days held in Fremont. In 1999 the event drew nearly 100,000. It honors the 1840 explorer who helped establish the Platte Valley route as the best way west.

remained unsold, John F. Kennedy was president. The special bond Nebraskans have with their Husker heroes is a strong unifying factor in such a large and diverse state, and Big Red spirit is reflected in the cordiality shown visitors. (In how many other sports venues does the home crowd give an end-of-game standing ovation, win or lose, to the visiting team?)

Football enthusiasm even has an impact on one of Nebraskans' other favorite pastimes, fishing. In 1999 Todd Weber of Lincoln caught a state record saugeye—eight pounds, nine ounces, 27 inches long—on the Saturday the Huskers played at Missouri. "On days when the Cornhuskers are playing is the best time to go fishing," he said, "because you have the lake to yourself. . . . Nobody else is out there." (The Huskers won, too, 40–10.)

As the 21st century began, Nebraska added another spectacular landmark, the Great Platte River Road Archway Monument. This epic construction spans the entire breadth of Interstate 80 just outside Kearney, its architecture and artwork paying tribute to the pilgrims who beat a historic path along the Platte, the settlers who stayed to forge a modern society, and the Native Americans whose sometimes tragic, sometimes inspiring stories are an integral part of the state's culture and traditions.

The monument is a guaranteed traffic-stopper, beckoning travelers to pause and experience what it was like for those who came before—on the road to Chimney Rock and beyond.

ABOVE: *Camping, theatrical productions, stage coach rides, historical tours, and other activities await visitors to Fort Robinson State Park near Crawford.* OVERLEAF: *Artist Jim Reinders created Carhenge from vintage American-made automobiles covered with gray spray paint. The unique sculpture, which is located along Highway 87 just north of Alliance, is a creative replica of Stonehenge, England's ancient mystical alignment of stones that chart phases of the sun and moon.*

MODERN ART ON THE PLAINS

If you like your artistic statements tongue in cheek, Carhenge needs to be on your Nebraska itinerary. In 1987 an imaginative citizen named James Reinders created an outdoor collage of old automobiles, arranged to resemble the ancient site of Stonehenge in England. One of Nebraska's favorite whimsies and sometimes interpreted as a sly poke at eastern artistic pretensions, it's just north of Alliance on U.S. 385.

HOSPITALITY>>

MARRIOT WORLDWIDE RESERVATIONS

A division of Marriott International, the world's largest provider of hospitality services, Marriott Worldwide Reservations, based in Omaha, continues to set sales records and raise the bar on industry standards.

In 1927 when J. Willard Marriott and his new bride, Allie, opened a nine-seat root beer stand in northwest Washington, D.C., few people could imagine that the business would someday become the world's largest provider of hospitality services. In March 1998, the family-owned business—now known as Marriott International—went public with a concentrated focus on lodging, senior living, and distribution services.

The Marriott Reservations Center, in Omaha, Nebraska, is one of the divisions of this vast enterprise. The Reservations Center was opened in 1971, receiving great fanfare by the Omaha business community. The reservations system—considered cutting-edge at the time—required that the reservations agent call each Marriott property directly for each booking. A new technological dimension was added one year later when reservations were transmitted by teletype to Key Bridge Hotel.

This Marriott Worldwide Reservations center is located in Omaha, Nebraska.

As the demand for hotel reservations increased, so did the workload at the Omaha center, and the center outgrew its building. Construction was started in 1981 for a new 30,000-square-foot building in Omaha. In just six years, sales again outpaced space and a second floor was added, doubling the size. As Marriott International expanded in the lodging industry and new venues were added, reservations grew accordingly. In 1987, reservations for Fairfield Inn by Marriott, Residence Inn by Marriott, and Courtyard by Marriott were added to the Omaha reservations center's responsibilities. In the years since, Marriott has continued to add to its portfolio of products, including Renaissance Hotels, SpringHill Suites, TownePlace Suites, Marriott Vacation Club International, Conference Centers, ExecuStay, Marriott Executive Apartments, Ritz-Carlton Hotels, and Marriott's newest innovation in vacation experiences, Horizons by Marriott Vacation Clubs.

More than 30 years since the first eight reservations agents began answering phones, Marriott Worldwide Reservations in Omaha continues to set sales records and raise the bar on industry standards. In 1999, the Omaha reservations center answered more than 12 million calls and generated more than $1 billion in revenue.

MOVING FORWARD

Today the reservations center in Omaha not only houses a significant number of sales professionals, it also is the home of Marriott's Guest Relations, National Group Sales Operations, and Travel Agents Support. In addition, it houses Worldwide Reservations Accounting, Telecommunications, Reservation Systems, and Internet Support for Marriott International's 12 worldwide reservations sites.

Sales responsibility for Fairfield Inn by Marriott, Residence Inn by Marriott, and Courtyard by Marriott was given to Marriott Worldwide Reservations in Omaha in 1987. Shown here is one of Marriott's Fairfield Inns.

WORLDWIDE RESERVATIONS CENTER

The Marriott Network Routing Center also is based in the Omaha office. With its state-of-the-art technology, this group is the central planning and operations group for Marriott's network of 12 reservations centers around the world. The Network Routing Center is responsible for managing call volume, operational analysis, and statistical reporting for each of the worldwide reservations centers.

A THREEFOLD MISSION

Marriott's primary mission as the world's largest provider of hospitality services is threefold: to provide excellent service to customers, to provide rewards to employees, and to provide significant returns to shareholders. Its motto of "creating significant value by aggressively growing its business" reflects these goals.

Providing excellent service to customers is the centerpiece of all Marriott endeavors. By using the best tools available, Marriott is able to deliver the lowest cost per reservation and maintains the highest productivity throughout the reservation industry. Marriott Rewards is a new program that highlights the innovation and the top quality of service delivered to customers. This program is the world's largest multibrand frequent guest program in the industry.

Marriott's founder, the late J. Willard Marriott, recognized that excellent employees are the main asset of any business. He often stated that "if you take care of your employees, they'll take care of you." The Marriott organization is able to attract and retain top-notch employees because the corporation puts them first. This philosophy was initiated in Marriott's early days, when the business was small and localized. It has continued to expand and now employs more than 145,000 people worldwide. In 2000, Marriott International was named for the third year in a row to *Fortune* magazine's "America's 50 Best Companies for Minorities." Marriott was also recognized among *Fortune's* "100 Best Companies to Work For" and "America's Most Admired Companies."

Marriott's goal of becoming every community's "best place to work" has been amply rewarded with very low employee turnover rates and high employee satisfaction survey scores.

Shareholders have also been the beneficiaries of Marriott strategies. In 1999, earnings per share increased 16 percent, and net income was up 15 percent compared to 1998. Net income increased to $424 million in 1999 from $390 million in the preceding year, and sales totaled $8.7 billion, up from $8 billion in 1998. Systemwide sales, which also include sales of managed and franchised properties, grew 11 percent to $17.7 billion in 1999.

Marriott International recognizes employees by celebrating Associate Appreciation Week every year in the spring. Marriott Worldwide Reservations in Omaha participates in the festivities with a barbecue, complete with food, games, and fund-raising for Children's Miracle Network. In 1999, the Omaha reservations center raised more than $10,000 toward this worthy cause.

FUTURE ENDEAVORS

Marriott International is well poised for the future. After going public, the corporation streamlined its efforts, focusing on the lodging, senior living, and distribution services industries. Marriott International's goal is to add 150,000 hotel rooms to its enterprise by the end of 2002. Clearly, the Omaha center for Marriott Worldwide Reservations will answer the demands placed by these additions.

RETAIL/SHOPPING>>

OAK VIEW MALL

Located on what was a cornfield just 10 years ago, Oak View Mall of Omaha has grown to become a prime

shopping destination with more than 100 stores and consistently increasing sales.

The setting sun silhouettes Oak View Mall's food court, outlining the natural beauty of the architecture.

Just 10 years ago, the intersection of 144th Street and West Center Road in Omaha was nothing more than a cornfield. Today, the area is developed as far as the eye can see. At the center is the reason this area has developed so extensively and so quickly: Oak View Mall.

Built in 1991, Oak View Mall is owned and operated by General Growth Properties of Chicago, Illinois. This shopping center giant also owns 140 other properties throughout the United States. Oak View Mall commands more than 875,000 square feet. The atrium-filled center features classical accents of cool creams and greens, marble flooring, pillars, and plants.

NUMBER ONE IN CONSUMER SURVEY

The 12-member management staff at Oak View Mall is committed to keeping the mall as it is now—the first choice in shopping for Omaha's residents. The mall was awarded this designation in the 2000 Consumer Preference Survey, published by the *Omaha World-Herald*. The survey asked the question, "At which mall have you spent the most money in the past 12 months?" Sarah Heinrich, marketing director, explains the success: "We have the stores people want and we are in a great, convenient location. Plus our stores have the selection people are looking for." The stores in the mall employ more than 900 people who work together to see that the mall continues to be the favorite shopping center in the Omaha area.

PRIME SHOPPING

Oak View Mall is special because of its merchant mix. The mall is home to more than 100 stores and four key anchors: Dillard's, JCPenney, Sears, and Younkers.

According to Heinrich, merchants are comprised of national chain apparel stores that sell either unisex or family apparel. The mall also features a wide variety of specialty stores offering personal and general services. The easily accessible food court, which hosts a vast selection of different types of food, also attracts people to Oak View Mall.

What else sets Oak View apart? "Oak View is fun, clean, safe, and prides itself on its family atmosphere,"

Night falls on Oak View Mall's center court, highlighting the feature elevator and fountain area.

Heinrich says. "We are a prime destination in the area. Whatever people want, they can find at 144th and West Center Road."

The mall appeals to everyone in the community. Weekday mornings, young mothers and children usually frequent the stores. By lunchtime, men and women from local businesses crowd the food court. Weekends find the mall filled with families and teens who enjoy shopping for the latest fashions. More than 11 million shoppers visit the mall annually.

COMMUNITY INVOLVEMENT

The Oak View Mall staff recognizes that the Omaha community and the surrounding area are vitally important. "We enjoy working with community groups. We currently work exclusively with the Make-A-Wish Foundation® of Nebraska. On major holidays, they offer gift-wrapping services to our customers. Make-A-Wish staffs the booth with volunteers from the community and uses all proceeds to benefit the children involved with the Make-A-Wish Foundation of Nebraska. We are pleased with the partnership," says Heinrich.

Oak View also sponsors a number of weekend events. "For approximately 40 weekends a year, the common areas of the mall are full of arts-and-crafts vendors

Oak View Mall's winning combination of an open and inviting atmosphere and a wide variety of shops and services provides a pleasurable and satisfying shopping experience.

and home-related events. The store managers like these family-related events. If one member is involved in the activity, the entire family comes and also shops and eats at Oak View. It is a nice arrangement," says Heinrich.

INCREASING SALES

Oak View Mall is in an enviable position, both literally and figuratively. It commands a massive and visible presence at a key intersection in southwest Omaha. "Our sales have increased each year we have been open. Initially our sales numbers were just meeting projections, but with the addition in 1996 of some high-profile stores such as Ann Taylor and Eddie Bauer, sales have skyrocketed and have made Oak View the most productive mall in the state. We are confident they will continue to increase as the neighboring area continues to develop," says Heinrich.

On a beautiful midwestern afternoon, sunshine filters through the dome-vaulted rotunda above the food court, beckoning customers to take a break and have a bite to eat.

Oak View Mall

144th Street and West Center Road
Open daily, 10 A.M.–9 P.M.;
Sunday, noon–6 P.M.
330-3332

ROCKBROOK VILLAGE

The multibuilding specialty retail complex of Rockbrook Village in Omaha is a popular and convenient area for

shopping, dining, and entertainment, with special events offered throughout the year.

Rockbrook Village was the vision of real estate developer Larry Myers and his wife, Virgie Myers. After moving to Omaha from Kansas City, they designed Rockbrook Village to match the multibuilding specialty retail concept of the Country Club Plaza shopping, dining, and entertainment district in Kansas City.

The Myers could see a bustling, prosperous suburban community nestled in the region, which was country then, with dirt roads and farms covering the hillsides. They first developed Countryside Village, at 87th and Pacific Streets, and then created Rockbrook Village, at 108th Street and West Center Road. Rockbrook Village now is the only community shopping center located on the Interstate highway system that encircles Omaha.

Since the death of Larry Myers, in 1986, daughter Sue Myers Daub and her husband, Russell Daub, have continued the Rockbrook Village portion of the family real estate business.

Rockbrook Village is a collection of more than 60 specialty stores and businesses, in 13 buildings, containing 150,000 square feet. In 1987, the property was substantially renovated, with the addition of a southwestern motif for the buildings and the creation of a central plaza.

Thirteen years later, that plaza is the home of many merchant activities and the summertime outpost of four fine restaurants. On Friday nights in the summer, families dine in the open-air restaurants and listen to music. Sometimes more than 800 friends and neighbors meet at

The Rockbrook Village shopping, dining, and entertainment complex, at 108th Street and West Center Road in Omaha, features various events, including the popular annual Art Fair, shown here, which attracts more than 10,000 visitors.

the central plaza, starting the weekend with music and pleasant conversation.

Rockbrook is like a village, and its business owners are the neighbors. An active Merchants Association develops annual themes and events that draw new customers as well as loyal friends. Perhaps the best-known event is the Art Fair, which annually attracts more than 10,000 art lovers and is one of the longest running art fairs in the Midwest.

People know Rockbrook Village as a great place to eat and to shop for home furnishings. Recently, a new emphasis on sports and fitness-related businesses has emerged. Rockbrook Village also is home for many established, successful retail and service merchants, including seven national/regional companies.

Businesses choose to locate in Rockbrook Village because of its tenant mix; its regional interest, with easy access to the Interstate highway system; its active marketing; and its Merchants' Association.

At Rockbrook Village on Friday nights in the summer, people attend live outdoor musical performances like this one, visit the shops, and dine in open-air restaurants.

BORSHEIM JEWELRY COMPANY, INC.

Borsheim's store in west Omaha's Regency Court is renowned locally, nationally, and internationally for its extra-

ordinary inventory of fine jewelry and gifts and for providing exceptional values with exemplary customer service.

A package wrapped in silver paper festooned with burgundy silk ribbons delights any bride or birthday celebrant. That distinctive wrapping characteristically means this is a gift from Borsheim's.

Borsheim Jewelry Company, Inc., one of the largest independent jewelry stores in the United States, is celebrating its 130th year in business. Founded in 1870 by Louis Borsheim, the company was purchased in 1947 by Louis Friedman and was shaped by his son, Ike Friedman, to become the phenomenon that it is today. The first small store, offering a wide variety of merchandise to shoppers, was located in downtown Omaha. In 1986, Ike Friedman moved Borsheim's into the specialty mall Regency Court, in west Omaha, and began a series of carefully planned expansions. Today, Borsheim's is a 45,000-square-foot enterprise, with more than 375 employees, including 15 graduate gemologists.

In 1989, Omaha investor Warren E. Buffett, through Berkshire Hathaway, Inc., acquired 80 percent of Borsheim's stock over a ten-minute conversation and a handshake. The simple transaction was based on mutual respect and trust. True to his style, Buffett gave Borsheim's management team laissez-faire directions: "Don't change a thing."

Borsheim's has distinguished itself among jewelers in its depth of product and its value-oriented prices: Borsheim's makes unbeatable deals. Because of this reputation for great deals, eager customers drive in and fly in, searching for something unique at a great price. More than 45 percent of Borsheim's customers are from places beyond Omaha, including all 50 states and five continents. Among the keys to success at Borsheim's are keeping expenses low, maintaining a huge inventory and selection, making conscientious purchases, and providing friendly customer service. The business is debt free, a rarity in the jewelry and giftware industry.

Borsheim's in Regency Court offers more than 100,000 pieces of fine jewelry, gifts, timepieces, and more.

In recent years, under the astute direction of Buffett-chosen president and CEO, Susan M. Jacques, Borsheim's has expanded in a number of ways, each bringing the same result: an increase in annual sales. One new emphasis has been on tabletop items, with a huge inventory to please any couple registering for wedding gifts. A strong business in corporate gifts brings even more customers, as do the exclusive offerings made by Borsheim's. In 1999, borsheims.com was launched, offering an extensive selection of products for on-line purchases.

With an inventory of more than 100,000 treasures —from simple diamond engagement rings to fine porcelain table settings to bejeweled watches to one-of-a-kind jeweler's masterpieces—there is simply no place like Borsheim's.

BORSHEIM'S.
Fine Jewelry and Gifts
A Berkshire Hathaway Company

The extensive selection at Borsheim's makes it easy to choose the perfect gift, for yourself or for someone you love.

PART THREE

REFLECTIONS & VISIONS

Innovation and good economic sense are hallmarks of the Cornhusker State, as they have been since the days when prairie schooners crossed the broad Platte Valley and settlers discovered some of the world's richest soil. Nebraska's strong, diverse economy springs not only from those two invaluable characteristics, but also from bountiful natural resources and their wise use. A highly educated citizenry, in partnership with its leaders, has crafted a state that stands out today as an example of livability.

In the following pages, leaders in a variety of Nebraska's economic sectors reflect on the achievements of their industries and offer their visions of the future. Just as the state pioneered the 9-1-1 emergency communications network now used throughout the country, so today it is utilizing the Internet to develop cutting-edge products. The same forward-looking spirit that motivated the public to take ownership of Nebraska's electric utilities in the 1930s and 1940s moves it to further develop renewable energy sources today.

Based on a competitive economic climate, an outstanding infra-structure, and the firmly established relationship between commercial success and higher education, Nebraska in the new century will be doing business as usual—spearheading change and thriving.

The sun sets on Johnson Lake, bringing with it quiet evenings and the possibility of dreams. Built in the 1930s, the 2,060-acre lake is the heart of one of Nebraska's premier recreation areas and site of the state's first recreational access road.

LIGHTING THE WAY

WILLIAM R. MAYBEN

President and Chief Executive Officer, Nebraska Public Power District (NPPD)

Prior to Bill Mayben's becoming president of NPPD in 1995, he held several positions with R. W. Beck, an engineering and management consulting firm. He currently serves on the board of the American Public Power Association and on the steering committee of the Large Public Power Council. He also is chairman of the dean's advisory board of the College of Engineering at the University of Nebraska.

The electrification of the cities, towns, and farms is considered by many to be the greatest improvement to the quality of life in Nebraska during the 20th century. • The populist movement of the 1930s and 1940s changed the ownership of Nebraska's electric utility systems from private stockholder companies to citizens. Nebraska is the

only state in the nation in which all the electric utilities are publicly owned.

While many individuals had strong roles in the development of public power, U.S. Senator George Norris of McCook, Nebraska, is recognized as the father of public power. Senator Norris authored federal legislation creating the Tennessee Valley Authority in 1933 and the Rural Electrification Administration in 1936, both major factors in the development of rural areas across the United States at the time. The year 1933 saw the passage of Nebraska legislation clearing the way for the creation of public power and development of three major hydro-electric projects.

With available, low-cost power, Nebraska attracted many branch plants of the nation's largest industries, resulting in continued rapid growth in the demand for electricity. Electric irrigation pumps, corn processing, and steel and meatpacking plants now consume large amounts of electric energy.

Nebraska's public power utilities use an efficient mix of coal, nuclear, hydroelectric, oil, gas, and wind-generation resources. We provide electricity at costs 20 percent less than the national average. These low electric rates stimulate economic development across the state by both expanding existing business and attracting new business to Nebraska.

Globalization has an enormous impact on the economy of our state. Nebraska ranks fifth in the nation in agricultural exports, and foreign markets are important for many of our manufacturers.

The Internet is changing the way we do business. High speed, broadband telecommunications will help our communities attract new types of businesses employing our highly educated workforce. Nebraska's electric industry is utilizing the Internet to buy and sell power. Utilities also use it to communicate with customers and to disseminate information worldwide about Nebraska's economic development opportunities. In turn, Nebraskans use it to learn about global markets.

In the future, Nebraskans will see further development of electric energy produced from renewable resources. The use of smaller generating units at individual businesses, known in our industry as "distributed generation," will grow.

The deregulation of the electric industry, too, will affect the way we do business in Nebraska. The wise development of resources in our citizen-owned utilities has kept electric costs low, contributing to the competitiveness of Nebraska's agricultural products and manufactured goods in the global marketplace. Keeping overall costs competitive is a good goal for Nebraska's electric utilities—and for all Nebraskans.

PHOTO: © Digital Stock

A CATALYST FOR DEVELOPMENT

BRUCE R. LAURITZEN
Chairman, First National Bank of Omaha

A graduate of Princeton University, Bruce Lauritzen received an MBA from the University of Virginia. He is president of the Omaha Development Council and Foundation, chairman of Clarkson Regional Health Services, a representative of the Financial Services Roundtable, and Nebraska consul for the Royal Danish Consulate. Lauritzen received the 1999 Headliner Award from the Omaha Chamber of Commerce.

Nebraska's banks have always been closely tied to the state's citizens. By lending Nebraskans the money to finance business, agriculture, manufacturing, real estate development, consumer goods, automobiles, and homes, the banking industry has served as a catalyst for the economic development of this great state.

The roots of Nebraska's financial success are found in the hundreds of independent banks that existed for more than a century in nearly every city, town, and village across the state. More recently, during the latter part of the 20th century, the United States' banking system saw dramatic consolidation, resulting in a handful of nationwide banks, several regional banks, and more than 5,000 local independent banks. Our state is served by a combination of all three, including more than 250 banks that are still headquartered in Nebraska.

The banking industry has changed dramatically over the past 100 years, but one thing that has remained constant is the desire to serve the consumer and build the state.

For much of the 20th century, bankers served their customers in person, over the teller line or in the lobby. After World War II, bank-by-mail advertising was introduced, and in the late 1950s, drive-through banks started to appear. Computers entered Nebraska's banks in the 1960s. In the 1980s, remote banking began in earnest with devices such as automated teller machines (ATMs), fax machines, toll-free numbers, and point-of-sale terminals for credit cards.

Today the Internet is furthering our ability to deliver banking products conveniently to customers wherever

they are located. In addition, with the passage in November 1999 of the Bank Modernization Act, banks can offer more financial products and services and compete fully in such areas as insurance and investments.

Bankers in the 21st century will need to remain technologically competent in order to compete locally and nationally. But the key to successful banking will be to realize that these communication devices are merely ways to enhance the delivery system and not substitutes for service. Fortunately, Nebraska's bankers remain close to the customer, believing that through competent personal service they will continue to be a catalyst for building this great state.

OUR INTELLECTUAL ADVENTURE

GLADYS STYLES JOHNSTON

Chancellor, The University of Nebraska at Kearney

Dr. Johnston assumed her current responsibilities at the University of Nebraska in 1993 after serving as provost and then executive vice president of DePaul University in Chicago. A published author, her scholarly recognition includes an appointment as Distinguished Commonwealth Visiting Professor at the College of William and Mary.

During the course of the 20th century, Nebraskans created a higher education enterprise that provides opportunities for its citizens to gain an affordable degree within a broad array of professions and disciplines. College and university facilities were distributed geographically to match the unusual population demographics. This enterprise is

widely supported as the state's single greatest investment, both for now and the future. Although part of a state with a limited population dispersed unevenly across the land, Nebraska's higher educational enterprise maintains a highly competitive edge with similarly situated states and serves its purpose successfully.

The greatest single impact on higher education during the 20th century was the introduction of scientific and scholarly research as a major component of the higher educational enterprise. This merger of teaching and learning with the creation of knowledge as a federally supported goal accelerated into full bloom during World War II, when universities and colleges became the intellectual focus of the nation's basic and applied research. This uniquely American effort brought federal capital and national guidance into all state higher educational enterprises on a limited-partnership basis. The fundamental principles of academic freedom remained intact and insured a faculty's independence in scholarly research and the discovery of new knowledge.

In the last half of the century, state higher education enterprises expanded rapidly, nurtured by an infusion of federal dollars. The freedom for open publication of scholarly efforts enhanced the globalization of new

knowledge, established an international scientific language based on English, and set into motion vast international technological development that was applied to commercially and socially useful outcomes. Commercial applications of electronic communications exploded, commercial productivity accelerated, and the relationship between commercial success and higher education was crystallized. As a new millennium dawns, the United States and its higher educational enterprise sit at the apex of worldwide admiration. Our freedom to inquire, grounded in state and federal cooperation, has provided educators the opportunity to create, discover, and transfer knowledge worldwide. This achievement demonstrates positively that an open democracy provides unlimited opportunity for intellectual development to all with the capacity and desire to learn.

As Nebraska further develops its higher education enterprise, its challenges include improving access to higher education for the underserved and continuing to provide the educated citizens needed in the state's commercial and nonprofit systems and to apply new technologies pertinent to the education and research process. The Nebraska Higher Education Enterprise, in turn, needs to improve efficiency in knowledge transfer and to assist the state in diversifying its commercial and fiscal base.

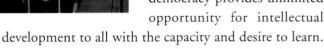

PHOTO: © *Corbis*

SHIFTING INTO OVERDRIVE

ANTHONY F. RAIMONDO/RICHARD F. CASEY

Chairman and Chief Executive Officer/Senior Vice President—Administration, Behlen Mfg. Co.

Tony Raimondo joined Behlen in 1982, when it was a division of the failing Wickes Corporation. He led a management buyout of the company in 1984, and in 1994, *Inc.* magazine selected Behlen and Raimondo as its Turn-Around Entrepreneur of the Year Award winner. Richard Casey joined Behlen in 1978, after working 12 years for Johnson & Johnson in various financial and IT positions.

Innovation, technology, and creative problem solving in the 20th century brought about a farming and manufacturing revolution that has changed the economic map of the United States. At the beginning of the 20th century, more than 50 percent of the country's population was needed to feed America. Today, fewer than 2 percent of the population is involved in production agriculture—and that 2 percent feeds not only our country, but also much of the world.

Agriculture and manufacturing have always been intertwined in Nebraska. Manufacturing companies in the state have mirrored the evolution of the farm economy. As companies recognized the need to serve the development of mechanized agriculture, they began manufacturing such items as corn cribs and mesh ventilators, storage facilities and grain handling/drying systems. The many changes in the farm economy, along with technology, resulted in the diversification of many of these companies.

Continued mechanization and automation brought new challenges and opportunities to the manufacturing sector later in the 20th century. Computer technology, globalization of the workforce and markets, and biotechnology have had a considerable impact on all areas of the economy, particularly agriculture and manufacturing. With open trade, the world is becoming a single community. The development and advancement of communication systems have shown us the needs of people worldwide. This has made it possible to broaden our markets by exporting American products and technology all over the world.

One of the factors fueling this success story is the American capitalistic system, in which people have the freedom to be innovative. They accomplish change and innovation by using cutting-edge technology to produce value-added products that support the customer and provide an understanding that the global economy is changing faster and more completely than ever before. Technology increases the transfer of information and becomes an integral way to develop and implement product designs. These designs in turn improve the product and customer satisfaction.

As we begin the 21st century, many challenges and opportunities lie ahead. Companies that are able to adapt and innovate, that can provide an environment encouraging new ideas and creative problem solving, that can provide high-quality products to their customers with on-time delivery, will be in a position to be successful.

The changes in the 20th century seemed rapid as we experienced them; however, those that lie ahead will occur at an ever-quickening pace. We must be prepared to make dramatic changes in our lives and in our way of doing business in order to survive and thrive in the 21st century. From evolution to revolution, change is a way of life, to be embraced and celebrated as we meet new challenges and accomplish goals that are still unimagined.

NEBRASKA ON THE MOVE

CLARENCE L. WERNER
Chief Executive Officer, Werner Enterprises

Clarence L. Werner began Werner Enterprises in 1956 with just one truck, hauling cargo in a six-state region. Today the company is one of the top five truckload motor carriers in the nation and employs more than 10,000 people. Werner Enterprises is a publicly owned business with strong family involvement; three of Werner's four children work in the business.

Transportation throughout the last two centuries has changed dramatically, from the covered wagons the pioneers used to transport all of their belongings when they headed west early in the 19th century to our present systems of modern transportation, among the best in the world.

Early on during the pioneer days, the railroad played a very important part in building what Nebraska is today. But as roads were built to replace rails in the late 19th century, motor trucks began to dominate our industry.

We now have all of our major county and state roads hard surfaced and developed to the point that most of our supplies and materials are delivered by truck.

Truck transportation is Nebraska's second largest industry, surpassed only by agriculture. Nebraska is also home to some of the largest trucking companies in America. A truck has brought every product you touch, see, or use in your home, no matter what part of the country you may live in. Truck transportation is a very vital part of Nebraska's, as well as America's, existence and well-being.

Of course, Nebraska business has many transportation options available, including such national and global companies as United Parcel Service and Federal Express, and other small companies that serve the entire state. In particular, Nebraska and the Midwest enjoy a large selection of companies that transport livestock. Numerous refrigerated trucking companies, too, are available, serving our large beef industry as well as the processed foods industry that is becoming more dominant in our state.

In support of our transportation infrastructure, manufacturers throughout the state build all types of trailers, including flatbed, refrigerated, dry van, and bulk tank trailers.

Massive amounts of imported coal arrive in Nebraska daily by rail, on coal trains. Our bulk agriculture commodities, such as supplies, grain, fertilizer, and feed travel to, from, and within the state by three modes of transportation: truck, railroad, and Missouri River barge.

Nebraska's central location has contributed to its excellent air transportation network. Both passengers and air freight are handled easily from the state's 94 public and 200 private airports, especially those in Omaha and Lincoln. Eppley Airfield in Omaha, in fact, which was just expanded, is one of the fastest growing airports in the country.

The 21st century promises an even better transportation network for Nebraska. The state highway department is doing major expansion on the most heavily traveled highways in the state, and a commission is studying the possibility of putting in high-speed rail service for passengers.

Nebraska's great transportation modes help make our state what it is today.

PHOTO: © Digital Stock

BIBLIOGRAPHY

American Automobile Association. *North Central TourBook.* Heathrow, Fla.: AAA Publishing, 1999.

Clerk of the Legislature. *Blue Book.* Lincoln: Nebraska Legislature, 1999.

Creigh, Dorothy Weyer. *Nebraska: A Bicentennial History.* New York: W. W. Norton & Co., 1977.

Dobler, William O.; Leslie Hewes; and James C. Olson. "Nebraska: The Cornhusker State," *World Book Encyclopedia,* vol. 12. Chicago: World Book, Inc., 1983.

Greater Omaha Chamber of Commerce. AccessOmaha. <http//www.accessomaha.com>

_____. *Cost of Living, Metropolitan Omaha Area.* Omaha: Greater Omaha Chamber of Commerce, 1999.

_____. *Guide to Greater Omaha 1999.* Omaha: Greater Omaha Chamber of Commerce, 1999.

_____. Memo to author, July 1999.

_____. *Metro Omaha Statistical Profile 1999.* Greater Omaha Chamber of Commerce, 1999.

Hastings Tribune. Hastings, Neb.: Seaton Publishing Co., editions of June 24 and August 7, 1999.

Hickey, Donald R. *Nebraska Moments.* Lincoln: University of Nebraska Press, 1992.

Hornor, Edith R., ed. *Almanac of the 50 States.* Palo Alto, Calif.: Information Publications, 1998.

McNally, Hannah. *Nebraska: Off the Beaten Path.* Old Saybrook, CT: Globe Pequot Press, 1997.

Microsoft Encarta Online Encyclopedia 2000. "Gibson, Bob." <http://encarta.msn.com> (April 21, 2000).

Morgan, Kathleen O'Leary, and Scott E. Morgan, eds. *Health Care State Rankings 1999.* Lawrence, Kan.: Morgan Quitno Press, 1999.

Moulton, Candy. *Roadside History of Nebraska.* Missoula, Mont.: Mountain Press Publishing, 1997.

Nebraska Department of Economic Development. "Nebraska Databook." <http//www.ded.state.ne.us>

Nebraska Division of Travel and Tourism. "Genuine Nebraska." <http//www.visitnebraska.org>

Nebraska Press Association. *Yearbook.* Lincoln: Nebraska Press Association, 1999.

Olson, James C. *History of Nebraska,* 2nd ed. Lincoln: University of Nebraska Press, 1966.

Omaha World-Herald. Nebraska Anthology. Omaha: World Publishing Co., 1982.

_____. *Famous Nebraskans.* Omaha: World Publishing Co., 1993.

_____. Editions of June 19 and 22, September 20, 29, and 30, and November 2, 1999.

Parks, Gabe C., comp. *Nebraska Trivia.* Nashville: Rutledge Hill Press, 1998.

Reilly, Robert T. *The Omaha Experience.* Omaha: Barnhart Press, 1990.

Van Noppen, Ina Woestmeyer. "Louisiana Purchase," *World Book Encyclopedia,* vol. 12. Chicago: World Book, Inc., 1983.

Winckler, Suzanne. *The Heartland—Nebraska, Iowa, Illinois, Missouri, Kansas.* The Smithsonian Guides to Natural America, ed. Sandra Wilmot. New York: Random House; Washington, D.C.: Smithsonian Books, 1997.

Wirth, Eileen. *The Omaha Experience.* Marietta, Ga.: Longstreet Press, 1996.

The Web sites of the following companies, places, organizations, and electronic publications also were consulted for this book: American Tool Cos.; Bahr Vermeer Haecker Architects; Behlen Mfg. Co.; Bozell Worldwide; Burlington Northern Santa Fe Corporation; California Institute of Technology; Commercial Federal Bank; ConAgra, Inc.; Creighton University Medical Center; Grand Island, Neb.; Iowa Beef Processors, Inc.; Kutak Rock; Lincoln Chamber of Commerce; McCook, Neb.; MDS Harris; National Commission on Educational Statistics; Nebraska Educational Television; Nebraska Health Systems; Nebraska Public Power District; Novartis AG; NP Dodge Real Estate; Scottsbluff, Neb.; Strategic Air Command Museum; University of Nebraska–Lincoln; University of Nebraska Medical Center; US Bank.

245

INDEX

Acceptance Insurance Companies, 156

Agate Fossil Beds National Monument, 44

Ag Processing, Inc. (AGP), 7, 54–55

Agriculture, 50–55, 241

Airports, 113, 242

Aldrich, Bess Streeter, 7, 70

Alegent Health, 153

Allereye, France, 138

Alliance, 46, 223

ALLTEL Corporation, 26

American Chamber of Commerce
    Researchers Association (ACCRA), 186

American Historical Society of Germans, 42

American Speech, 5

American Tool Companies, 38, 82, 87

Ameritas Life, 156

Angus Automobile Company, 86

Arbor Day, 6, 36, 69

Arbor Lodge, 36

Arnold, 34

Arthur Bowring Sandhills Ranch State
    Historical Park, 34

Ashfall Fossil Beds State Historical Park, 18

Ash Hollow State Historic Park, 46

Astaire, Fred, 4

Austerlitz, Frederick, 4

Back to the Bible, 78

Bahr Vermeer Haecker Architects, 191

Bancroft, Dr. William, 134

Banking industry, 156–60, 239

Bank Modernization Act, 240

Base Hospital, 49, 138

Beadle, Dr. George W., 6, 139

Beatrice, 36

Behlen Mfg. Co., 82–83, 108–09

Bellevue, 16, 190

Bellevue University, 207

Benkelman, 40

Big Rodeo, 34

Black Elk Speaks, 7

Blair, 17

Blair Memorial Community Hospital and
    Health System, 152

Blue Cross and Blue Shield of Nebraska, 156

Bodmer, Karl, 16

Bond, Ward, 40

Boosalis, Helen, 7

Boot Hill, 30

Borsheim Jewelry Company, Inc., 220, 235

Borsheim's, 220

Boston Central Artery, 189

Bowring, Eve, 34

Boys Town, 6, 24, 205

Boys Town National Research Hospital,
    137, 205

Bozell Worldwide, 161

Bradbury, John, 53

Brokaw, Tom, 69

Brooks, Ralph, 42

Brown, Dee, 70

Brown, John, 36

Brownville, 7, 36, 38, 69

Bryan, Gov. Charles W., 6

Bryan, William Jennings, 4

BryanLGH Medical Center, 150–51

Buffett, Warren, 7, 14, 21

Bureau of Business Research, 87

Burlington Northern and Santa Fe Railroad,
    26, 38, 112, 113

Burwell, 34

Cabela's, 46

California Trail, 3, 26

Campos, Robert, 189

Campos Construction Co., 189

Capt. Meriwether Lewis, 36

Cargill Corn Milling, 58–59, 83

Cargill Dow LLC, 60, 82, 83–84

Cargill, Incorporated, 22, 55, 83

Carhenge, 223

Carson, Johnny, 4–5, 67

Casey, Richard F., 241

Cather, Willa, 7, 40, 70

CBSHOME Real Estate, 186

Center for Information Technology, 207

Central High School, 202

Central Park Plaza, 20

Central States Health and Life Co., 159

Chadron, 205

Chadron State Park, 44, 47

Chase 3000, 68

Cherry County, 32

Cheyenne Autumn, 7

Chicago Central and Pacific, 112

Chief Industries, Inc., 104–05

Children's Hospital, 137

Children's Museum, 30

Children's Rights Council, 86

Chimney Rock, 44, 218

City of Omaha, The, 168

Clarkson College, 154

Clarkson Hospital, 7

Clay County, 221

CliffsNotes, 69

Cody, William F. "Buffalo Bill," 5, 30, 40,
    157

College of Agriculture, 51

Columbus, 17, 82

Commercial Federal Bank, 21, 172–73, 160

Community-Oriented Primary Care
    Program, 134

Comstock, Bill, 5

ConAgra, Inc., 8, 20, 54, 64–65

Controller, 70

Cooper Nuclear Power Plant, 38

Cope Memorial Fountain, 204

Cornhuskers, 7, 221–22

Cornhusker State, 3, 4, 49, 50, 237. See
    also Nebraska.

Coronado, Francisco Vásquez de, 54

Council Bluffs Bugle, 69

Court House Rock, 44

Cowboy Recreation and Nature Trail, 15,
    32

Cowboy Triathlon, 34

Cox Communications, 69

Cozad, 30

Crawford, 44

Crazy Horse, 7

Crazy Horse, Chief, 5, 44

Creighton, Edward, 66

Creighton University, 5, 12, 134, 205, 206,
    214–15

Creighton University Institute of Technology, 207

Creighton University Medical Center, 137

Creighton University School of Medicine, 134, 207

Crossroads Mall, 22

Custer, Lt. Col. George A., 5, 40

Cuthills Vineyards 18

Cycle of the West, A, 7

Dakota City, 16

Daly, Leo A., 188

Dana College, 17

Data Documents, 82

Dawes, Charles G., 6

Death Comes for the Archbishop, 7

Deshler, 84

Deshler Broom Factory, 84

Devaney, Coach Bob, 7

DeWitt, 38, 87

Dismal River, 32

DLR Group, 84, 166, 190–91

Dobie, J. Frank, 70

Douglas, 86

Dow Chemical Company, 83

Dundy, Judge Elmer S., 5

Durham, Charles W. and Marge, 190

Durham Western Heritage Museum 10, 23

Education, 202–07, 240

Electricity, 42, 113–17, 238

Elkhorn River Valley, 15 19

Energy, 113–17

Enron Corp., 128–29

Eppley Airfield, 113, 242

EIII, Inc., 68

Excel Corporation, 61, 84

Farmers Mutual Insurance Company of Nebraska, 182–83

Farmland Foods, 54

Federal Express, 242

First Charge, 6

First Data Corporation, 19, 176–77, 206

FirsTier Bank, 158

First National Bank of Omaha, 6, 8, 20, 157, 174–75

First National of Nebraska, 157

Fitch, Val L., 6

Flanagan, Father Edward, 6, 24

Fonda, Henry, 5

Food processing, 53–55

Forbes magazine, 7

Ford, Gerald, 5

Fort Atkinson, 17–18, 137

Fort Hartstuff, 34

Fort Kearny, 30

Fort Niobrara National Wildlife Refuge, 32

Fort Omaha, 5

Fort Robinson, 5

Fort Robinson State Park, 44, 47, 218, 223

Freeman, Agnes, 36

Freeman, Daniel, 36

Fremont, 19, 222

Fuller car, 86

Furnas, Robert W., 69

Gale, John, 137

Gallup Organization, 26

Garwood and Offner, 42

Gene Leahy Mall, 17

George W. Beadle Center for Genetics and Biomaterials Research, 139

Gerald R. Ford Conservation Center, 189

German Heritage Days, 42

Gibbon, 52

Gibraltar Packaging Group, Inc., 39, 96–97

Gibson, Bob, 5

Girls and Boys Town, 6, 24, 205

Godfather's Pizza, 7

Golden Spikes, 12

Goodhue, Bertram G., 29, 188

Goodyear Tire and Rubber, 26

Gothenburg, 30

Grand Duke Alexis Recreation Area, 40

Grand Island, 5, 26, 30, 54, 69, 188

Great American Cattle Drive, 26

Great Plains Blizzard of 1888, 204

Great Platte River Road, 26, 30

Great Platte River Road Archway Monument, 223

Groundwater Foundation, 55

Grubb & Ellis/Pacific Realty, 186, 200–01

Guarantee Life, 156

Handcart Pioneers, 8

Harlem Globetrotters, 5

Harold Warp Pioneer Village, 40

Hastings, 26, 86

Hastings College, 5

Hastings Museum/Lied IMAX Theater, 218

Hawthorne, Nathaniel, 69

Haymarket district, 30

HDR, Inc., 189–90, 198–99

Health care, 134–39

Health Care State Rankings, 134

Heartland of America Foundation, 8

Henry Doorly Zoo 10, 218

Hickock, James Butler "Wild Bill," 220

High Plains Museum, 42

Hillegass, Clifton K., 69

Historic Winter Quarters, 8

Hitchcock, Gilbert M., 70

Home for Homeless Boys, 6

Homestead Act, 36

Homestead National Monument of America, 36

Hoover, President, 189

Hormel, 55

Hudson-Meng Bison Bone Bed, 44

Hyannis, 32, 34

Hyatt, 218

IBP, Inc., 55

Insul-8 Corporation, 90–91

Insurance industry, 156

International Mathematics Olympiad, 207

Interstate highways, 6, 112, 114

In-WATS calling service, 6

Iowa Beef Processors, Inc., 16

Irrigator, center-pivot, 6, 54

ISDN, 67

ITI, 68

Jail Rock, 44

Jensen, Dr. John, 69

Johansen, Franz, 8

John Brown's Cave and Historical Village, 36

John C. Fremont Days, 222

John Day Company, 13, 62–63

Johnson, Joseph E., 69

Johnson, Philip, 188

Johnson Lake, 237

Johnston, Gladys Styles, 240

Joslyn, George A. and Sarah H., 13

Joslyn Art Museum 10, 13, 188, 190, 218

Kansas-Nebraska Act, 69, 190

Kawasaki Motors Manufacturing Corp.
   U.S.A., 82, 106–07
KCAJ, 69
KCRO, 69
Kearney, 26, 30, 223
KFAB, 69
Kids Count Data Book, 86
Kimball County, 46
Kincaid, Rep. Moses P., 4
Kincaid Act, 4
Kingsley Dam, 6
Kirkpatrick Pettis, 156
Kizer, William, 159
Klein, Lawrence R., 6
KMMJ, 69
KMTV, 68, 69
KN Energy, 115
Kool-Aid, 6
Kountze, Herman and Augustus, 156–57
Kountze Bros. Bank, 157
KUON-TV, 68
Kuralt, Charles, 32
Kutak Rock, 157, 160
Lake Crescent National Wildlife Refuge, 47
Lake McConaughy, 6, 30, 220
Landmark Center, 67, 186
Lauritzen, Bruce R., 239
LaVista, 139
Lawrie, Lee, 49
Lee Enterprises, 69
Leo A Daly, 20, 188–89, 194–95
Lewis and Clark, 14, 19, 24
Lexington, 26
Liberty Bonds, 5
Lied Center for the Performing Arts, 26
Lied Jungle, 218
Lied Transplant Center, 136–37
Lincoln, 4, 7, 26, 30, 69, 70, 82, 138, 156,
   159, 188, 189, 191, 242
Lincoln, Abraham, 4, 66, 189
Lincoln County Historical Museum, 220
Lincoln Electric System, 30, 115, 122–23
Lincoln Journal-Star, 70
Lincoln Lightning, 30
Lincoln Stars, 30
Lincoln Telephone, 6
Linweld, 31, 82, 98–100

Little Big Horn, 5, 40
Long, Maj. Stephen, 50, 53
Louisiana Purchase, 186, 188
Louisville, 36
Loup River, 32, 51
Lozier Corporation, 82, 86
Lucent Technologies, 87
MacDonald, Alan, 188
Machinery Trader, 70
Mahoney State Park, 218
Makhpiyaluta, 5
Malnove Incorporated, 16, 94–95
Mannheim Steamroller, 7
Manufacturing, 82–87, 241
Marriott, 218
Marriott Worldwide Reservations, 228–29
Massacre Canyon Pow-Wow, 40, 42
Mattes, Merrill, 70
Mayben, William R., 238
McCanles, David C., 220
McCook, 42, 137–38
McKinley, President William, 8
MDS Harris, 138–39
MDS Pharmaceuticals, 139
Memorial Community Hospital and Health
   System, 134
Memorial Stadium, 221
Mennonites, 46
Merriman, 34
Merritt Reservoir State Recreation Area, 32
Methodist Health System, 14, 144–45
Methodist Hospital, 137
Metropolitan Community College, 216
Metropolitan Utilities District, 115, 126–27
MFSA Network Technologies, 186
Midlands Packaging Corporation, 110
Mientka, Walter, 207
Milford, 86
Millard Lumber Inc., 18, 196–97
Miller, George L., 70
Minden, 40
Mirage Flats, 7
Miss Bishop, 7
Missouri River, 8, 14, 24, 26, 186
Missouri River barge, 112, 113, 242
Mormon Trail, 3, 26, 30
Mormon Trail Center, 8

Morrison, Frank, 42
Morton, J. Sterling, 6, 36, 69, 191
Mother Mason, 7
Mutual of Omaha Companies, 8, 156, 158,
   184
Mutual of Omaha's Wild Heritage Center,
   161
Mutual of Omaha's Wild Kingdom, 7, 161
My Antonia, 7
National Bank of Commerce, 159
National Cancer Institute, 136
National Czech Capital of the United
   States, 39
National Geographic, 18
National Institutes of Health, 137
National Museum of American History, 84
National Parent-Teacher Association, 7
Nature Conservancy, 222
NatureWorks PLA, 82, 83
NBC News, 69
NCAA, 7
NCAA College World Series, 12, 13
Nebraska, 3–7
   agriculture and, 50–55
   communications and, 66–71
   education and, 202–07, 240
   energy and, 113–17
   health care and, 134–39
   manufacturing and, 82–87, 241
   real estate and, 186–91
   tourism and 218–25
   transportation and 112–13, 242
Nebraska Advertiser, 69
Nebraska City, 6, 36
Nebraska City News, 69
Nebraska Consolidated Mills, 54
Nebraska Department of Economic
   Development, 167
Nebraska Educational Telecommunication
   (NET), 68
Nebraska Educational Telecommunications
   Commission, 68
Nebraska Health System, 12, 136, 142–43
Nebraska Higher Education Enterprise, 240
Nebraskaland Days, 30
Nebraska National Forest, 6, 32

Nebraska Palladium, 190

Nebraska Press Association, 70

Nebraska Public Power District, 114, 130–31

Nebraska Shakespeare Festival 10

Nebraska Sports Hall of Fame, 5

Nebraska State Bar Association, 159

Nebraska Territory, 69, 157, 158, 160, 190

Nebraska Wesleyan University, 69

Neihardt, John G., 7, 14, 70

Nelson, Ben, 42

Niobrara River, 32, 34

Niobrara Valley Preserve, 222

Nobel Prizes, 6, 139

Norbest Turkey, 52

Norfolk, 4, 17, 67, 69, 86

Norris, George W., 5, 42, 238

Northern Natural Gas, 115

North Omaha Power Station, 117

North Platte, 26, 86

North Platte River, 30, 46

Norwest Bank Nebraska, 157

Novartis Consumer Health, 138

NP Dodge Real Estate, 186

Nuclear power plant, 7

Oakland, 16–17

Oak View Mall, 22, 232–33

Offutt Air Force Base, 66

Ogallala, 6, 26, 30, 46, 50

Ogallala Aquifer, 32, 51

Ogallala-Texas Cattle Drive, 26

Oglala National Grassland, 44

Oglala Sioux, 5

Old Jules, 7

Old Market, 3, 11

Omaha, 3, 4, 5, 7, 8–13, 20, 26, 54, 66, 67, 68, 69, 82, 86, 87, 112, 113, 115, 117, 134, 156, 159, 186, 188, 189, 191, 218, 220, 242

Omaha Arrow, 69

Omaha Beef, 12

Omaha Building, 157

Omaha Community Playhouse, 5, 10

Omaha Daily Herald, 70

Omaha Evening World, 70

Omaha Lancers, 12

Omaha National Bank, 157

Omaha Printing Company, 70

Omaha Public Power District, 114, 115, 124–25

Omaha Symphony Orchestra 10, 14

Omaha World-Herald, 8, 70

Omni, 218

OMNI Behavioral Health, 148–49

One Box Pheasant Hunt, 34

On Golden Pond, 5

O'Neill, 17

One of Ours, 7

O! Pioneers, 7

Oregon Trail, 3, 26, 30, 218

Orr, Kay, 7

Osborne, Tom, 5

Overland Stage route, 220

Panhandle, 44–47

Panhandle Mental Health Center, 138

Pawnee Killer, 40

Paxton & Vierling Steel, A Division of Owen Industries, Inc., 15, 92–93

Peoples Natural Gas, 115, 132

Perkins Products Co., 6

Pershing, John J., 5

Peru, 205

Peter Kiewit Institute of Science, Technology and Engineering, 206–07

Petersen, William, 87

Pfizer Inc, 102–03

Phelps County, 42

Physician's Mutual, 156

Picotte, Susan La Flesche, 5

Pierce, President Franklin, 69

Pine Ridge, 44

Platte River, 26, 29, 51, 221

Platte River State Park, 36

Platte River Valley, 26, 30, 50, 66, 112, 116, 222, 237

Plazzotta, Enzo, 24

Poncas, 14

Ponca State Park, 17, 24

Pony Express, 26, 30, 66

Poppleton, Andrew J., 160

Pound, Louise, 5

Prairie Lakes Country, 40, 42, 137–38

Public Broadcasting System, 68

Qwest Communications, 66, 67, 186

Railroads, 112, 113, 115, 242

Raimondo, Anthony F., 241

Reading Rainbow series, 68

Real estate, 186–91

Red Cloud, 5, 7, 40, 42

Reinders, James, 223

Republican Party, 69

Republican River, 40, 42, 51

Republican River Valley, 40

Ricketts, J. Joe, 7

Rim of the Prairie, 7

Rockbrook Village, 22, 234

Rock Creek Station State Historical Park, 220

Rogers, Ginger, 4

Roller Skating National Museum, 30

Rosenblatt Stadium, 12, 13

Rural Electrification Administration, 42, 238

Rural Health Education Network, 134

Russell, Majors, and Waddell, 66

Russell, William H., 66

Sacramento, 66

St. Joseph, MO, 66

Saint Joseph Hospital, 17, 134, 137, 146–47

St. Louis Cardinals, 5

Sandhill cranes, 29, 30, 221

Sandhills, 32, 34

Sandhills Publishing Company, 29, 70, 74–77

Sandoz, Mari, 7, 34, 70

Sandoz Sandhills ranch, 7

Saugeye, 223

Scarlet Letter, The, 69

"Schoolchildren's Blizzard," 204

"Scopes Monkey Trial," 4

Scott, Walter Jr., 7

Scottsbluff, 46, 86, 138, 218

Scotts Bluff National Monument, 3, 44, 218

Scout's Rest Ranch, 30

Seacrest, Susan, 55

Sheldon Memorial Art Gallery and Sculpture Garden, 26, 188

Sheridan, Gen. Philip, 40

Sidney, 46

SITEL, 7, 68

Sitting Bull, 5

Skelton, Red, 4

Slogum House, 7

Smart Computing, 70

Smith Falls, 32

Smithsonian Institution, 84

Snake River, 32

Sod houses, 44

Southeast Community College, 217

South Sioux City, 17

Sower, The, 49

Standard Digital Imaging, 79

Standing Bear, 5, 160

STARS (School-based Teacher-led
   Assessment and Reporting System), 206

State Bank Building, 42

State capitol, 5, 29, 188

State Fair, 30

State Highway 2, 32

State Historical Society, 44

State Museum of Natural History, 26

Sterling Software Information Technology
   Division, 80

Stone, Edward Durrell, 188

Stone Creek, 36

Stonehenge, 223

Strategic Air Command (SAC), 66

Strategic Air Command Museum, 10, 188

Streck Laboratories, 139

Stromsburg, 16

Stuhr Museum of the Prairie Pioneer, 30,
   188

Swanson Foods, 6

Swift and Armour, 6

Tashunca-Utico, 5

Tennessee Valley Authority, 5, 42, 238

Texas longhorns, 50

Theisen, Willy, 7

Thomas, Gerry, 6

Toadstool Geologic Park, 44

Tonight Show, The, 5

Tourism, 218

"Tower on the Plains," 5

Trails West, 44, 46

Transcontinental telegraph, 66

Trans-Mississippi and International
   Exposition, 4, 8, 49

Transportation, 112–113, 242

Treaty of Fort Laramie, 5, 46

Trenton, 40

Trinity Lutheran Church, 220

Trucking, 242

Truck Paper, 70

Truman, President, 189

Turkey Red winter wheat, 53

TV dinners, 6

Two Brothers, 24

Underground Railroad, 36

UneMed Corp., 136

Union Pacific Railroad, 8, 11, 26, 50, 112,
   113, 114

Union Station, 23

United Parcel Service, 242

University of Nebraska, 204–05, 207,
   210–13

University of Nebraska at Kearney (UNK),
   204, 205

University of Nebraska at Omaha (UNO),
   8, 12, 51, 205, 206, 207

University of Nebraska College of
   Medicine, 138, 205

University of Nebraska–Lincoln, 4, 5, 7, 26,
   30, 68, 69, 87, 139, 202, 205, 207, 221

University of Nebraska Medical Center
   (NMC), 134, 136

University of Nebraska Press, 69, 70

University of Nebraska's Center for Human
   Molecular Genetics, 7

UNMC Eppley Institute for Research in
   Cancer and Allied Diseases, 137

USBancorp, 158

US Bank, 157–58

U.S. News & World Report, 206

US West, 66, 67, 186

Valentine, 32, 34

Valentine National Wildlife Refuge, 32

Valley, 82

Valmont Industries, Inc., 82, 84, 87, 101

Victoria model broom, 84

VISE-GRIP pliers, 38, 82, 87

Wagon Train, 40

Wayne, 17, 205

Wayne, John, 40

Weber, Lucas, 16

Weber, Todd, 223

Webster, John L., 160

Wellness Councils of America (WELCOA),
   159

Wells Fargo, 157, 159

Werner, Clarence L., 242

Werner Enterprises, Inc. 23, 112, 120–21

West, 68

Western Exchange Fire and Marine
   Insurance Co., 160

Westin, 218

Westroads Mall, 22

West TeleServices Corporation, 164–65

Who Do You Trust?, 5

Wilbur, 39

Willa Cather Foundation, 42

Wilson, President Woodrow, 4

Winnebago Indian Reservation 19

Wisner, 14

WJAG, 69

Woodmen of the World, Omaha Woodmen
   Life Insurance Society, 156, 157, 180–81

Woodmen Tower, 156, 157

WOW, 69

WOWT, 67, 68

Zyback, Frank, 6